TMH Professional: Cracking the IT Interview Series

Cracking the IT Interview

Jump-start your CAREER with CONFIDENCE

Second Edition

Other Titles in this Series

- **Cracking IT Campus Interviews**
  Deepa Jain
- **Cracking the C, C++ and JAVA Interview, 2e**
  SG Ganesh and Subhash KU
- **Cracking the QTP Interview**
  Siva Koti Reddy K
- **Cracking the System Software Interview**
  Sandya Mannarswamy and SG Ganesh

TMH Professional: Cracking the IT Interview Series

Cracking the IT Interview

Jump-start your CAREER with CONFIDENCE

Second Edition

BALASUBRAMANIAM

K. R. BAALAJI

KIRAN G. RANGANATH

RAVINDRA K. NANDAWAT

SELVAGURU M.

SUBASH T. COMERICA

VENKAT RAGHAVAN S.

VIKRAM SATHYANARAYANA A.

Tata McGraw Hill Education Private Limited

NEW DELHI

McGraw-Hill Offices

New Delhi New York St Louis San Francisco Auckland Bogotá Caracas
Kuala Lumpur Lisbon London Madrid Mexico City Milan Montreal
San Juan Santiago Singapore Sydney Tokyo Toronto

Tata McGraw-Hill

Published by Tata McGraw Hill Education Private Limited,
7 West Patel Nagar, New Delhi 110 008

ISBN (13): 978-1-25-906133-2
ISBN (10): 1-25-906133-7

Vice President and Managing Director—Asia-Pacific Region: *Ajay Shukla*
Publishing Manager—Professional: *Praveen Tiwari*
Asst. Sponsoring Editor—Science, Technology and Computing: *Simanta Borah*
Sr. Copy Editor: *Neha Sharma*
Sr. Production Executive: *Rita Sarkar*
AGM—Sales and Business Development: *S Girish*
Deputy Marketing Manager—Science, Technology and Computing: *Rekha Dhyani*
General Manager—Production: *Rajender P Ghansela*
Manager—Production: *Reji Kumar*

Typeset at Text-o-Graphics, B-1/56, Arawali Apartment, Sector 34, Noida 201 301 and printed at Rajkamal Electric Press, Plot No. 2, Phase-IV, Kundli, Haryana.

Cover Printer: Rajkamal Electric Press

Cover Design: Mukul Khattar

The McGraw·Hill Companies

To

Our Parents

Preface to the Second Edition

Indian IT industry has seen many down-turns, recessions and challenges over the past 14 years. The Dot Com bust of 2000, the Telecom recession of 2004 and, more recently, the worldwide economic slowdown of 2008–2011, where every global company was forced to re-think their technology outsourcing strategy.

Every recession has resulted in a greater need for IT professionals in low-cost countries like India—the need of the hour being "Productive IT professionals" with the right technology skills.

Following the tremendous success and appreciation for the First Edition of this book, which sold over 50,000 copies, we decided to re-look at the latest trends in Technology hiring and interviewing. The Second Edition is a combination of additional new topics and refining of existing topics.

We realise that while hiring for software engineers with upto 3 years of experience, the emphasis is on:

- Understanding of the software fundamentals
- Breadth of software technologies candidate is comfortable with
- Attitude to problem solving and
- Interviewing skills

In this edition, we have focused on equipping you with these skills.

In addition to revising all the existing chapters, we have enhanced the interviewing tips and soft-skills section and added a section on real-time operating systems.

Even though you may have a thousand books that go to greater detail, we believe that this is the one book which will help you CRACK THAT IT INTERVIEW !

Authors

Preface to the First Edition

This book took its birth from our experiences as interviewers and also as interviewees. It is an effort to assist and advise prospective employees of software companies across the globe. The book addresses some of the "must-haves" and bare minimum aspects of software along with some advanced strategies and guidelines to be followed in a technical interview.

There are several compelling reasons that have inspired and motivated us to pen this book.

Firstly, India is fast being recognized as a global source for extremely talented, English-speaking knowledge workers. This is driving the market for graduates aspiring to be software engineers. But, alas, there are more than a million graduates walking out of colleges every year, and only the best few manage to snap up the available jobs. This fierce competition is driving students to persevere and companies to innovate.

Cracking the IT Interview attempts to provide an insight into what different companies look for in a prospective employee and their innovative approaches to net the very best from a huge talent pool.

Secondly, many software companies recruit graduates with different backgrounds—computer engineers, electrical engineers, civil engineers, mechanical engineers, MScs, MCAs, MBAs, etc. Well, that is the need of the hour; the Indian IT market is poised to touch the $50 billion by 2007, employing a million graduates! But that does not mean that the selection process is going to get any easier. Our book caters to people from any of the above diverse streams and more!

Thirdly, it has been observed that there are technical books in the market which delve into subjects with varying degrees of detail. There are books on operating systems, data structures and algorithms, programming languages, quality procedures, software engineering models, testing methodologies... the list goes on and on. This book seeks to address the obvious need for a single source of information that can be used as a reference. At the same time care has been taken to keep the book concise and focused towards taking an interview.

Finally, attending and successfully clearing an interview is by no means an easy task. Employers are very demanding and set tough measurement criteria for interviewees. This book is therefore presented from the interviewer's perspective.

Having described the motivation, we would like to share some other salient features of our book:

- Provides an end to end blueprint—right from resume presentation to volleying the interview questions.
- Presents a comprehensive question bank on the different aspects of Software Engineering covering Programming Languages, Operating Systems, Data Structures, Java & J2EE, Object Oriented Design, Networking and Database ensuring a combination of standard time-tested technologies with bleeding edge technologies to ensure effectiveness in the long term with special emphasis on practical application.
- Contains an exhaustive list of interview questions with varying levels of difficulty.
- Sets out important guidelines on some implicit behavioural aspects of an interview, which are usually under emphasized/neglected by aspirants.
- Provides a "Thinker's Choice" for the opportunity to further one's understanding on a particular technology or language.
- Contains a reference section on each topic for general guidance.

A word of caution—This book should not be construed as the sole source of information on the above mentioned subjects. It is merely a framework on which you need to build the necessary competency levels with further reading of the books mentioned in the References.

Feedback—We will appreciate receiving your comments, criticism and feedback at http://www.facebook.com/#!/CrackingTheITInterview.

For more question tips and suggestions for Cracking the IT Interview please visit our website www.crackinginterviews.com

Authors

Acknowledgements

Our Special thanks to:

Anuradha T. *Technical Lead, Wipro Technologies*

Chandra Mohan *Software Engineer, Wipro Technologies Ltd.*

Chaturbhuj Kalro *Gangarams Book House, Bangalore*

Clettas Chacko *Technical Lead, Lucent Technologies*

Diwakar Vishwanathan *Staff Engineer, Infineon Technologies*

Madhusudhan K. *Software Engineer, Tata Infotech Limited*

Premraj Duraivelu *Software Engineer, Cisco Systems*

Sitaram, P. Katti *Manager-Software Development, Cisco Systems Inc.*

Apart from these core reviewers, there are many other people who helped us fine tune this book. Without their help, this book would not be in the shape it is now. Our heart felt thanks to each and every one associated with this book—both directly and indirectly.

Authors

Contents

Introduction

As the world recoups from the economic downturn, it has become more evident than ever that outsourcing and off-shoring are here to stay and India is in the best position to help global companies cut costs. All companies are out looking for one kind of employee– "A *technically capable* engineer with good *communication skills*".

Are you ready to impress the interviewers on both these aspects?

A class topper with an 80+ aggregate percentage, who always has the answers for all the tough mathematical problems and has an unblemished academic scoreboard, cruises his/her way through the technical written test of every software company coming to the campus for recruitment **but** is unable to crack the interview.

Does this seem to be a familiar story?

Every class has its set of interview-bloopers and all of them could have been avoided with a little preparation and adherence to a few fundamental rules of communication!

It is not necessarily the 'Most Intelligent' but the 'Best Prepared' candidate who lands the job. In this book, we have emphasized the importance of good preparation on all aspects of a recruitment cycle—*Technical* and *Soft-Skills*, based on our experiences in the industry.

The first section we shall try to explain some of the common questions broached in most interviews as well as learn how to avoid potential potholes in an interview. This section will be relevant for any interview irrespective of your experience level!

The technical topics of the book have been revised taking into consideration the changing technology arena as well as additional topics, which have been gaining importance in the industry.

After 12 years in the software industry and having sold over 50,000 copies of the previous edition of this title, we realize that this book is as relevant to a college fresher as it is to a software engineer looking for a new job with 5 years of experience.

PRE-INTERVIEW PREPARATION

From the ocean of programmers competing for the job, soft-skills and good presentation are often the main differentiators in an interview. This section gives us an insight into some of the psychological aspects of interview handling, which are as important as technical expertise.

RESUMÉ PREPARATION

With the automation of the hiring process in most companies, resumés will be shortlisted using **specialized software** in few minutes. Tacky resumés could unwittingly doom your job search. So, writing an 'ideal resumé' for a job is the most important and perhaps the only tool to getting a foot through the door.

Verify the following points before you dispatch your resumé to any companies:

1. Size: Make sure your resumé does not span more than two to three pages. No one likes to read lengthy articles on your achievements. They would prefer to get it from you in person.

2. Format: Any good resumé should not have a confusing/fuzzy look.

- ➢ Use a standard and easily readable font consistently in the document.
- ➢ Have proper and meaningful headings.
- ➢ Italicize characters judiciously and avoid excessive colors.
- ➢ Give the resumé an overall 'Professional Look'.

3. No Grammatical Errors: Most resumés have grammatical errors that are easily visible through any Word editor. Avoid them as much as possible. For example, if you use MS-Word, make sure you do not see any red or green waved underlines on your resumé. Make sure you run Spell Check before dispatching any correspondence to the companies.

4. Contact Details: Provide your contact details clearly at the top of the resumé. Do not forget to mention your email-id and phone number; preferably a mobile number—ensuring you never miss a call from the HR when he/she is looking for you.

5. Multiple resumés: It pays to customize your resumé according to the company's requirement.

For example, you might need to sell yourself for an 'embedded programmer' job with your C knowledge and for an 'application programmer' job, you may need to emphasize visual packages like VB, VC++, etc.

POINTS TO REMEMBER

- Make sure you are familiar with what you write in your resumé; and ensure that you are well prepared on all the facets of the topics you have touched upon. Your resumé is the only source of information for the interviewers and all questions would invariably be directly linked to what you have mentioned.
- Be crisp and clear. In the project details section, it is recommended that you write about the responsibilities you handled in the project and what you have **accomplished** in this project rather than a lengthy essay about the nitty-griity of the project.
- Highlight any technical accomplishments like certifications obtained, training attended, etc.
- Limit or avoid writing excessively about your personal details.
- You ***do not need*** to have a ***declaration***. Remember it is a resumé and not a legal affidavit.

SAMPLE RESUMÉ

There is a lot that can be written about a perfect resumé. We believe that this sample resumé can enlighten you as to how a good resumé should look. Spend enough time and put in all your creativity into your resumé.

James Bond

#007, 7th F Cross, 4 T Block, Times Square,
Bangalore, India–560 007
Mobile: +91-12345-12345
Res: +91-80-12345678
E-mail: james007@xyz.com

Objective: Seeking a challenging career in the field of Software Design and Development.

Professional Profile

- ✓ Experience in Software development on C and C++ during my Academic project
- ✓ Effective team worker

Technical Skills/Key Software Skills

- ✓ Programming Languages : C, C++, JAVA
- ✓ Operating Systems : UNIX
- ✓ Scripting Language : PERL, TCL / TK

- ✓ Database : Oracle 11i
- ✓ Front-end tools : Visual Basic 5.0

Experience: XYZ India Pvt. Ltd. (Academic Project)

- ✓ Title : Design and Development of a Retail Banking Solution
- ✓ Technology : C, Visual Basic, Oracle

Description: Designed and developed a banking software solution for XYZ India Pvt. Ltd. The retail sector of the banking was automated including the Savings bank and the Over-draft functionalities. Operating in a team of 3 members, we were exposed to some of the various aspects of the software development life cycle including Requirements.

- ✓ Collection, Design, Coding, Testing and delivery to client
- ✓ Module ownership and on-time delivery
- ✓ Won "Spot" award for excellence
- ✓ Won "feather in the hat" award for innovation

Bachelor of Engineering in Electronics and Communication Engineering, Bangalore University (1995–1999) with First Class with distinction. (75%)

Semester 1	*Semester 2*	*Semester 3*	*Semester 4*
74 %	75 %	76 %	75 %
Semester 5	*Semester 6*	*Semester 7*	*Semester 8*
74 %	75 %	76 %	75 %

Pre-University Course:
The International College of Science, Bangalore
Aggregate Percentage: 92%

School: ICSE (Class X):
St. James Bond School, MI6, Roger Moore Nagar, Bangalore
Aggregate Percentage: 90%

Certifications: Java , Microsoft , CCNA, CCNP

Interests: Sports, reading and traveling

Skills: Fast learner, good communication and listening skills

POINTS TO PONDER

- As in any market situation, the best way to guarantee success is to cater to the commodity in demand. Similarly, the world of Software Technology is always in a constant churn with technologies changing by the season. Be abreast with the latest technologies.
- Most companies assume that freshers recruited would have to be trained before introduction into the mainstream. With this assumption, they shortlist students with a good academic background and percentage, this cut-off being a first filter. But all students selected in the percentage band always stand an even chance in the interview.
- This is where other characteristics of the candidate's personality are brought to the fore and the better the attitude, the better the chances.
- It is very important for the candidate to do his/her homework about the background of the company he/she is applying to before proceeding to the interview. This would help in asking more informed questions as well as emphasizing the right aspects of his/her skill-set.

SOFT SKILLS

Interview Presentation and Handling

Most interviewers try to comfort the candidates during the initial session of the interview; hence they try to talk about personal details about which candidates are pretty comfortable talking about. This also opens up a channel of communication at a personal level. If you could impress the panel with well prepared/rehearsed crisp answers, your chances of success are assuredly better.

It is a scientifically proven fact that only about 10–20% of your communication depends on the words you speak and its content. Over 80% of communication hinges on other neuro-linguistic attributes like the tone of speech, fluency of expression and body language while delivering the content. Hence, to get comfortable in such situations, organize/attend mock interviews among your peers and host group discussions to improve your communication skills.

Some of the MUST-DO items PRIOR to your interview are as follows:

- **Do your *homework*:** Check out the company's website. Ask around; find out as much as possible about the company before your interview. Prepare answers to commonly asked interview questions. This will make you feel mentally prepared.
- **Feel good:** Bring your best attitude. Get a good sleep.
- **Dress smart:** Everything counts when you are making a first impression. Dress conservative and professional. Hair should be well groomed. Your face should be preferably clean-shaven.

- **Arrive early plan**: to arrive 15–20 minutes before your scheduled interview. Additionally, give yourself a little extra time for your commute just in case traffic is bad. In total, build in an extra half hour for yourself; 15 minutes for commute "what ifs" and 15 to be sure that you're early.

Turn your cell phone off.

Some of the MUST-DO items DURING to your interview are as follows:

- **Greet with confidence:** Direct eye contact, a firm handshake and a smile. Show enthusiasm! Sure they are looking for someone who can do the job. Be that person. Be yourself. Sell yourself on that interview as a person qualified and eager to take on the task at hand. Express your interest. Be pleasant. Be positive. Be sure to sit with your best posture.
- **Listen:** The interviewer will tell you everything you need to know to get this job if you are careful to actively listen. Do not give the interviewer the impression that you are not paying attention. It is important to engage the interviewer in a meaningful discussion than to have a monologue to an audience who are switched-off.
- **Answer the questions directly**: It is important that you answer the questions crisply without rambling and going off on a tangent.

Some of the common ice-breakers are as follows:

- **Tell me something about your background**

  Give a brief introduction about your educational background and your passionate hobbies. Even before the actual tech interview begins you can strike a very positive chord with your interviewers by answering confidently and putting forth a concisely prepared brief. Keep it short and to the point. Never elaborate unless requested.
- **What are your plans for pursuing higher education?**

  Such questions are aimed at probing into your future retention value to the company. Companies would like to weed out any candidates who are looking at a stop-gap arrangement before they proceed on to their foreign universities.
- **What has been the toughest challenge you have faced in your life so far?**
- **Describe your most successful moment in life.**

  If you could give an interesting situation, which you faced in your life and how you overcame adversity, it could help the panel in understanding your personality better. In all personal questions, truth and honesty is best adhered to.
- **What are your strengths and weaknesses?**

  Do enumerate both aspects of your personality preferably stressing on your strengths with examples.

Also show how you are working to improve on your weaknesses.

- **Why do you want to switch from your field (electronics/mechanical) to computers? Do you think you can cope with the pressures of learning a new domain?**

  Any non-computer science student is bound to be asked this question. But giving a positive answer to this is very important. If you try to show that you are not interested in your own area of specializations and wish to move just because Software looks rosy on the outside, you could be caught off-guard with a follow-up question like "After attending our training sessions if you suddenly realize that Software is not the place for you, what will you do". Try to depict your versatility and readiness to adapt to changes if necessary.

- **Give me an example where you have taken initiative in College? Have you ever organized a college tour or event? Give a brief account of your extracurricular life in College.**

  Such questions are posed to test the leadership traits displayed by the candidates in their academic lives and would definitely go a long way in scoring extra points in your overall tally.

  This opportunity should be used to highlight any leadership initiative you have taken in leading a group towards a common goal.

Some of the TRAP QUESTIONS are as follows:

- **Are you willing to travel outside Bangalore (any city) if placed in some other part of the country?**

  Requirements to travel are very dynamic in the software industry and every candidate is expected to accord priority to project requirements. Unless you have serious traveling limitations this issue is best postponed to when the actual travel need arises.

- **Do you have any strong likes/dislikes with respect to Technology? Do you mind working on maintenance projects?**

  If you have a passion for a specific technology or domain, it wouldn't harm in letting them know about your interests and how your learning curve would be steeper if assigned to these assignments.

- **Do you have any problems staying up late in office or working on holidays as required?**

  The late hour working and holidays skipping is an intrinsic part of the software professional's life. As freshers, all candidates are expected to understand and consent to this.

Some other questions to test your emotional maturity!

- **We see that your marks have not been very consistent through your semesters. Can you tell us why?**

- **Which do you think is more important: individual brilliance, team effort or hard work? Rank them in your order of importance.**
- **A lot of candidates with much better marks have also applied for this job, why should we consider you instead of them?**

  All projects, software or otherwise, require us to work in groups and be capable of dealing with the complexities arising from it. Coming out of academic life we often see that highly individualistic or uncommunicative people are not preferred everywhere. As always, virtues like hard work, perseverance, honesty, truthfulness and helpfulness are highly respected.

Some of the possible questions in which you could portray some of the high points of your academic career are as follows:

- **What do you consider to be your most significant achievement so far?**
- **In the software industry what do you think is the most important characteristic of a Software professional?**
- **How do you see your career growth in this organization? Where do you see yourself three years from now?**

  You are the best person to answer these questions about yourself and the better you portray yourself the better it is for you. As these questions are about incidents in life you have experienced you should always have a couple of ready answers to these questions rather than thinking about them while on the hot-seat!
- The **MOST IMPORTANT** question you need to prepare for are as follows: **Do you have any questions for us?**

  This is usually the final question in the interview and should be seized by the candidate to show his/her interest in knowing the organization better and clarify any concerns he/she has.

Some Pointers on good open-ended questions are in the following:

- **About the company**
  - Who are your main competitors?
  - "I saw in your web site that …."
  - How do you distinguish yourself from competitors?
  - How would you describe your company culture, philosophies?
- **About the position**
  - Describe the job cycles—weekly, quarterly, annually.
  - In what technology area am I likely to be working (for freshers)?

- Describe your expectations of the right person in this job technically? Personally?
- How could someone exceed them?
- Has anyone who worked for you really been a super star? Why?
- Has anyone who worked for you really failed? Why?
- What do you find to be the most challenging aspect of the job?

What training programs will the company organize?

➢ **About the interviewer or group**
- Do you mind if I ask your background?
- How long have you been with the company?
- What do you like most about the company? Least?
- What are your "secrets" about how to do well here?

➢ **Remain Flexible**: It is advisable to defer the discussions around benefits, salary, international travel, etc., until after you have convinced the interviewers that you are the right person for the job.

Networking

➢ No, this is not the networking of routers and switches. This is the network you build for yourself of people in different companies, which will help you forward your resumé around companies and get you an opportunity to appear for tests and interviews at reputed firms. So it is very important that you make a lot of people and keep in touch.

➢ Subscribe to various mailing lists and keep in touch with your fellow interviewees.

➢ That will help you to understand the interview process better, get to know a company's requirement and the kind of questions a company expects its prospective employees to answer.

➢ Almost all companies have 'Employee referral, which means that there is enough incentive for both the candidate and the reference to push your resume through.

How NOT to get hired ....

➢ Poor personal appearance: *Outright shabby*

➢ Lack of interest and enthusiasm: *Passive and indifferent*

➢ Over emphasis on money: *Interested only in the best offer*

➢ Condemnation of past employers: *Strict no-no*

➢ Failure to look at interviewer when conversing: *Shows poor self-confidence*

- Limp, fishy handshake
- Unwillingness to go where sent: *Very strong preferencesis not always a good virtue*
- Lack of courtesy: *Ill-mannered/Rude*
- Lack of maturity: *Very critical to leave your college attitude at home*
- Lack of energy: *Can be a key differentiator*
- Late for interview: *Important to apologize if it is your fault*
- Ask no questions about position/job: *Shows introvert tendencies*
- Vague responses to questions: *Might indicate you are lying*
- Over-aggressive, loud with superiority complex
- Inability to express self clearly: *Language can be improved but not attitude*
- Lack of planning for career: *No purpose or goals*
- Lack of confidence and poise: *Nervous*
- Failure to participate in activities: *Group discussions are used to weed out passive/non-communicative candidates*
- Unwilling to start at the bottom, expects too much, too soon
- Makes excuses; evasive; hedges on unfavorable factors
- Indecision
- Merely shopping around: *Not interested in the job*
- No interest in company
- Low moral standards/Virtues
- Lazy
- Intolerant (Strong prejudices)
- Inability to take criticism
- Excessively emotional

Here is an interview checklist, something that almost every IT company has. It lays down the blueprint for any interview and provides a framework on which most interviewers assess the interviewees. Getting to understand the way the Interview panel is documenting their assessment gives you pointers on how to prepare better for the interview.

SAMPLE INTERVIEW CHECKLIST

Candidate's Name:

Education:

Experience:

Current Company:

Subject	Rating	Comments
Operating Systems		
C		
C++		
Java		
Data Structures		
Database		
Networking		
Software Engineering		
Quality		
Testing		
Communication Skills		
(Behavioural)		
Others		

Result	Hire	Reject	WaitList
☐	☐	☐	☐

Rating:

1- Poor

2- Average

3- Good

4- Very Good

5- Excellent

CONCLUSION

This introduction would have given you a peek into the interview process and gives an idea on the ground work you will have to do before you start thinking about applying for a job. But this has been limited to the non-technical aspects.

The forthcoming chapters will give you an insight into the technical aspects of the interview, which are, of course, equally important.

1

C Programming

INTRODUCTION

C language, being one of the earliest computing languages, is commonly considered as the basic requirement for any aspiring software professional. All interviews invariably start with questions in C language and it is imperative for every individual to master C language. A collection of C language FAQs (Frequently Asked Questions) and solutions are presented in this chapter.

STORAGE CLASS

1. What are local and global variables?

Local

- These variables only exist inside the specific function that creates them.
- They are unknown to other functions and to the main program.
- Local variables are allocated *memory on the stack* and they cease to exist once the function that created them has completed execution.
- They are recreated each time a function is executed or called. Local variables are not initialized automatically.
- Their scope and life is limited to the function in which they are declared.

Global

- These variables can be accessed (i.e., known) by any function contained in the program.
- These variables are visible (scope) throughout the program from the point of their declaration.
- They do not get recreated if the function is recalled.

- To declare a global variable, declare it outside all the functions.
- If a local variable is declared with the same name as a global variable, then the function will use the local variable that was declared within it and ignore the global variable.
- Global variables are normally initialized to 0 by default.
- Global variables are allocated *memory on the Data Segment.*

2. What is the scope of `static` variables?

The storage class, `static`, has a lifetime lasting the entire program. `Static` storage class can be specified for automatic (local) as well as global variables.

Static automatic variables continue to exist even after the block in which they are defined terminates. Thus, the value of a static variable in a function is retained between repeated function calls to the same function. Static variables are *allocated on the heap.* The scope of static automatic variables is identical to that of automatic (local) variables, i.e., it is local to the block in which it is defined; however, the storage allocated becomes permanent for the duration of the program. On the other hand, static variables may be initialized in their declarations; however, the initializers must be constant expressions, and initialization is done only once at compile time when memory is allocated for the static variable.

The scope of a static global variable is only within the file in which it is declared. A user cannot use extern in a different file and access the static global variable.

3. What is the difference between static and global variables?

While the life of an object determines whether the object is still in the memory (of the process), scope of the object decides whether the variable can be accessed at that point in the program. Static variables are local in scope to the block or file in which they are defined, but their lifespan is throughout the program. For instance, a static variable inside a function cannot be called from outside the function (because it is not in scope) but is alive and exists in memory. It retains its old value between function calls.

Global variables persist (life) throughout the program; scope is also throughout the program. It means that global variables can be accessed from any function, any file (unless declared static) in the program.

4. What are volatile variables?

The `volatile` keyword acts as a data type qualifier. It alters the default way in which the compiler handles the variable and does not attempt to optimize the storage referenced by it. The `volatile` keyword means the storage is likely to change anytime by code outside the control of the user program. This means that if you reference a variable, the program should always read from the physical address and not its cached value.

A `volatile` keyword is an instruction to the optimizer to make sure that the variable or function is not optimized during compilation.

Example 1

```
...
...
int flag = 1;
while (flag);
...
...
```

In the above example, on compilation, the compiler assumes that the value of the flag will not be changed during the execution of the program. So the compiler is free to ignore the `while (flag)` loop instructions during optimization. However, if the `flag` variable is changed outside this program control (say by an interrupt routine or by some other thread) then it is advisable to declare the flag as a volatile variable.

Example 2

In multithreaded applications, thread P might change a variable being shared with thread Q. Since the compiler does not see any code that changes the value in thread Q, it could assume that Q's value has remained unchanged and store it in a CPU register instead of reading it from the main memory. But, if thread P changes the variable's value between two invocations of thread Q, the latter will have an incorrect value. To force the compiler not to store a variable in a register, declare it volatile.

Q 5. What is the use to 'auto' keyword?

The `auto` storage-class specifier declares an automatic (local) variable, a variable with a local lifetime. It is the default storage-class specifier for block-scoped variable declarations. An `auto` variable is visible only in the block in which it is declared.

Since variables with auto storage class are not initialized automatically, you should either explicitly initialize them when you declare them, or assign initial values to them in statements within the block. The values of uninitialized auto variables are undefined.

Q 6. What is the use to 'register' keyword in the context?

The `register` keyword specifies that the variable is to be stored in a CPU register, if possible. Variables are usually stored in stack and passed to and from the computers processor, as and when required, the speed the data is sent at is pretty fast but can be improved on. Almost all computer processors contain CPU registers, these are memory slots on the actual processor, and storing data there gets rid of the overhead of retrieving the data from the stack. This memory (in registers) is quite small compared to the normal memory, therefore, only a few variables can be stored there. Having a `register` keyword for variables and parameters also reduces code size, which is important in embedded systems. The number of available CPU registers (and their uses) is strictly dependent on the architectural design of the CPU itself. The number of CPU registers is 32 in most cases.

7. How do we make a global variable accessible across files? Explain the extern keyword?

If a variable is declared (with global scope) in one file but referenced in another, the `extern` keyword is used to inform the compiler of the variable's existence. Note that the keyword `extern` is for declarations, not definitions. An extern declaration does not create any storage. Variable initializations should not be done with extern.

FUNCTIONS

8. What is a function prototype?

A function prototype is a declaration similar to variable declarations. Function declarations are generally placed in header files. Specifically, it tells the compiler (and the programmer)

- the name of the function
- the type of the output returned by the function
- the number of types of inputs (called arguments), if any, the function expects to receive and the order in which it expects to receive them

To understand why function prototypes are useful, enter the following code and run it:

```
#include <stdio.h>
void main()
{
    printf ("%d\n",add(99));
    return;
}
int add(int x, int y)
{
```

```
    return x+y;
}
```

This code compiles on many compilers without giving you a warning, even though add expects two parameters but receives only one. It works because many C compilers do not check for parameter matching either in type or count. To solve this problem, C let us place function prototypes at the beginning of (actually, anywhere in) a program. If you do so, C checks the types and counts of all parameter lists. Try compiling the following:

```
#include <stdio.h>

/* function prototype for add */
int add (int,int);

void main()
{
    printf("%d\n",add(20));
    return;
}
int add(int x, int y)
{
    return x+y;
}
```

This code gives compiler error as it expects add function to have two parameters. Replace `add (20)` with `add(20,40)` it works.

9. What does the keyword '`extern`' mean in a function declaration?

Use the `extern` modifier in a method declaration to indicate that the method is implemented externally. Similarly, when you declare a variable as `extern` your program does not actually reserve any memory for it; `extern` emphasizes that the variable already exists external to the function or file.

If you want to make a variable available to every file in a project you declare it globally in one file, that is, not inside any function, and add an `extern` declaration of that variable to a header file that is included in all the other files.

10. How do you write a function that takes a variable number of arguments? What is the prototype of `printf()` Function?

The presence of a variable-length argument list is indicated by an ellipsis in the function prototype. For example, the prototype for `printf()` function, as found in `<stdio.h>`, looks something like this:

```
extern int printf(const char *, ...);
```

Those three dots "..." is the ellipsis notation. This is the syntax that C uses to indicate the presence of a variable-length argument list. This prototype conveys that `printf()` function's first argument is of type const `char *`, and that it takes a variable (and hence unspecified) number of additional arguments.

11. How do you access command-line arguments within the code?

A program is started by the operating system by calling a program's `main()` function. `main()` function is the only function in C that can be defined in multiple ways. It can take no arguments, two arguments or three arguments. The two and three argument forms allow it to receive arguments from the shell (command-live). The two-argument form takes an `int` and an array of strings. When defining `main()` function arguments any name can be given but it is convention to call them `argc` and `argv[]`. The first argument `(argc)` holds a count of how many elements there are in the array of strings passed as the second argument `(argv)`. The array is always null terminated so **`argv [argc]`** = NULL.

Here is a short program demonstrating the use:

```
int main(int argc, char *argv[])
{
    int i;
    for(i = 0; i < argc; i++)
    printf("argv[%d] == %s\n", i, argv[i]);
    return 0;
}
```

The integer, `argc`, is the argument count (hence argc). It is the number of arguments passed into the program from the command line, including the name of the program.

The array of character pointers is the listing of all the arguments. `argv [0]` is the name of the program. After that, every element number less than `argc` is command line arguments. You can use each `argv` element just like a string, or use `argv` as a two dimensional array.

12. How can the environment list be passed to a C Program?

The environment list is passed to the C program using the third argument of `main()` function.

Here is a short program demonstrating it:

```
#include <stdio.h>

void main(
   int argc, /* Number of strings in array argv */
   char *argv[]/* Array of command-line argument strings */
   char **ppenv /* Array of environment variable strings */
)

{
   int count;

   /* Display each command-line argument. */
   printf( "\nCommand-line arguments:\n" );

   for( count = 0; count < argc; count++ )
      printf( " argv[%d] %s\n", count, argv[count] );

/* Display each environment variable. */
printf( "\n Environment variables : \n" );

while( *ppenv != NULL )
   printf( " %s\n", *(ppenv++) );
   return;
}
```

```
Output of the above program when called as. /a. out a b

Command-line arguments:
argv[0] ./a.out
argv[1] a
argv[2] b
```

```
Environment variables:

...(The environment variables with their values are displayed here).
```

PREPROCESSOR

13. What does '#include <stdio.h>' mean?

If a line starts with a hash, denoted by #, it tells the compiler that a command should be sent to the C PREPROCESSOR. The C preprocessor is a program that is run before compilation takes place (hence the name). The '`#include`' is one of the many C preprocessor commands we use.

Basically, when the preprocessor finds `#include` it looks for the file specified and replaces #include with the contents of that file. This makes the code more readable and easier to maintain if you needed to use common library functions.

Header files have the extension `.h` and the full filename follows from the `#include` directive. They contain declarations to certain functions that you may or may not have used in your program.

For example, the `stdio.h` file is required if you have used functions like `printf()` and `scanf()` in your program.

14. What is the difference between `#include<...>` and `# include "..."`?

There are two ways to include a header file:

```
#include "stdio.h" and
#include <stdio.h>
```

If you use the double quote marks, it means that the directory you are currently in, will be searched first, for the header file, before any other directories (mentioned in the `INCLUDE_PATH`) are searched.

When you use the angled brackets, directories other than the one you are currently in, will be searched for the header file. The system dependent directories are searched. Usually this will be the default directory for header files specified in your compiler, so you'll probably be using square brackets all the time.

15. What are `#pragma` statements?

Each implementation of C and C++ supports some features unique to its host machine or operating system. Some programs, for instance, need to exercise precise control over the memory areas where data may be stored or to control the way certain functions receive parameters. The `#pragma` directives offer a way for each compiler to offer machine and operating system-specific features while retaining overall compatibility with the C and C++ languages. Pragmas are machine- or operating system-specific by definition, and are usually different for every compiler.

Pragmas can be used in conditional statements, to provide new preprocessor functionality, or to provide implementation-defined information to the compiler.

16. What is the difference between an enumeration and a set of preprocessor `#defines`?

An enumeration consists of a set of named integer constants. An enumeration type declaration gives the name of the (optional) enumeration tag and defines the set of named integer identifiers (called the enumeration set, enumerator constants, enumerators or members). A variable with enumeration type stores one of the values of the enumeration set defined by that type.

Variables of `enum` type can be used in indexing expressions and as operands of all arithmetic and relational operators.

Enumerations provide an alternative to the '`#define`' preprocessor directive with the advantages that the values can be generated for you and hence obey normal scoping rules.

In ANSI C, the expressions that define the value of an enumerator constant always have `int` type; thus, the storage associated with an enumeration variable is the storage required for a single `int` value. An enumeration constant or a value of enumerated type can be used anywhere the C language permits an integer expression.

17. What is the most appropriate way to write a multi-statement macro?

The usual goal is to write a macro that can be invoked as if it were a statement consisting of a single function call. This means that the 'caller' (point where the macro is being used) will be supplying the final semicolon, (denoting end of statement) so the macro body should not. The body of the macro cannot therefore be a simple brace-enclosed compound statement, because syntax errors would result if it were invoked (apparently as a single statement, but with a resultant extra semicolon) as the '`if`' branch of an '`if/else`' statement with the explicit '`else`' clause.

Therefore, it is recommended to use

```
#define MACRO(arg1, arg2) do {\
   /* declarations */ \
   statement1; \
   statement2; \
   /* ... */ \
   } while(0) /* (no trailing ; ) */
```

When the caller appends a semicolon, this expansion becomes a single statement regardless of context.

18. What are the disadvantages of using macros?

Two disadvantages are as follows:

- Macro invocations do not perform type checking.
- `#define MULTIPLY(a, b) a * b`

```
void main()
{
    printf( "%d", MULTIPLY(1+2,3+4));
}
```

In the above example, the answer will be `11` and not `21`. Because the macro will be expanded as: `1+2*3+4`. Since the * operator has higher precedence than the + operator, the value will be `11` instead of `21`. To get the correct answer the macro should be declared as:

```
#define MULTIPLY(a, b) (a) * (b)
```

STRUCTURES AND UNION

19. Why does the 'sizeof' operator sometimes report a larger size than the calculated size for a structure type?

The **sizeof** operator gives the amount of storage, in bytes, required to store an object of the type of the operand. When we apply the **sizeof** operator to a structure type name, the result is the number of bytes in the structure including internal and trailing padding. This size may include internal leading and trailing padding used to align the members of the structure on memory boundaries. Thus, the result may not correspond to the size calculated by adding up the storage requirements of the individual members.

For example, `struct xyz {int x; char y[2];};` The `sizeof struct xyz` is returned as 8 and not as 6 bytes.

20. What are the properties of union? What is the sizeof a union variable?

- Union allows same storage to be referenced in different ways.
- The **`sizeof`** applied on a union gives the size of its biggest member.
- There is no standard way of initializing a union. Each initialization will over write the previous one.
- Syntax, format and use of tags and declarators are like `struct`, but members overlay each other, rather than following each other in memory.

For instance:

```
union rk
{
   short shvar;
   long lovar;
   char chvar;
   long double dovar;
};
```

Here, variable 'rk' will be of the size of dovar.

21. What is a self-referential structure?

If a structure contains a member that is 'pointer to the same structure' then the structure is called self-referential structure.

```
struct list
{
   int nodedata;
   struct list *next;
};
```

22. Can a Union be self-referenced?

No. Because union allocates a single shared memory for all of its data member. Consider an example:

```
union list
{
    long nodedata;
    union list *next;
};
```

For the above union type, only 8 bytes of memory will be allocated (for long) that will be shared by both the 'next pointer' and nodedata member. Here, there are high chances that the value of these members can overlap which leads to data corruption.

POINTERS

23. What is a pointer?

A pointer is a special kind of variable. Pointers are designed for storing memory address, i.e., the address of another variable. Declaring a pointer is the same as declaring a normal variable except that an asterisk `'*'` is placed in front of the variables identifier. The 'address of' operator `'&'` and the 'dereferencing' operator `'*'` are available for working with pointers. Both are prefix unary operators. An ampersand in front of a variable gets its address; this can be stored in a pointer variable. Whereas an asterisk in front of a pointer gets the value at the memory address pointed to by the pointer.

Example

```
int x;
int *pointer_to_x;
pointer_to_x = &x;
```

24. What is LValue and RValue?

Expressions that refer to memory locations are called *l-value expressions.* An l-value represents a storage regions locator value, or a left value, implying that it can appear on the left of the equal sign (=).

Expressions referring to modifiable storage locations are called *modifiable l-values.* A modifiable l-value cannot have an array type or a type with the `const` attribute.

The name of the identifier denotes a storage location, while the value of the variable is the value stored at that location. An identifier is a modifiable l-value if it refers to a memory location.

The term *r-value* is sometimes used to describe the value of an expression and to distinguish it from an l-value. The r-value is the data value of the variable, that is, what information it contains. All l-values are necessarily r-values but not all r-values are l-values.

Here is an example.

```
int a;

/* This is fine, 5 is an rvalue, a can be an lvalue.*/
a = 5;

/* This is illegal. A literal constant such as 5 is not
    addressable. It cannot be a lvalue */
5 = a;
```

25. What is the format specifier for printing a pointer value?

`%p` format specifier displays the corresponding argument that is a pointer. `%x` can also be used to print any value in a hexadecimal format.

26. What is the difference between these initializations?

```
char a[] = "String";
char *p = "Literal";
```

A string literal can be used in two slightly different ways. As an array initializer (as in the declaration of `char a []`), it specifies the initial values of the characters in that array. Anywhere else, it turns into an unnamed, static array of characters (here "Literal"), which may be stored in read-only memory, which is why you cannot safely modify it. In an expression context, the array is converted at once to a pointer, so the second declaration initializes `p` to point to the unnamed array's first element.

The first declares a character array and the second declares a pointer to char array. The program might crash if `p[i]` is modified.

27. Does `*p++` increment `p`, or what it points to?

Unary operators like `*`, `++`, and `--` all associate (group) from right to left. Therefore, `*p++` increments `p` and returns the value pointed to by `p` before the increment. To increment the value pointed to by p, use `(*p)++`.

28. What is a void pointer?

When a variable is declared as being a pointer to a variable of type `void` it is known as a generic pointer. Since we cannot have a variable of type `void`, the pointer will not point to any data and therefore cannot be de-referenced. It is still a pointer though; to use it we have to cast it to another kind of pointer first. Hence, the term Generic pointer.

This is very useful when you want a pointer to point to data of different types at different times.

Here is an example code using a `void` pointer:

```
int main()
{
    int i;
    char c;
    void *the_data;

    i = 7;
    c = 'a';

    the_data = &i;
    printf("the_data points to the integer value %d\n",
    *(int*) the_data);

    the_data = &c;
    printf("the_data now points to the character %c\n",
    *(char*) the_data);

    return 0;
}
```

29. Why arithmetic operation can't be performed on a void pointer?

C language does not allow pointer arithmetic on `void` pointers. The argument being that we do not know the size of what's being pointed to with a `void *` and therefore can't know how far to seek the pointer to get to the next valid address.

30. Differentiate between const `char *a; char* const a;` and `char const *a`.

1. 'const' applies to `char *` rather than 'a' (pointer to a constant char)

```
*a='F' : illegal
a="Hi" : legal
```

2. 'const' applies to 'a' rather than to the value of a (constant pointer to `char`)

```
*a='F' : legal
a="Hi" : illegal
```

3. Same as 1.

By checking whether the `const` appears before or after the asterisk, we can tell a const pointer from a const variable. The sequence `"* const"` indicates a const pointer; by contrast, if const appears **before** the asterisk, the object bound to the pointer is const.

31. Compare array with pointer.

Arrays automatically allocate space, but cannot be relocated or resized. Pointers must be explicitly assigned to point to allocated space but can be reassigned (i.e., pointed at different objects) at will, and have many other uses besides serving as the base of blocks of memory.

32. Declare a pointer to an array of (size 10) integers and an array of pointers to integers.

```
int (*x)[10];
x is a pointer to array of (size 10) integers.

int *x[10];
x is an array(size 10) of pointers to integers.
```

33. State the declaration for a pointer to a function returning a pointer to char.

```
char *(*f)();
```

34. What does the following program do? Is there an error?

```
int main()
{
    char src[]= "This is an excellent book for attending
    interviews";
    char tar[80];
    char *x,*y;
    x = src;
    y = tar;
    while(*y++ = *x++) ;

    printf("\n %s", tar);
    return 0;
}
```

The program works very well. The body of the program above is basically doing a string copy of 'src' into 'tar'. The output of the above code is

"This is an excellent book for attending interviews"

The 'while' loop in the program does the core work. It is assigning the value stored at location 'x' to the location 'y'. 'x' and 'y' are initialized with the base addresses of 'src' and 'tar', respectively. 'x' and 'y' are incremented and the loop continues. The decision to continue in the loop is based on the expression `*y`. When the end of string 'x' is reached the value '\0' with ASCII value 0 is stored in location `*y`. This value evaluates the while condition to "**false**" and the while loop terminates.

35. What is the value of the expression 5["INTERVIEW"]?

The value of the expression `5["INTERVIEW"]` is **'V'.**

The string literal `"INTERVIEW"` is an array, and the expression is equivalent to `"INTERVIEW"[5]`. The inside-out expression is equivalent because `a[b]` is equivalent to `*(a + b)` which is equivalent to `*(b + a)` which is equivalent to `b[a]`.

36. What is a NULL pointer?

A NULL pointer is conceptually different from an uninitialized pointer. A NULL pointer is known not to point to any object or function; an uninitialized pointer might point to anywhere.

In `'stdio.h'` `NULL` is defined as 0. Whenever a program tries to access 0th location the operating system kills the program with runtime assignment error because the 0th location is in the operating systems address space and operating system does not allow access to its address space by user programs.

37. What does 'Segmentation Violation' mean?

These generally mean that a program tried to access memory it should not have, invariably as a result of improper pointer use. The most likely causes could be inadvertent use of null pointers or uninitialized, misaligned, or otherwise improperly allocated pointers, corruption of the malloc area and mismatched function arguments, especially involving pointers; two possible cases are `scanf("%d", i)` (without ampersand) and `fprintf (invalid FILE *argument).`

A segmentation violation occurs when an attempt is made to access memory whose address is well-formed, but to which access cannot be granted. This might be due to either a protection fault or an invalid page fault.

38. What does 'Bus Error' mean?

Bus Error is a fatal failure in the execution of a machine language instruction resulting from the processor detecting an abnormal condition on its bus. The most likely causes for such conditions include invalid address alignment (accessing a multi-byte number at an odd address), accessing a physical address that does not correspond to any device, or some other device-specific hardware error. A bus error triggers a processor-level exception, which the OS translates into a `"SIGBUS"` signal, which, if not caught, will terminate the currently running process.

FUNCTION POINTERS

39. Define Function Pointers.

Function Pointers are pointers, i.e., variables, which point to the address of a function. A running program gets a certain space in the main-memory. Both the executable compiled program code as well as the used variables are put inside this memory. Thus, a function in the program code is like a character field, nothing else than an address.

In C, each function has an address in the code segment. This address may be stored in a pointer (function pointer), and later invoked from this pointer. This is the mechanism that is commonly used in callbacks and virtual function tables.

40. How do you initialize a function pointer? Give an example.

```
int display( ) ;
int ( *func_ptr )( ) ;

void main( )
{
   func_ptr = display ; /* assign address of function */
   printf ("\nAddress of function display is %u", func_ptr );
   (*func_ptr )(); /* invokes the function display( )*/
   return;
}

int display( )
{
   printf ( \nHello World!!" ) ;
}
```

The output of the program would be:

Address of function display is 67188 Hello World!!

In this program, we declare the function `display()` as a function returning an int. `int (*func_ptr )( ) ;`

In this statement, we are declaring a function pointer by name `func_ptr`, which returns an int. If we glance down a few lines in our program, we see the statement,
`func_ptr = display;`

Here, func_ptr is being assigned the address of `display ()` function. To invoke the function we are just required to write the statement,
`(*func_ptr)();`

41. Where can function pointers be used?

Function pointers can be used to replace `switch/if`-statements, to realize late-binding (virtual function tables) or to implement callback function primitives.

BIT OPERATIONS

42. What are bitwise shift operators?

Bitwise Left-Shift is useful when we want to multiply an integer (not floating point numbers) by a power of 2.

The left-shift operator, like many others, takes 2 operands like this:

```
a << b
```

This expression returns the value of `'a'` multiplied by 2 to the power of `b`.

If you are wondering why it is called a left shift, then consider the binary representation of a, and add b number of zeros to the right, consequently "shifting" all the bits b places to the left.

Example: `4 << 2.`

4 is 100 in binary. Adding 2 zeros to the end gives 10,000, which is 16, i.e., $4*2^2 = 4*4 = 16$.

What is `4 << 3`? Simply add 3 zeros to get 1,000,00, which is $4*2^3 = 4*8 = 32$.

Notice that shifting to the left multiplies the number by 2. Multiple shifts to the left, results in multiplying the number by 2 over and over again. In other words, multiplying by a power of 2.

More examples:

$5 << 3 = 5*2^3 = 5*8 = 40$
$8 << 4 = 8*2^4 = 8*16 = 128$
$1 << 2 = 1*2^2 = 1*4 = 4$

Bitwise Right-Shift does the opposite, and takes away bits on the right.

Suppose we had:

```
a >> b
```

This expression returns the value of '`a`' divided by 2 to the power of '`b`'.

43. What are bit fields? What is the use of bit fields in a Structure declaration?

Bit fields allow the packing of data in a structure. This is especially useful when memory or data storage is at a premium. Typical examples:

Bit fields can be used for packing several objects into a machine word. For example, 1 bit flags can be compacted as in Symbol tables in compilers.

C let us do this in a structure definition by putting: bit length after the variable, i.e.,

```
struct packed_struct
{
    unsigned int f1:1;
    unsigned int f2:1;
    unsigned int f3:1;
    unsigned int f4:1;
    unsigned int type:4;
    unsigned int funny_int:9;
} pack;
```

Here the `packed_struct` contains 6 members: Four 1 bit flags `f1`...`f3`, a 4 bit type and a 9 bit `funny_int`.

C automatically packs the above bit fields as compactly as possible, provided that the maximum length of the field is less than or equal to the integer word length of the computer. If this is not the case then some compilers may allow memory overlap for the fields whilst other would store the next field in the next word. Access members as usual via:

```
pack.type = 7;
```

MISCELLANEOUS

44. What is the size of an Integer variable?

The size of an integer variable depends on the processor and the operating system, e.g., in a 32 bit operating system it is 4 bytes.

45. What are the files which are automatically opened when a C file is executed?

`stdin, stdout, stderr` (standard input, standard output, standard error).

46. What do you mean by little endian and big endian processors?

Endianness is the attribute of a processor that indicates whether integers and other data types are represented from left to right or right to left in the memory.

'Little Endian' means that the low-order byte of the number is stored in memory at the lowest address, and the high-order byte at the highest address. (The little end comes first.) For example, a 4 byte `longvariable`

Byte3 Byte2 Byte1 Byte0

will be arranged in memory as follows:

Base Address+0 Byte0

Base Address+1 Byte1

Base Address+2 Byte2

Base Address+3 Byte3

Intel processors (those used in PC's) use 'Little Endian' byte order.

'Big Endian' means that the high-order byte of the number is stored in memory at the lowest address, and the low-order byte at the highest address. (The big end comes first.) Our `longvariable`, would then be stored as:

Base Address+0 Byte3

Base Address+1 Byte2

Base Address+2 Byte1

Base Address+3 Byte0

Q 47. How to determine the endianness at run time?

```
#define BIG_ENDIAN      0
#define LITTLE_ENDIAN   1

int TestEndian(void)
{
    short int word = 0x0001;
    char *byte = (char *) &word;
    return(byte[0] ? LITTLE_ENDIAN : BIG_ENDIAN);
}
```

This code assigns the value 0001h to a 16-bit integer. A `char` pointer is then assigned to point at the first (least-significant) byte of the integer value. If the first byte of the integer is 01h, then the system is little-endian (the 01h is in the lowest or least-significant address). If it is 00h then the system is big-endian.

48. What is the use of `fflush()` function?

The standard input-output functions (like `printf()` and `scanf()`) are buffered, i.e., each device has an associated buffer through which any input or output operation takes place. After an input operation from the standard input device, care should be taken to clear the standard input buffer lest the previous contents of the buffer interfere with subsequent input operations. The function `fflush()` clears the buffer associated with a specified input/output device(`stdin` or `stdout`).

49. What is the difference between `exit()` and `_exit()` functions?

- The `exit` (status) function causes normal program termination and the value of status is returned to the parent. All functions registered with `atexit()` are called in the reverse order of their registration, and all open streams are flushed and closed.
- The `_exit()` function does not call any functions registered with the ANSI C atexit function and does not flush standard I/O buffers. The `_exit()` function terminates the calling process immediately.

50. Where does `malloc()` function get the memory?

The pool of memory from which dynamic memory is allocated is separate, and is known as the *heap*. The `malloc()` and `free()` functions are simple library routines to manage the heap. The `malloc()` function dynamically allocates a block of at least size (given as function parameter) bytes suitably aligned for any use. This dynamic memory allocation is made from the heap.

51. What is the difference between `malloc()` and `calloc()` function?

The prototypes for `malloc()` and `calloc()` functions are as follows:

```
void *malloc(size_t size);
```

where `size` is the number of bytes that we want to be assigned to the pointer.

```
void *calloc(size_t nelem, size_t elsize);
```

The two parameters of `calloc()` function are multiplied to obtain the total size of the memory block to be assigned. Usually, the first parameter `(nelem)` is the number of elements and the second parameter `(elsize)` serves to specify the size of each element.

Another difference between `malloc()` and `calloc()` is that `calloc()` function initializes all its elements to 0.

`calloc()` function expects the total expected memory to be continuous, whereas `malloc()` function allocates memory as chained link.

52. What is the difference between postfix and prefix unary increment (decrement) operator?

- If the unary increment operator, ++, is used after the operand, e.g., x++, it is called a **postincrement operator**.
- If the unary increment operator, ++, is used before the operand, e.g., ++x, it is called a **preincrement operator**.

The unary decrement operator, --, also has two forms:

- postdecrement, x--
- predecrement, --x

The difference between the postdecrement and predecrement operators is the same as the difference between the postincrement and preincrement operators.

It is important to note that when incrementing or decrementing a variable in a statement by itself, there is no difference between the pre and post forms of the operator.

It is only when a variable occurs in the context of a larger expression that the pre and post forms of the operator, have a different effect.

This effect can be explained as follows:

Preincrementing (predecrementing) a variable causes the variable to be incremented or decremented by 1, and then the new value of the variable is used in the expression in which it appears.

Postincrementing (postdecrementing) a variable causes the current value of the variable to be used in the expression in which the variable resides. The variable is then incremented (decremented) by 1.

An example should make this clearer. Look at these two statements:

```
x = 10;
y = x++;
```

After these statements are executed, x has the value 11, and y has the value 10. The value of x was assigned to y, and then x was incremented. In contrast, the following statements result in both y and x having the value 11. x is incremented, and then its value is assigned to y.

```
x = 10;
y = ++x;
```

53. What is the difference between `strcpy()` and `memopy()` function?

The `strcpy()` function copies character(s) in the source string to the destination string till it reaches the source string's NULL character. Then it adds the terminating NULL character in the destination string.

```
char *strcpy(char *dst, const char *src);
```

The `memcpy()` function copies `character(s)` in the source string to the destination string till the given length. Also, memcpy can be used on any similar data type.

```
char memcpy(void *s1, void *s2, int num);
```

PROBLEMS AND SOLUTIONS

54. What is the output of the statement 'print(f)("%",-1<<4);'?

The output of the statement 'print(f)("%",-1<<4);' is in the following:

```
fff0
```

Explanation

`-1` is internally represented as all 1s. When left shifted four times the least significant 4 bits are filled with 0s.The `%x` format specifier specifies that the integer value be printed as a hexadecimal value.

55. Will the following program compile?

```
int i;
scanf("%d", i);
printf("%d",i);
```

Explanation

The code has a bug. The `scanf()` function expects pointer arguments indicating where the input should be stored. In the above code the variable "`i`" is used as it is. The correct syntax is

```
scanf("%d", &i);
```

The program will compile with no errors. But when we enter a value using `stdin`, the system tries to store the value in location with address "`i`". Since "`i`" may be an invalid address, the program will crash and core dump.

56. Write a string copy function routine.

```
void my_strcpy(char *target, char *source)
{
    while(*source != '\0')
    {
        *target = *source;
        source++;
        target++;
    }
    *target = '\0';
}
```

57. Write a function routine to find string length.

```
int my_strlen(const char *str)
{
    int count = 0;
    while(*str != '\0')
    {
        count++;
        str++;
    }
    return count;
}
```

58. Swap two integer variables without using a third temporary variable.

There are many ways to solve the above problem. Two of the most frequent answers are given in the following:

Option 1

```
a^=b^=a^=b
```

which is

```
a = a xor b
```

```
b = b xor a

a = a xor b
```

Option 2

```
a=a+b;

b=a-b;

a=a-b;
```

59. How do you redirect `stdout` value from a program to a file?

There are two ways to implement the above program:

First Solution

The system call `'dup'` is used in the program.

`int dup(int fd)`—Makes a copy of the given `fd` in the first available `fd` table slot.

Algorithm

The parent process opens file `a.out` and forks a child. Recall that a child gets a copy of the parents file descriptors. The parent can fool the child by redirecting stdout. The child process closes `stdout`. It uses `dup(fd)` system call. Dup creates a copy of the given `fd` in the first available file descriptor table slot. The dup call uses the old (now empty) file descriptor of `stdout`. The child process then closes the original `fd`, basically to keep it clean.

```
#include <stdlib.h>
#include <sys/types.h>
#include <sys/wait.h>
#include <unistd.h>
#include <fcntl.h>

int main(int argc, char **argv)
{
   pid_t id;int fd;
   if ((fd = open("out", O_CREAT | O_WRONLY, 0644)) < 0)
   {
      printf("cannot open out\n");
      exit(1);
   }
```

```
    id = fork();

    if (id == 0)
    {
       /* we are in the child */
       /* close stdout in child */
       close(1);
       /* replace stdout in child with "out" */
       dup(fd);
       close(fd);
       execl("/bin/date", "date", NULL);
}
       /* we are in the parent */
       close(fd);
       id = wait(NULL);

       return 0;
    }
```

Output

```
$ cc -o redirect redirect.c
$ ./redirect
$ cat out
$ Sat Nov 20 04:00:00 IST 2004
$
```

Second solution:

```
#include <stdio.h>

void main(void)
{
   FILE *stream;
   if((stream = freopen("book.txt", "w", stdout)) == NULL)
      exit(-1);

   printf("this is stdout output redirected to book.txt \n");
    stream = freopen("/dev/tty", "w", stdout);
```

```
    printf("And now back to the console once again\n");
    return;
}
```

60. Write a program that finds the factorial of a number using recursion (The program should not have any new function defined).

```
#include <stdio.h>
void main()
{
   static int var = 5;
   static int result = 1;
   result *=var;
   printf(" \n %d ",var--);
   printf(" \n Result is %d", result);
   if(var)
   {
      main();
   }
   return;
}
```

Answer

```
5
Result is 5
4
Result is 20
3
Result is 60
2
Result is 120
1
Result is 120.
```

Explanation

When `static` storage class is given, it is initialized once. The change in the value of a static variable is retained even between the function calls. `Main` is also treated like any other ordinary function, which can be called recursively.

61. Write a "Hello World" program in 'C' without using a semicolon.

```
#include <stdio.h>

void main()
{
    if(printf("Hello World \n"))
    {}
}
```

Explanation

`printf()` is a function that returns the number of characters it is able to print. This return value can be used in the "`if`" conditional expression. With this combination, we can print the required string without using a semicolon.

62. Give a method to count the number of ones in a 32 bit number.

```
int bitcount (unsigned int n)
{
    int count=0;
    while (n)
    {
        count += n & 0x1u ;
        n >>= 1 ;
    }
    return count ;
}
```

Iterated '`count`' runs in time proportional to the total number of bits. It simply loops through all the bits, terminating slightly earlier because of the while condition. Useful, if 1's are sparse and among the least significant bits.

63. Write a program that prints itself even if the source file is deleted.

```
#include <stdio.h>
int main ()
{
    int c;
```

```
    FILE *f = fopen (__FILE__, "r");
    if (!f) return 1;

    for (c=fgetc(f); c!=EOF; c=fgetc(f))
        putchar (c);

    fclose (f);
    return 0;
}
```

This works if the source code exists.

The following code works even if the source is deleted.

```
char *p="char *p=%c%s%c;main(){printf(p,34,p,34);}";
main(){printf(p,34,p,34);}
```

Another implementation:

```
#include<stdio.h>
main(){char*c="\\\"#include<stdio.h>%cmain(){char*c=%c%c%c%.102s%
cn%c;printf(c+2,c[102],c[1],*c,*c,c,*c,c[1]);exit(0);}\n";printf(
c+2,c[102],c[1],*c,*c,c,*c,c[1]);exit(0);}
```

Q 64. Given an unassigned integer, find it the number is power of 2.

Answer

```
unsigned int x; /* we want to see if x is a power of 2 */
bool result; /* True if x is a power of 2. */
result = (x & (x - 1)) == 0;
```

Explanation

If x is 8

8 in binary is 1000 and x-1 in binary is 0111. Therefore `(x & (x-1))`evaluates to 0. The comparison `(x & (x-1))`= = 0 returns true and hence result is true.

Note that 0 is incorrectly considered a power of 2 here. To remedy this, use:

```
result = !(x & (x - 1)) && x;
```

Q 65. Predict the output in the following snippet.

```
int main()
{
   char s[]="SEA";
   int i;
   for(i=0;s[i];i++)
      printf("\n%c%c%c%c",s[i],*(s+i),*(i+s),i[s]);
   return 0;
}
```

Answer

SSSS

EEE

AAA

Explanation

`s[i], *(i+s), *(s+i), i[s]` are all different ways of expressing the same idea. Generally, array name is the base address for that array. Here, '**s**' is the base address. '**i**' is the index number/displacement from the base address. So, indirecting it with `*` is same as `s[i]`. `i[s]` may be surprising. But in the case of C, it is the same as `s[i]`.

Q 66. Predict the output in the following snippet.

```
int main()
{
   char *p;
   printf("%d %d ",sizeof(*p),sizeof(p));
   return 0;
}
```

Answer

1 4

Explanation

The '`sizeof`' operator gives the number of bytes taken by its operand. `p` is a character pointer, which needs one byte for storing its value (a character). Hence, `sizeof(*p)` gives a value of `1`. Since it needs four bytes to store the address of the character pointer `sizeof(p)` gives `4`.

67. Predict the output in the following snippet.

```
int main()
{
    int i=3;
    switch(i)
    {
        default:printf("zero");
        case 1: printf("one");
        break;
        case 2: printf("two");
        break; case 3: printf("three");
        break;
    }
    return;
}
```

Answer

three

Explanation

The default case can be placed anywhere inside the loop. It is executed only when all other cases does not match.

68. Predict the output or error in the following snippet.

```
int main()
{
    printf("%d", out);
    return 0;
}
int out=100;
```

Answer

Compiler error: undeclared symbol out in function main.

Explanation

The rule is that a variable is available for use from the point of declaration. Even though "`out`" is a global variable, it is not available for main. Hence, an error results.

```
int main()
{
    extern out;
    printf("%d", out);
    return 0;
}
int out=100;
```

This is the correct way of writing the program.

69. Predict the output or error in the following snippet.

```
int main( )
{
    int a[ ] = {1,2,3,4,5},j,*p;
    for(j=0; j<5; j++)
    {
        printf("%d" ,*a);
        a++;
    }
    p = a;
    for(j=0; j<5; j++)
    {
        printf("%d " ,*p);
        p++;
    }
    return 0;
}
```

Answer

Compiler error: lvalue required.

Wrong type argument to increment.

Explanation

Error is in line with statement `a++`. The operand must be an lvalue and may be of any scalar type. Array name only when subscripted is an lvalue. Just the array name is a non-modifiable lvalue.

The right way to scan through the array is shown in the second '*for*' loop in the program.

70. Predict the output or error in the following snippet.

```
int main()
{
    int rk;
    /* value 10 is given as input here */
    printf("%d",scanf("%d",&rk));
    return 0;
}
```

Answer

1

Explanation

`scanf()` function returns the number of items successfully read and not `10`. Here `10` is given as input, which should have been scanned successfully. So number of items read is `1`.

71. Predict the output or error in the following snippet.

```
int main()
{
    main();
    return 0;
}
```

Answer

Runtime error: Stack overflow.

Explanation

`main()` function calls itself again and again. Each time the function is called its return address is stored in the call stack. Since there is no exit condition to terminate the function call, the call stack overflows at runtime. So it terminates the program and results in an error.

72. Predict the output or error in the following snippet.

```
int main()
{
    char *str1="abcd";
    char str2[]="abcd";
    printf("%d %d %d",sizeof(str1),sizeof(str2),sizeof("abcd"));
    return 0;
}
```

Answer

4 5 5

Explanation

In first `sizeof`, `str1` is a character pointer so it gives you the size of the pointer variable. In second `sizeof` the name `str2` indicates the name of the array whose size is 5 (including the '\0' termination character). The third `sizeof` is similar to the second one.

73. Predict the output or error in the following snippet.

```
void main()
{
    printf("sizeof (void *) = %d \n", sizeof( void *));
    printf("sizeof (int *) = %d \n", sizeof(int *));
    printf("sizeof (double *) = %d \n", sizeof(double *));
    printf("sizeof(struct unknown*)=%d\n",sizeof(struct
    unknown *));
}
```

Answer

```
sizeof (void *) = 4
sizeof (int *) = 4
sizeof (double *) = 4
sizeof(struct unknown *) = 4
```

Explanation

The pointer to any type is of the same size.

74. Predict the output or error in the following snippet.

```
void allocate(int *p);
int main ()
{
    int *p;
    allocate(p);
    *p = 20;
    printf("%d",*p);
    return 0;
}

void allocate(int *p)
{
    p = (int *)malloc(sizeof(p));
}
```

Answer

Core Dump

Explanation

When pointer `'p'` allocates memory in allocate function, it needs to be a double pointer and the caller should pass `'&p'` instead of `'p'`.

75. Predict the output or error in the following snippet.

```
void main()
{
    int a[10], b[10];
    ...
    a = b;
}
```

Answer

Incompatible types in assignment.

You cannot assign arrays to each other.

Explanation

Base pointer of an array cannot be changed.

76. Predict the output or error in the following snippet.

```
void check()
{
    static int i=1;
    i++;
    printf("Value of i is %d\n", i);
}
void main()
{
    check();
    check();
}
```

Answer

```
Value of i is 2
Value of i is 3.
```

Explanation

`static` variables are allocated in the heap and their value will be persisted till the end of the program.

77. Predict the output or error in the following snippet.

```
void test (int a, int a1)
{
    printf("In test %d %d \n",a,a1);
}
int main(int argc, char* argv[])
{
    int a = 20;
    test (a,++a);
    printf(" In main %d %d ",a,++a);
```

```
    return 0;
}
```

Answer

```
In test 21 21
In main 22 22
```

Explanation

For any 'C' function call; arguments will be passed from right to left. Thus, `test ()` function gets and prints `a`, `a1` values as `21`. After the `test ()` function, statement executed value of `a` is `21`. When `printf ()` function is being executed, value of `a` will be `22`.

78. Predict the output or error in the following snippet.

```
int main ()
{
    int arr[] = { 0,1,2,3,4 };
    unsigned int i;
    int *ptr;
    for (ptr = arr + 4, i=0; i<=4;i++)
        printf("%d ",ptr[-i]);
}
```

Answer

```
4 3 2 1 0
```

Explanation

The `printf()` prints out the value of `ptr[-i]`. `ptr[-i]` is nothing but `*(ptr-i)`. And since `i` loops from `0 to 4`, the value `ptr[-i]` prints the numbers in the array in reverse.

79. Predict the output or error in the following snippet.

```
int main ()
{
    int n[3][3] = {
        1,2,3,
        4,5,6,
```

```
        7,8,9
    };
    printf(" %u %u %d", n , n[2], n[2][2]);
}
```

Assuming that the array begins at address 1000.

Answer

```
1000 1024 9
```

Explanation

The 2-D array is stored in memory in continuous locations. There are no rows and columns in memory. A 2-D array is nothing but an array of several 1-D arrays. Here, the 1-D array `n[2]` starts at location which is 6 integers away from the base. `n[2][2]` is the normal indexing into the 2-D array.

80. Predict the output or error in the following snippet.

```
void main()
{
    char *p1="name";
    char *p2;
    p2=(char*)malloc(20);
    memset (p2, 0, 20);
    while(*p2++ = *p1++);
        printf("\n%s",p2);
}
```

Answer

Empty String.

Explanation

The pointer `p2` moves ahead of the string `"name"`.

81. Predict the output in the following snippet.

```
void main()
{
```

```
    int x=5;
    printf("%d,%d,%d \n",x,x<<2,x>>2);
}
```

Answer

5,20,1

82. What happens if this code snippet is executed?

```
#define TRUE 0 /* some code... */
while(TRUE)
{
    /* some code... */
}
```

Answer

Execution will not go into the loop as `TRUE` is defined as 0.

83. Predict the output in the following snippet.

```
void main()
{
    int a=0;
    if(a=1)
        printf("Never let yesterday use up your today \n");
        printf("Never let yesterday use up your today ");
}
```

Answer

Never let yesterday use up your today
Never let yesterday use up your today

Explanation

In the `'if'` statement the value of `'a'` assigned to `'1'`, so the `'if'` statement will return true and the next statement is executed.

84. Predict the output or error in the following snippet.

```
void main()
{
    int p = 20;
    char *c1 = &p;
    /*.........*/
}
```

Explanation

Compiler throws a warning: 'initializing': incompatible types - from `'int *'` to `'char *'`

Pointer type should match the data type it points to or else it produces undesirable result. In this case, since the variable `'c'` points to integer variable `'p'`, it can access only the first byte of the variable `'p'`.

85. Predict the output or error in the following snippet.

```
void main()
{
    unsigned long a = 100000;
    long b = -1;
    if (b>a)
    printf("yes\n");
    else
    printf("no\n");
}
```

Answer

yes

Explanation

Try yourself

86. Predict the output or error in the following snippet.

```
float t=1.0/3.0;
if (t*3 == 1.0)
```

```
    printf("yes\n");
else
    printf("no\n");
```

Answer

no

Explanation

Try yourself

THINKER'S CHOICE

87. What is the use of a 'conditional inclusion' statement?

88. Write a function that counts the number of ones in an unsigned integer (Not the one mentioned in this book).

89. Find the size of an integer variable without using 'size of' operator.

90. Given an array x[100] which contains numbers between 1..99. Return the duplicated value. Try on both o(n) and o(n2).

91. Write a function to print 123 using putchar(...) function without using temp variable (Hint: Use recursion).

92. Give a fast way to multiply a number by 7.

93. Reverse a string without using a temp variable.

94. Write a function that accepts characters of undefined length and print it as a String (Hint: Use recursion).

95. Implement malloc(...) and free(...) function routine.

96. Write a function to print Fibonacci series and Tribonacci series.

97. **Implement String manipulation function routine for strstr (...) and strtok (...).**

98. **What does calling convention mean? What is the calling convention C language follows during function invocation?**

99. **What are near, far and huge pointers?**

100. **Write a function to check if an integer is signed or unsigned.**

101. **Write a function to find the second largest number in an array of 100 integers in a single array traversal.**

102. **How are va-list, va-start, va-end, va-arg used for variable number of arguments manipulation?**

REFERENCES

1. Brian Kernighan and Dennis Ritche, *C Programming Language*, 2nd edition, Prentice Hall Software Series.
2. Byron Gottfried, *Schaums Outline of Programming with C*, Mc-Graw-Hill.
3. Yashwant Kanetkar, *Pointers in C*, BPB Publications.

2

Data Structures and Algorithms

INTRODUCTION

This chapter is by far the most important chapter for any IT aspirant.

Most interviewers would like to test the 'Basic concepts' and foundations of Logic and algorithms and what better way than a few tricky questions from Data structures.

In this chapter, we have captured aspects of the following points:

- Arrays
- Stacks
- Queues
- Linked List
- Trees
- Sorting and Searching
- Socket Programming

There are many variations of trick questions in data structures, and the easiest way to come up on top is to invest time in understanding the basic concept and logic behind these 'elegant solutions'.

Questions around search and sort algorithms are asked even to industry veterans of 12–15 years experience in their interviews just to test the sharpness of the mind. You will do well to give it your full attention.

CONCEPTS OF DATA STRUCTURES

The heart of any computing system is the data and the logic embedded in it. And the logic is conceived through a set of many established computing constructs, such as Data Structures and Algorithms. Interviews definitely have questions on this area to access one's analytical and logical reasoning skills. This chapter presents basic and advanced 'Frequent Interview Questions' on data structures and algorithms.

Q 1. Define data structures.

An organization of information, usually in memory, for better algorithm efficiency, such as queue, stack, linked list, heap, dictionary and tree, or conceptual unity, such as the name and contact details of a person. It may include redundant information, such as length of the list or number of nodes in a sub-tree. Most data structures have associated algorithms to perform operations, such as search, insert or delete that maintain the properties of the data structure.

Q 2. What is an algorithm?

A computable set of steps to achieve a desired result is known as an algorithm. Algorithms have the following properties: each operation must be definite, that is, it must be crisp and each operation must be effective or, in other words, each step must be such that it can, at least in principle, be done by a person using pencil and paper in finite amount of time. An algorithm produces one or more outputs and may have zero or more inputs, which are externally supplied. An Algorithm needs to terminate after a finite number of operations.

Q 3. Describe briefly the Big O notation.

A function F(N) is O(G(N)) (read of the order) if for some constant k and for values of N greater than some value N_0:

$F(N) <= k^* G(N)$ for $N>N_0$

The idea is to arrive at the upper bound of the function F(N).

For example:

- a constant-time method is "order 1": O(1)
- a linear-time method is "order N": O(N) _ a quadratic-time method is "order N squared": $O(N^2)$
- a logarithmic-time method is "order log N": O(Log(N))

4. What is recursion?

Recursion occurs when a piece of code is executed before a previous execution of the same code has terminated; for example, when a program calls itself either directly or indirectly. Code that is capable of being executed in this way is called re-entrant; it must define its variables in local-storage (typically saved in a stack) so that data from one instance of the code does not interfere with data from another instantiation.

A simple example of recursion would be as follows:

```
int main()
{
   main (); //Sets off the recursion
}
```

However, this program will not continue forever. The computer keeps function calls on a stack and once too many are called without ending, the program will crash throwing a stack overflow error. Some problems, such as evaluating the Nth Fibonacci number, factorial of a positive integer are inherently recursive in nature, which can be easily solved using recursion noting the property that factorial(N) = N*factorial(N-1) where N>0 and if N=0 factorial(N) = 1.

5. For free construction which is the most efficient data structure that can be used?

(a) Array (b) Linked list (c) Stack (d) Queue (e) none

Using linked list for tree construction comes with the following advantages:

- Overflow never occurs unless the memory is actually full.
- Insertions and deletions are easier than for contiguous (array) lists.
- With large records, moving pointers is easier and faster than moving the items themselves.

6. What is backtracking? Explain the 8-Queens problem and brief an approach to solve it.

The backtracking method is based on the systematical inquisition of the possible solutions where, through the procedure, a set of possible solutions are rejected even before they are completely examined so the number of possible solutions gets a lot smaller.

Backtracking is used to solve problems like 8-Queens problem.

The 8-Queens problem is to place eight queens on an 8 × 8 chessboard so that no two 'attack', that is no two of them are in the same row, column or diagonal.

Solution

Let us number the rows and columns of the chessboard 1 through 8 as shown in the figure below. The queens may also be numbered 1 through 8. Since each queen must be on different row we can, without loss of generality assume queen i is to be placed on row i. All solutions to the 8-Queens problem can, therefore, be represented as 8-tuples (x1, ..., x8) where xi is the column on which queen i is to be placed.

- ➢ Start with one queen in the first column, first row.
- ➢ Start with another queen in the second column, first row.
- ➢ Go down with the second queen until you reach a permissible situation.
- ➢ Advance to the next column, first row and do the same thing.
- ➢ If you cannot find a permissible situation in one column and reach the bottom of it, then you have to go back to the previous column and move one position down there. (This is the backtracking step.)
- ➢ If you reach a permissible situation in the last column of the board, then the problem is solved.
- ➢ If you have to backtrack BEFORE the first column then the problem is not solvable.

Please fix the figure below.

	1	2	3	4	5	6	7	8
1				Q				
2						Q		
3								Q
4		Q						
5							Q	
6	Q							
7			Q					
8					Q			

ARRAYS

7. Give an array of integers, move all the zeroes to the bottom of the array.

Traversing every element of the input array in linear order and copying the elements into another array only if the element is non-zero is one of the solutions to the problem. For every copy made to the output array advance the indexes of both the arrays or else if the element is zero then advance just the index of the input array. Repeat the above steps until the end of the input array is reached. Fill in the remaining slots of the output array with appropriate number of zeroes.

The algorithm is of O (N) since we traverse every element of the array before copying into the other array.

Input: Array of integers with zeroes scrambled here and there all across the array and its size.

Output: The same array with all the zeroes at the bottom of the array with the relative order of the other elements of the array being preserved.

```
void compress(int *arr,int size)
{
    int *result;
    int i,j=0;
    result = (int *)malloc(size*sizeof(int));
    for(i=0;i<size;i++)
    {
        if (arr[i]!=0) result[j++]=arr[i];
    }
    for(i=0;i<j;i++)
    {
        arr[i]=result[i];
    }
    for(i=j;i<size;i++)
    {
        arr[i]=0;
    }
    free(result);
}
```

8. Determine the efficient code for extracting unique elements from a sorted array list, e.g., (1, 1, 3, 3, 3, 5, 5, 5, 9, 9, 9, 9) -> (1, 3, 5, 9).

Take a new array (O) and maintain two indexes, one for the new array (O) and another for the input array (I). Simply copy the first element of I into O. Advance the index of the array O. Compare the current indexed element of I with its next element in I itself and if these are not identical then copy it into O and advance both the indexes otherwise just advance the index of I. Repeat the steps until the end of I is reached.

The algorithm is of O (N) since we traverse every element of the array before copying into the other array.

Input: Array of sorted integers with some repeated elements and its size.

Output: Pointer to array with all the distinct elements in their sorted order.

```
int *unique(int *arr,int size)
{
    int *result;
    int i,j=0;
    result = (int *)malloc(size*sizeof(int));
    result[j++]=arr[0];
    for(i=0;i<size-1;i++)
    {
        if (arr[i]!=arr[i+1]) result[j++]=arr[i+1];
    }
    return result;
}
```

9. Explain the algorithm used to merge two sorted arrays.

The merging of sorted arrays can be explained as follows:

Maintain three indexes `ai`, `bi`, `ci` for the two input arrays and one output array viz., `a`, `b` and `c`, respectively. Compare `a[ai]` and `b[bi]` and copy the smaller of the two to `c[ci]` and advance index `ci` and (`ai` or `bi`), whichever of the indices has the smaller element. Repeat the steps until one of the input array's end point is reached, upon which just copy the remaining elements of the other input array directly into the output array `c`.

The algorithm is of O (M+N) since we traverse every element of both the arrays before copying into the third array.

Input: Two sorted arrays of integers and another third array (empty), which can hold the elements of the first two arrays combined and their corresponding sizes.

Output: The third sorted array contains the elements of the first two input arrays combined.

```
void merge(int a[],int b[],int c[],int asize,int bsize,intcsize)
{
int
ai,bi,ci;
csize=asize+bsize;
   while ((ai < asize) && (bi < bsize))
   {
      if(a[ai] <= b[bi])
      {
         c[ci] = a[ai];
         ci++; ai++;
      }
   else
      {
         c[ci] = b[bi];
         ci++; bi++;
      }
   }
   if (ai >= asize)
      for (i=ci;i<csize;i++,bi++)
         c[i] = b[bi];
   else if (bi >= bsize)
      for (i=ci; i<csize;i++,ai++)
         c[i] = a[ai];
}
```

Q 10. Explain the procedure to insert into a sorted array.

Insertion in a sorted array is a very time consuming operation. This is because to retain the order, the chunk of data just below the point of insertion has to be displaced, which is typically an O (N) operation.

Input: A sorted array and its size along with the item to be inserted.

Output: The sorted array with the item inserted at its right place in the sorted array.

```
void insert(int array[],int *size,int item)
{
int i=1,j;
if (size <= 0) return;
//Check if the element is less than the first one in the
//array
if (item < a [0]) i = 0;
else
      {
      for(i=1;i<*size;i++)
         if (array[i]>item && array[i-1]<item) break;
      }
      for(j=*size;j>i;j—)array[j]=array[j-1];
      array[i]=item;
      (*size)++;
}
```

11. Explain deletion procedure from a sorted array.

Deletion in a sorted array is also a time consuming operation. This is because to retain the order, the chunk of data just below the point of deletion has to be displaced, which like insertion again, an O (N) operation.

Input: A sorted array and its size along with the item to be deleted.

Output: The sorted array with the item deleted from its place in the sorted array.

```
int delete(int array[],int* size,int item)
{
   int i;
   while(array[i]!=item && i<*size) i++;
   /* failure - could not find the element */
   if (i==*size) return(-1);
   for(;i<*size-1;i++)
   array[i]=array[i+1];
   (*size)--;
```

```
    return 0; /* success */
}
```

STACK AND QUEUE

12. What is the data structure used to perform recursion?

Stack is the data structure that is used to perform recursion. Its LIFO (Last In First Out) property is used to store return addresses of the 'caller' or invoker of the recursive function and its successions in recursion to know where the execution control needs to return on completion of execution of the current function call. Every recursive function has its equivalent iterative (non-recursive) function. Even when such equivalent iterative procedures are written, explicit stack is to be used.

13. Explain the Basic Stack Operations.

Stack is a FILO (First In Last Out) or LIFO (Last In First Out) data structure. Stack permits two operations—push and pop. Two other common stack status checking methods implemented are `empty()` and `full()` to check if the stack is empty, full, respectively.

Input: Push method takes an integer and also a pointer to integer to return the method's status. Pop just takes a pointer to integer to return the method's status.

Output: Push pushes the element into the stack unless stack overflows. Pop removes the element from the top of the stack and returns it unless stack underflows.

```
int stack[100];
int top=-1;
void push(int item,int *error)
{
    if (top=99)
    {
        *error = 1;
        return;
    }
    top++;
    stack[top] = item;
    *error = 0;
}
int pop(*error)
```

```
{
    int item;
    if (top=-1)
    {
        *error = 1;
        return -1;
    }
    item = stack[top];
    top—;
    *error = 0;
    return item;
}
```

14. Explain the Basic Queue Operations.

Queue is a FIFO (First In First Out) or LILO (Last In Last Out) data structure. Queue permits two operations—enqueue and dequeue. Two other common queue status checking methods implemented are `empty()` and `full()` to check if the queue is empty, full, respectively.

The following algorithm implements a circular queue using linear array:

Input: `enqueue` method takes an integer and also a pointer to integer to return the method's status. `dequeue` just takes a pointer to integer to return the method's status.

Output: `enqueue` queues the element at the rear of the queue unless queue overflows. `dequeue` removes the element from the front of the queue and returns it unless queue underflows.

```
int front=0, rear=-1;
int SIZE = 100;
void enqueue(int item, int *error)
{
    if ((rear+2)%SIZE!=front))//queue full
    {
        rear = (rear+1)%SIZE;
        array[rear] = item;
        *error = 0;
        return
    }
    else
```

```
        *error = 1;

    return;
}
int dequeue(int *error)
{
    int item;
    if ((rear+1)%SIZE!=front)//queue empty
    {
        item = array[front];
        front = (front+1)%SIZE;
        *error = 0;
        return item;
    }
    else
        *error = 1;
    return -1;
}
```

15. What are Priority Queues?

A priority queue is essentially a list of items in which each item has a priority associated with it. In general, different items may have different priorities and we speak of one item having a higher priority than another. Given such a list we can determine, which is the highest (or the lowest) priority item in the list. Items are inserted into a priority queue in any, arbitrary order. However, items are withdrawn from a priority queue in order of their priorities starting with the highest priority item first. Priority queues efficiently support finding the item with the highest priority across a series of operations. The basic priority queue operations are: insert, find-minimum (or maximum) and delete-minimum (or maximum). Some implementations also efficiently support join two priority queues (meld), delete an arbitrary item and increase the priority of an item (decrease-key).

16. Implement queue using stacks.

The trick is, for enqueue, to keep pushing into one stack and when dequeue starts first pop all elements one-by-one from this stack and push into another stack before popping it out finally to the user. If enqueue resumes again the popstack shall pop all elements one-by-one before pushing it back into the pushstack. And then the new element is pushed into the pushstack.

There are 2 stacks pushstack, popstack and so two tops of these stacks, pushtop, pop-top. Also let us assume there are simple stack push and pop functions, which modifies the pushtop and poptop global variables accordingly.

Input: `enqueue` method takes an integer and also a pointer to integer to return the method's status. `dequeue` just takes a pointer to integer to return the method's status.

Output: `enqueue` queues the element at the rear of the queue unless queue overflows. `dequeue` removes the element from the front of the queue and returns it unless queue underflows.

```
void enqueue(int item)
{
    while(poptop!=-1) push(pushstack,pop(popstack));
    push(pushstack,item);
}
int dequeue()
{
    while(pushtop!=-1) push(popstack,pop(pushstack));
    return(pop(popstack));
}
```

Q 17. Implement stack using queues.

Make two queues, queue1 and queue2. For 'push', just enqueue into queue1. For 'pop', first dequeue all except one element one-by-one from queue1 and enqueue into queue2. The one remaining element in the queue1 shall be popped as stack's pop. If 'push' resumes, just enqueue in queue2 itself. Assume queue1 and queue2's 'fronts' as front1 and front2.

Input: Push method takes an integer and also a pointer to integer to return the method's status. Pop just takes a pointer to integer to return the method's status.

Output: Push pushes the element into the stack unless stack overflows. Pop removes the element from the top of the stack and returns it unless stack underflows.

```
void push(int item)
{
if (sizeof(queue1)==0)&&(sizeof(queue2)==0)
enqueue(queue1,item);
if (sizeof(queue1!=0) enqueue(queue1,item);
else enqueue(queue2,item);
}
```

```
int pop()
{
    if (sizeof(queue1)!=0)
    {
        while(sizeof(queue1)!=1) enqueue(queue2,dequeue(queue1));
        return(dequeue(queue1));
    }
    if (sizeof(queue2)!=0)
    {
        while(sizeof(queue2)!=1)enqueue(queue1,dequeue(queue2));
        return(dequeue(queue2));
    }
}
```

18. Implement two stacks using single array efficiently.

The aim of the problem is to implement two stacks using an array. The simple solution to the problem is to let two stacks grow in the reverse directions, one starting from the lower bound of the array and another starting from the upper bound of the array. Either of the stacks will overflow only when both the stack top pointers meet. Underflows can be checked by the lower and upper bounds of the array itself. The stacks grow in the opposite directions as illustrated in the figure.

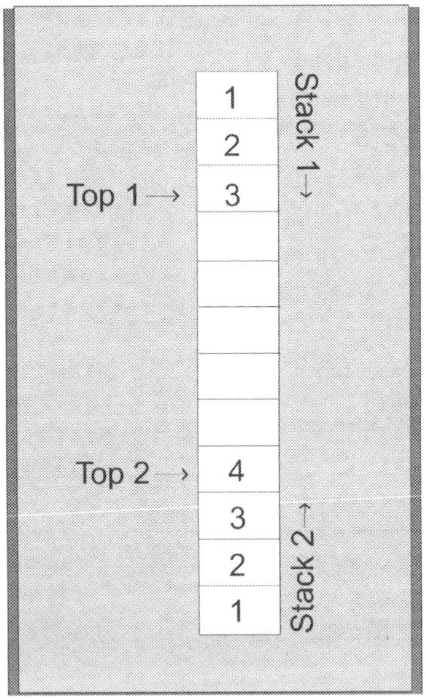

Input: push1 and push2 methods take an integer and also a pointer to integer to return the method's status. pop1 and pop2 just take a pointer to integer to return the method's status.

Output: push1 and push2 push the elements into the stack1 and stack2, respectively unless the two tops collide. pop1 and pop2 remove the elements from the tops of the stack1 and stack2, respectively and returns it unless stack under-flows.

```
#define SIZE 100;
int top1=-1,top2=SIZE;
int array[SIZE];
void push1(int item, int *error)
{
   if (top2-top1!=1)
   {
      top1++;
      array[top1] = item;
      *error = 0;
      return;
   }
   *error = 1;
   return;
}
int pop1(int *error)
{
   int item;
   if (top1!=-1)
   {
      item = array[top1];
      top1—;
      *error = 0;
      return item;
   }
   *error = 1;
   return;
}
void push2(int item, int *error)
```

```
{
    if (top2-top1!=1)
    {
        top2--;
        array[top2] = item;
        *error = 0;
        return;
    }
    *error = 1;
    return;
}
int pop2(int *error)
{
    int item;
    if (top2!=SIZE+1)
    {
        item = array[top2];
        top2++;
        *error = 0;
        return item;
    }
    *error = 1;
    return;
}
```

LINKED LIST

Q 19. Explain the singly linked list insertion procedure.

The code snippet inserts the new node as the successor to the node pointed to by 'after'.

Input: Pointer to the node to which the element has to be inserted as the successor in the linked list.

Output: The linked list rendered with the item inserted as the successor to the node pointed to by 'after'.

```
typedef struct node {
                 int data;
                 struct node *next;
                 } link;
void insert(link *after, int item)
{
   link *newnode = (link *) malloc(sizeof(link));
   newnode->data = item;
   newnode->next=after->next;
   after->next=newnode;
}
```

20. Explain the singly linked list deletion procedure.

The following code snippet deletes the node whose predecessor is pointed to by 'before'.

Input: To be deleted node's predecessor node from the linked list.

Output: The linked list rendered with the item deleted from the linked list. It returns the pointer to the deleted node.

```
link *deletion(link *before)
{
   link *deleted=NULL;
   deleted = before->next;
   before->next=before->next->next;
   return(deleted);
}
```

21. How do you reverse a singly linked list?

There are two ways of reversing a singly linked list viz., using recursion and using iteration.

Reversing it using recursion uses the simple concept of breaking down the problem, which can also be illustrated using string reversal, e.g., reverse (abcdef) =reverse (bcdef).a where '.' means string concatenation. Both the algorithms are of O (N).

Using Recursion

Input: Pointer to the head of the linked list to be reversed.

Output: The pointer to the head of the reversed linked list.

```
typedef struct list *listptr;
struct list {
      int data;
      listptr next;
      };
static listptr head = curp;
//Initialized to input linked list's header
static listptr revHead = NULL;
listptr recursiveReverse(listptr curp)
{
   if (curp == NULL)
      return NULL;
   if (curp->next == NULL) //This is the new linked list's
      revHead = curp;      // head, so save it in revHead.
   else
      reverse(curp->next)->next = curp;
   if (curp == head) { // The head of the input linked list
      curp->next = NULL; // will become the last node
      return revHead;
      }
   else
      return curp;
}
```

Using Iteration

Input: Pointer to the head of the linked list to be reversed.

Output: Pointer to the head of the reversed linked list.

In linked list reversal using iteration, three pointers are needed.

For example, let us assume the following linked list.

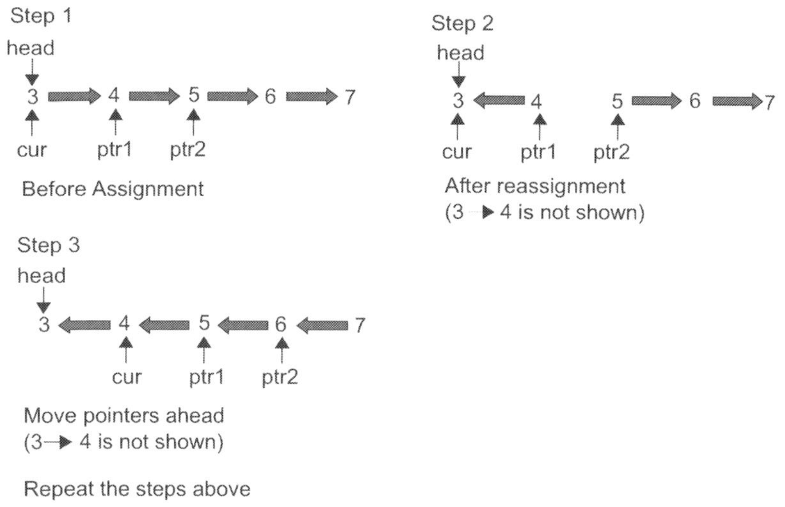

The pointer ptr1→ next is made to point at cur and this is done iteratively after moving all the pointers one step ahead, until ptr2= =NULL when all the iterations are complete the last node is made to point to its earlier predecessor and the head is now made to point to this last node.

```
//This function assumes there are atleast 2 nodes in the
//linked list to be reversedvoid iterativeReverse (listptr*head)
{
   listptr cur,ptr1,ptr2;
   cur = *head;
   ptr1 = cur->next;
   ptr2 = ptr1->next;
   while (ptr2!=NULL)
   {
      ptr1->next = cur;
      cur = ptr1;
      ptr1 = ptr2;
      ptr2 = ptr2->next;
   }
   ptr1->next = cur;
   *head = ptr1;
}
```

22. Given a singly linked list, determine whether it contains a loop or not without using temporary space.

To detect a loop inside a linked list:

- make a pointer to the start of the list and call it the hare
- make a pointer to the start of the list and call it the tortoise
- advance the hare by two and the tortoise by one for every iteration
- there is a loop if the tortoise and the hare meet
- there is no loop if the hare reaches the end

This algorithm is particularly interesting because it is O (n) time and O (1) space, which appears to be optimal;

Input: Pointer to the head of the linked list for which loop has to be checked.

Output: 1 for true—indicating there is a loop or 0 for false otherwise.

```
int containsLoop(listptr head)
{
   listptr hare,tort;
   tort = head;
   if(head!=NULL)hare=tort->next;
   while(hare!=tort && hare!=NULL)
   {
      tort = tort->next;
      if (hare->next!=NULL) hare = hare->next->next;
      else return(0);
   }
      if (hare==tort) return(1);
      else return(0);
}
```

23. Given a pointer to a linked list node, explain how you will delete the same node.

This is a tricky problem since a node cannot be deleted unless the predecessor node's pointer is known. The problem can be solved only if there a successor node for the current node to be deleted.

The data of the successor node is copied onto the current node and the successor node is deleted to make the linked list look exactly as it would look on a normal deletion of the current node.

The algorithm is of O (1) since we traverse just 1 node of the list.

Input: Pointer to the node whose data is to be deleted.

Output: Renders the linked list without the node (data).

```
int delete(link *ptr)
{
    link *deletednode;
    /* failure - cannot be deleted. */
    if (ptr->next==NULL) return(-1);

    /* copy the next node's data into current node */
    ptr->data = ptr->next->data;

    deletednode = ptr->next;
    ptr->next = ptr->next->next;

    return 0; /* success */
}
```

Q 24. Given a singly linked list, find the middle of the list in a single traversal without using temporary memory.

To find the middle node in a linked list:

- ➢ make a pointer to the start of the list and call it single.
- ➢ make a pointer to the start of the list and call it double.
- ➢ advance single by one and double by two till double reaches the end of the list.
- ➢ single shall be at middle of the list when double reaches the end.

The algorithm is of O(N).

Input: Pointer to the head of the linked list whose center is to be found.

Output: Pointer to the middle node of the linked list.

```
listptr findMiddle(listptr head)
```

```
{
    listptr single,double;
    single = head;
    if (head->next!=NULL)
        double=head->next->next;
    else
        return(head);
    while(double!=NULL)
    {
    if (double->next!=NULL)
        double = double->next->next;
    else
        return(single);
    single = single->next;
    }
    return(single);
}
```

25. Explain how in a singly linked list you can get to (n-k)th node, where (k<n), in a single traversal.

To get to the (n-k)th node of a linked list, maintain two pointers, ptr1 and ptr2. Initialize both to point to the header node. Move ptr2 by k nodes. Now move both ptr1 and ptr2 simultaneously one node at a time until ptr2 reaches the last node. When ptr2 is at the last node ptr1 will be pointing to the (n-k)th node.

Input: Pointer to the head of the linked list and the integer 0<k<n.

Output: Pointer to (n-k)th node, if 0<k<n otherwise NULL.

```
link *traversenk(link *head, int k)
{
    link *ptr1,*ptr2;
    int i=0;
    ptr1=ptr2=head;
    while(i<k && ptr2!=NULL)
    {
```

```
    ptr2=ptr2->next;
    i++;
    }
    if (ptr2==NULL) return (NULL); /* k>n so returning NULL */
    while(ptr2->next!=NULL)
    {
    ptr2=ptr2->next;
    ptr1=ptr1->next;
    }
    return ptr1;
}
```

26. Given a singly linked list, state how to print out its contents in reverse order without using any extra space.

The logic that is applied here is to make use of recursion to print out the linked list in the reverse when recursion is unwinding back. Make recursive calls passing the next node before printing the current node's data. The terminating condition checks if next node is Null then prints this node's data.

The algorithm is of O (N) since we traverse every node of the list.

Input: Pointer to the header node whose contents are to be printed in the reverse order.

Output: The linked list data is printed in the reverse order.

```
void PrintReverse(link *head)

{
    if (head==NULL) return;
    if (head->next != NULL)
    PrintReverse(head->next);
    printf("%d\t",head->data);
}
```

27. What is a circular singly linked list?

A circular linked list is a normal singly linked list, whose last node points back again to its header node. The advantage of such a linked list is that it can be traversed completely from any known pointer in it.

28. Explain the doubly linked list insertion procedure.

The code snippet inserts the new node as the successor to the node pointed to by 'after'. In addition to what done for the singly linked list, the reverse links are also properly changed.

Input: Pointer to the node to which the new element has to be inserted as the successor in the linked list.

Output: The linked list rendered with the item inserted as the successor to the node pointed to by 'after'.

```
typedef struct dnode{
                int data;
                struct dnode *prev,*next;
                } dlink;


void insert(dlink *after, int item)
{
   dlink *newnode = (dlink*) malloc(sizeof(dlink));
   newnode->data = item;
   newnode->prev = after;
   newnode->next = after->next;
   after->next->prev = newnode;
   after->next = newnode;
}
```

29. Explain the doubly linked list deletion procedure.

The following code snippet deletes the node pointed to by 'ptr'. The 'ptr' node's predecessor node can be reached through the reverse link and so the linked list is modified to make the 'ptr' node's successor node to become the 'ptr' node's predecessor's immediate successor, in the process of detaching the node pointed to by 'ptr'. The reverse links are also changed appropriately.

Input: Pointer to the node to be deleted from the linked list.

Output: The linked list rendered with the item deleted from the linked list. It returns the pointer to the deleted node.

```
dlink *delete(dlink *ptr)
{
   dlink *deleted=NULL;
```

```
    deleted = ptr;
    deleted->prev->next = deleted->next;
    deleted->next->prev = deleted->prev;
    return(deleted);
}
```

TREES

Q 30. List out some of the applications of the Tree data-structure.

- Some of the Tree data-structure are as follows: For the representation and evaluation of Arithmetic expressions.
- Symbol Table construction at the lexical analysis phase of Compiler.
- Syntax analysis.

Q 31. Explain an algorithm to find the depth of a binary tree.

The depth of any tree is the longest path from root to any of its leaf nodes. It is evaluated by incrementing the larger depth among its left and right sub-tree by 1.

For example:

The depth of the following tree is evaluated as below:

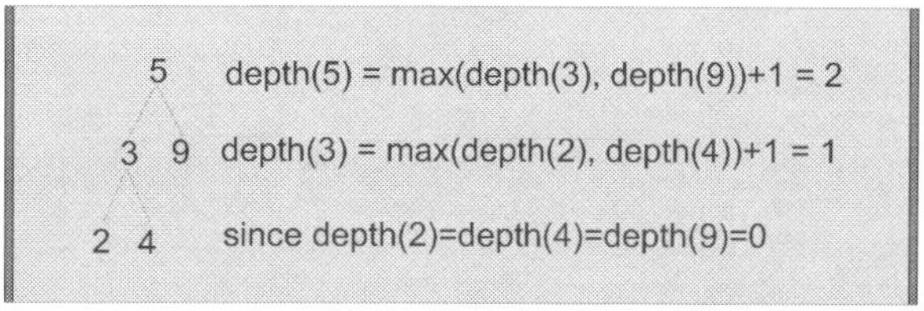

The algorithm is of O (N) since we traverse every node in the tree atleast once.

Input: Pointer to the root node of the tree whose depth has to be evaluated.

Output: The depth of the tree whose pointer to root was supplied.

```
typedef struct tnode *treeptr;
struct tnode {
      int data;
      treeptr left,right;
```

```
    };

int depth(treeptr root)
{
    int leftdepth=-1,rightdepth=-1;
    if (root==NULL) return(-1);
    if (root->left!=NULL) leftdepth= depth(root->left);
    if (root->right!=NULL) rightdepth= depth(root->right);
    if (leftdepth>=rightdepth) return(1+leftdepth);
    else return(1+rightdepth);
}
```

32. Discuss the algorithm that returns the mirror image of the input of the input binary tree.

The mirror image of any tree with root as ROOT is obtained by swapping the left and right sub-trees with roots as ROOT->left and ROOT->right. But just before swapping them, the left and right sub-trees in turn must be already 'mirrorized'. This can be easily achieved using recursion.

For example: The tree's mirror image is obtained as described below:

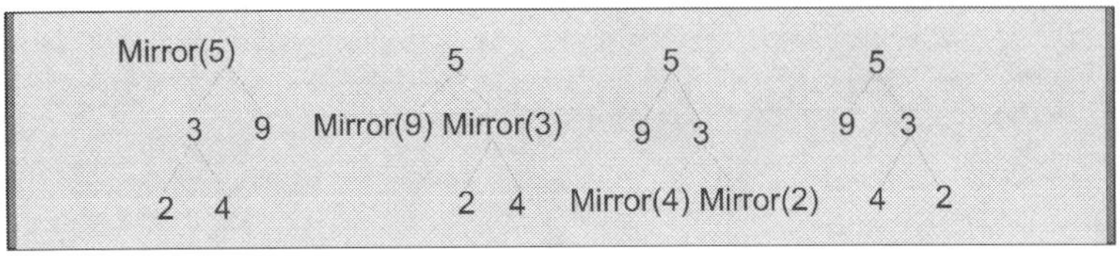

Mirror of leaf nodes are obtained by simply swapping their null pointers and returning the same node. The algorithm is of O (N) since we traverse every node in the tree atleast once.

Input: Pointer to the root node of the tree, which has to be mirror-imaged.

Output: The pointer to the root node of the tree, which is the exact mirror image of the tree supplied earlier.

```
treeptr mirror(treeptr root)
{
    treeptr ltree=NULL,rtree=NULL;
    if (root==NULL) return root;
    if (root->left!=NULL) ltree = mirror(root->left);
```

```
    if (root->right!=NULL) rtree = mirror(root->right);
    root->right=ltree;
    root->left=rtree;
    return(root);
}
```

33. State the algorithm to check if two trees are identical assuming integer data.

To check if two trees are identical (given their root nodes), first check if both the root's data are the same AND again check the same condition for the root's left and right sub-tree. If during the course of comparison if at least any of the pointers do not match, i.e., one node has left sub-tree as null and other does not or vice versa, then we can say they are not-identical. If not then we need to drill deep down till its leaf nodes comparing every node's data. This can be easily achieved by Boolean AND operation where if any condition fails, it returns false and if everything is true then true is returned as result.

The algorithm is of O (N) since we traverse every node in the tree at least once unless the tree is not identical.

Input: Pointers to the root nodes of the two trees, which need to be checked for identicalness.

Output: true—if both the trees are identical, false otherwise.

```
int checkIdentical(treeptr root1, treeptr root2)
{
        if(((root1!=NULL)&&(root2==NULL))
            ||((root2!=NULL)&&(root1==NULL)))
    return(0);
    if ((root1==NULL)&&(root2==NULL)) return(1);
    else return((root1->data==root2->data)&&
                checkIdentical(root1->left,root2->left)&&
                checkIdentical(root1->right,root2->right));
}
```

34. Explain Pre-order Tree Traversal.

In the pre-order tree traversal, first the node is traversed, followed by the node's left sub-tree and finally its right sub-tree (NLR).

Input: Pointer to the root of the tree to be pre-order traversed.

Output: Pre-order traversal of the tree pointed to by root.

```
void preorder(treeptr root)
{
    if (root!=NULL)
    {
        printf("%d",root->data);
        if (root->left!=NULL) preorder(root->left);
        if (root->right!=NULL) preorder(root->right);
    }
}
```

For example

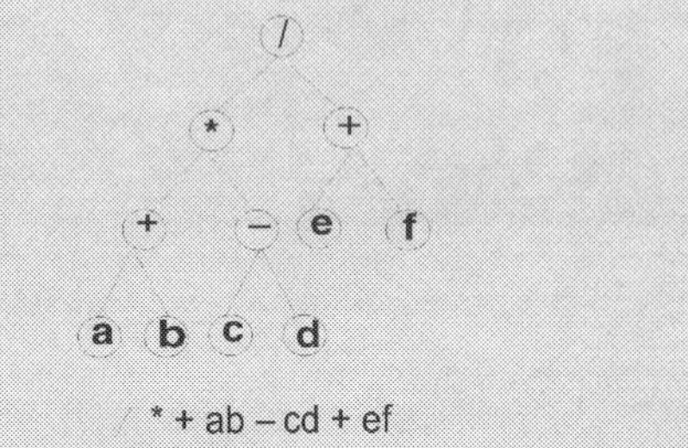

Preorder traversal is used to obtain the prefix form of an expression

35. Explain In-order Tree Traversal.

In the in-order tree traversal, first the node's left sub-tree is traversed, followed by the node and finally the right sub-tree (LNR).

Input: Pointer to the root of the tree to be in-order traversed.

Output: In-order traversal of the tree pointed to by root.

```
void inorder(treeptr root)
{
    if (root!=NULL)
    {
```

```
    if (root->left!=NULL) inorder(root->left);
       printf("%d",root->data);
    if (root->right!=NULL) inorder(root->right);
    }
}
```

For example

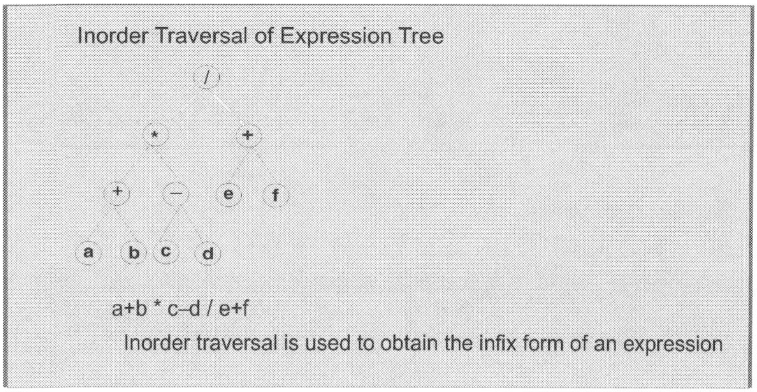

Q 36. Explain Post-order Tree Traversal.

In the post-order tree traversal, first the node's left sub-tree is traversed, followed by the node's right sub-tree and finally the node (LRN).

Input: Pointer to the root of the tree to be post-order traversed.

Output: Post-order traversal of the tree pointed to by root.

```
void postorder(treeptr root)
{
    if (root!=NULL)
    {
       if (root->left!=NULL) postorder(root->left);
       if (root->right!=NULL) postorder(root->right);
       printf("%d",root->data);
    }
}
```

For example

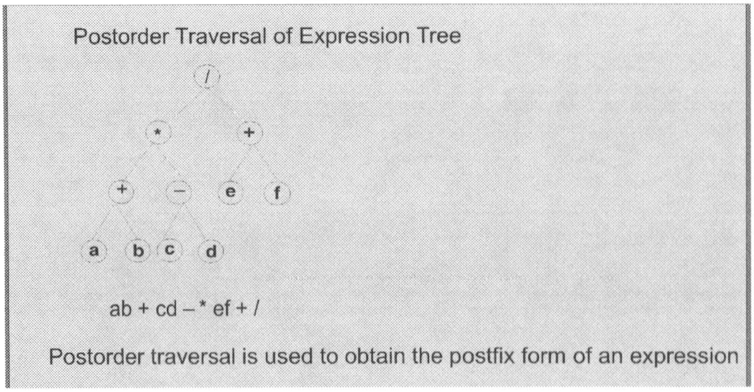

37. Explain the procedure to print tree levelwise.

Tree can be displayed levelwise by using recursion. The tree is printed as it would look like when rotated 90 anti-clockwise. The tree is oriented on the screen with the root at the far left and children thereon to the right.

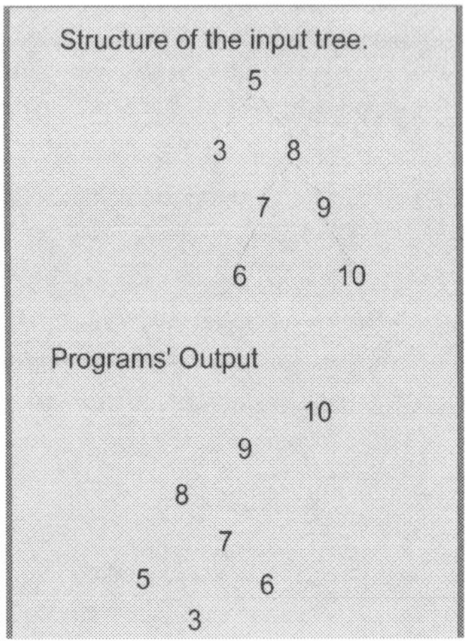

Input: Pointer to the root of the tree to be levelwise traversed.

Output: Levelwise traversal of the tree pointed to by root, but rotated anti-clockwise by 90 degrees.

```
void PrintTree(treeptr root, int depth)
{
```

```
    int i;
    if (root !=NULL)
    {
        PrintTree(root->right, depth+1);
        for(i=0;i<depth*6+4;i++)
            printf(" ");
        printf("%d\n",root->data);
        PrintTree(root->left, depth+1);
    }
}
```

The procedure should be first called PrintTree(root, 0).

38. Discuss the array representation of a binary tree.

Starting the root node's data from index 1 and every node's left child at index 2*n and right child at index 2*n+1, where 'n' stands for root node index.

As an illustration consider the following binary tree:

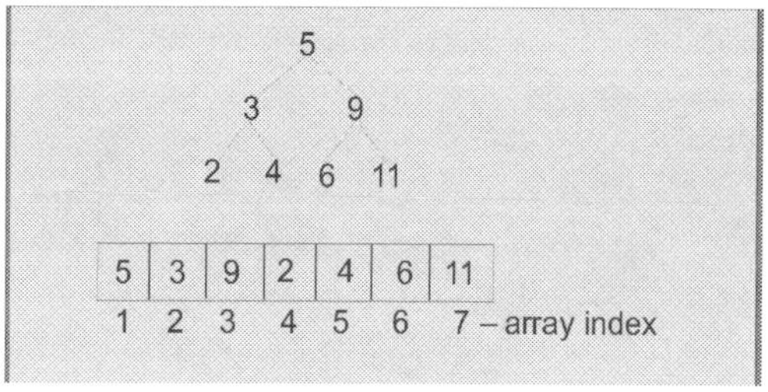

Left child of 9(at index n=3) is the node at index 2*3= array[6] = 6 and right child is the node at index 2*3+1=array[7]=11.

39. What is a binary height balanced tree?

Binary height balanced tree is a binary tree in which for every node the heights of its left sub-tree and its right sub-tree differ by not more than 1, i.e., height(left-sub-tree)height(right-sub-tree) = ±1.

40. How do you represent a ternary tree?

A ternary tree is a tree in which a node can have zero or more child nodes. Ternary nodes can be represented as a tree comprising of nodes, which can be defined as follows:

```
typedef struct node
{
    int data;
    struct node *sptr;/* sibling pointer */
    struct node *cptr;/* child pointer */
}treenode;
```

Consider the representation of the following ternary tree:

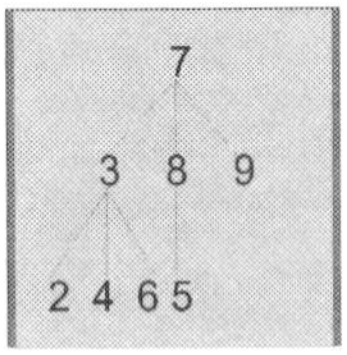

The ternary tree representation shall look like

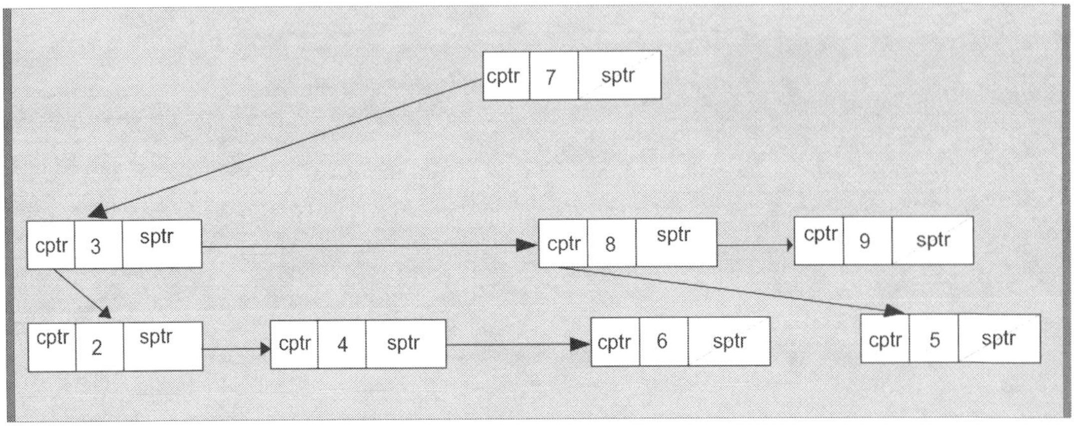

In the above figure, a pointer field with a stroked-out line over it indicates that it is NULL.

The root node has its sibling pointer NULL since there is no other node at the same level and the root's child pointer points to node with data 3. Similarly, this node has its sibling pointer pointing to its sibling node with data 8 and that node in-turn has its sibling pointer pointing to its sibling node with data 9. The node with data 3 has its child pointer pointing to the node with data 2. The node with data 8 has its child pointer pointing to the node with data 5. The node with data 2 has its sibling pointer pointing to the node with data 4, which again has its sibling pointer pointing to its next sibling with data 6. The node with data 5 has both its child and sibling pointer as NULL.

Q 41. Distinguish amongst full, complete and perfect binary trees.

In a full binary tree, each node is either a leaf or internal node with exactly two non-empty children.

In a complete binary tree of height d, every level, except possibly the deepest, is completely filled. At depth d, all nodes must be as far left as possible.

In a perfect binary tree of height n, every internal node has two children and all the leaf nodes are at the same level and there are exactly $2^{n+1}-1$ nodes.

Q 42. How many nodes does a perfect binary tree on n levels have and how many leaves?

A perfect binary tree has $2^{n+1}-1$ nodes and 2^n leaf nodes.

Q 43. What are the red–black trees?

A red–black tree is a binary search tree, which has the following red–black properties:

- Every node is either red or black.
- The root is black—every leaf (NULL) is black.
- If a node is red, then both its children are black.
- All internal nodes have two children.
- Every simple path from a node to a descendant leaf contains the same number of black nodes.

Q 44. What are splay trees?

Splay Trees were invented by Sleator and Tarjan in 1985. A splay tree is a self-adjusting binary search tree. These trees have the wonderful property to adjust optimally to any sequence of tree operations. Every time we access a node of the tree, whether for retrieval, insertion or deletion, we perform radical surgery on the tree, resulting in the newly accessed node becoming the root of the modified tree. This surgery will ensure that nodes that are frequently accessed will never drift too far away from the root whereas inactive nodes will get pushed away farther from the root. The surgery on the tree is done using rotations, also called splaying steps. There are six different splaying steps: Zig Rotation (Right Rotation), Zag Rotation (Left Rotation), Zig-Zag (Zig followed by Zag), Zag-Zig (Zag followed by Zig), Zig-Zig and Zag-Zag.

A sequence of m operations on a tree with initially n leaves takes time $O\ (n \log_n + m \log_n)$

45. What is a Big B-tree?

B-trees were introduced by Bayer and McCreight. They are a special m-ary balanced tree used in databases because their structure allows records to be inserted, deleted and retrieved with guaranteed worst-case performance. An n-node B-tree has height O(log n). The Apple Macintosh HFS filing system uses B-trees to store disk directories. A B-tree satisfies the following properties:

- The root is either a tree leaf or has at least two children.
- Each node (except the root and tree leaves) has between ceil(m/2) and m children, where ceil is the ceiling function.
- Each path from the root to a tree leaf has the same length.

46. What is a B+ tree?

A B+ tree is a variant of B-tree with the following properties:

- A B+ tree of order v consists of a root, internal nodes and leaves.
- The root may be either leaf or an internal node with two or more children.
- Internal nodes contain between v and 2v keys, and a node with k keys has k + 1 pointers (children).
- Leaves are always on the same level and are the only nodes containing data pointers, and are also chained using sequence pointers.

47. What are threaded binary trees?

A Threaded Binary Tree is a binary tree in which every node that does not have a right child has a link (called, a thread) to its INORDER successor. By doing this threading, we avoid the recursive method of traversing a tree, which makes use of stacks and consumes a lot of memory and time.

48. What is a binary search tree? Explain its various operations.

A binary search tree is a binary tree with the following properties:

- The data stored at each node has a distinguished key, which is unique in the tree and belongs to a total order. (That is, for any two non-equal keys, x,y either $x < y$ or $y < x$.)
- The key of any node is greater than all keys occurring in its left sub-tree and less than all keys occurring in its right sub-tree.

One property of a binary search tree is that an in-order traversal walks over the nodes in order of their keys (thus, the name in-order). Data maintained in a binary search tree is sorted by the key value in each of its node.

The operations that can be performed on a binary search tree (BST) are as follows:

- Search—look up an item in the BST by its key
- Insert—add an item and its key to the BST
- Remove—delete an item/key from the BST by its key

BST Search Algorithm

Input: Pointer to the root of the BST and key to be searched.

Output: Pointer to the node if item is found else NULL if item is not found.

- if this node is NULL then return NULL
- if this node's key matches the search key then return pointer to this node
- if this node's key is less than the search key then recursively search the right sub-tree
- recursively search the left sub-tree

```
/* assume item itself is the key here */
treeptr search( treeptr root, int key)
{
   /* not found just return NULL */
   if (root==NULL) return root;
   if (root->data == key) return (root);
   if (root->data > key) return(search(root->left,key));
   if (root->data < key) return(search(root->right,key));
}
```

BST Insertion Algorithm

The insertion of a key, item pair is performed by searching for the key and inserting it as either left child or right child, respectively based on whether we hit NULL while accessing the left sub-tree or while accessing the right sub-tree during the course of the recursion as explained in the steps below.

Input: Pointer to the root of the BST and (key,item) to be inserted into the BST.

Output: The root of the BST, rendered with the item inserted appropriately without breaking the BST's property.

- If this node is NULL then allocate a new node, copy the key, item and return this node (This is for empty tree).

- If this node's key is less than the search key then recursively search the right sub-tree, if right sub-tree is NULL then allocate a new node, copy the key, item and make this node as its right child.
- Recursively search the left sub-tree, if left sub-tree is NULL then allocate a new node, copy the key, item and make this node as its left child.
- The insert algorithm assumes there is no node in the tree with the same key that is being inserted now.

```
/* assume item itself is the key here */
treeptr insert( treeptr root, int key)
{
   treeptr parent, newnode;
   if (root==NULL)
   {
      root = (treeptr) malloc(sizeof(treenode));
      root->data = key;
      root->left=root->right=NULL;
      return root;
   }
   parent = ParentSearch(root, key);
   newnode = (treeptr) malloc(sizeof(treenode));
   newnode->data = key;
   newnode->left=newnode->right=NULL;
   if (parent->data > newnode->data) parent->left=newnode;
   else parent->right=newnode;
   return root;
}

treeptr ParentSearch(treeptr root, int key)
{
   if ((root->data < key) && (root->right == NULL))
      return(root);
   if ((root->data < key) && (root->right != NULL))
      return(ParentSearch(root->right,key));
   if ((root->data > key) && (root->left == NULL))
      return(root);
```

```
    if ((root->data > key) && (root->left != NULL))
        return(ParentSearch(root->left,key));
}
```

BST Deletion Algorithm

Input: Pointer to the root of the BST and key to be deleted from the BST.

Output: The root of the BST, rendered with the item deleted appropriately without breaking the BST's property.

Deletion again uses the BST search to first locate the item. Then three cases may arise for deletion:

- Deleting a leaf -> simply remove it:

  For example, consider the deletion of 17 happens as below

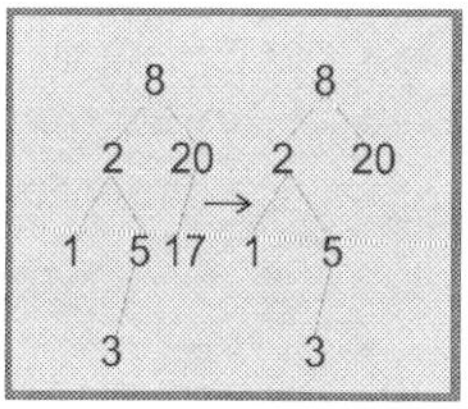

- Deleting a node with one child -> remove it and move its child (the sub-tree rooted at its child) up:

  For example, consider the deletion of 20 happens as below

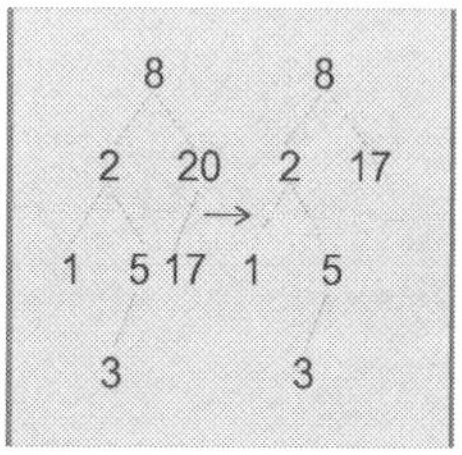

- Deleting a node with two children ->

  (a) copy the (key, item) of its in-order predecessor and remove its in-order predecessor. For example consider the deletion of 3 happens as below

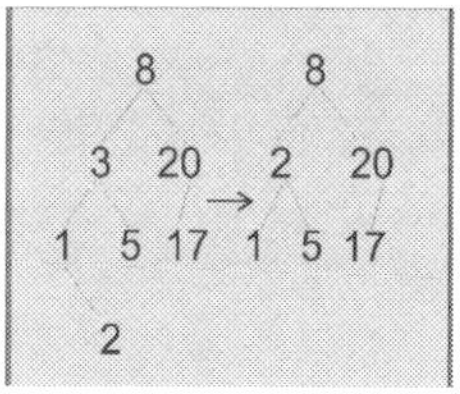

(b) copy the (key, item) of its in-order successor and remove its in-order successor.

For example, consider the deletion of 2 happens as below

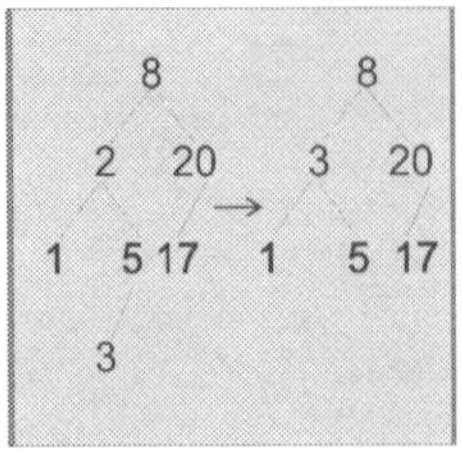

Q 49. AVL Trees operations—insert, delete, search.

AVL trees are height-balanced binary search trees, in which every node has the property that its height of the left and right sub-trees, differ in height by at most 1. The advantage of AVL trees over normal BSTs are, AVL trees store the tree nodes with minimum number of NULL pointers, thus saving memory space. In AVL trees, the access for any node is of the order of Log N where N is the total number of nodes in the tree.

The operations that can be performed on an AVL tree are as follows:

- Search—look up an item in the AVL tree by its key
- Insert—add an item and its key to the AVL tree
- Remove—delete an item/key from the AVL by its key

AVL Search Algorithm

The AVL tree search algorithm is exactly the same as in for the BST, the only difference being that even the worst case order of search algorithm in an AVL tree being Log N, where N is the total number of nodes in the AVL tree.

AVL Insertion Algorithm

AVL insertion is performed by initially adding the new node into the AVL tree as per the BST insertion algorithm and following it up with an act of height-balancing of the tree, since the insertion could have unbalanced the tree. Height-balancing of the tree is performed by means of rotations to balance the trees without losing their BST property. Sometimes the trees may require a couple of AVL rotations called a double rotation otherwise single rotations suffice to balance the tree. These rotations are performed around the Pivot node. There are two types of single AVL rotations:

- LL Rotation
- RR Rotation

Double rotations are of two types:

- ➢ LR Rotation
- ➢ RL Rotation

LL rotation

The figure below portrays the state of the AVL tree before and after the insertion of the key '1' in the AVL tree.

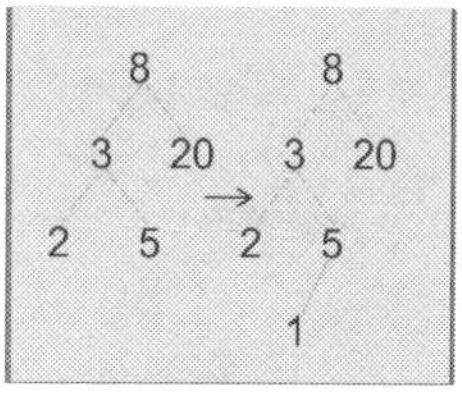

The above insertion unbalances the AVL tree at the node 8. Performing a LL rotation centered at the pivot node 8 balances the tree as shown below.

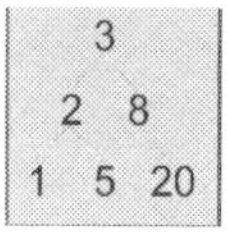

RR rotation

RR rotation in an AVL tree is performed when an insert happens in a way symmetric to the LL rotation as illustrated using the figure below. Consider the insertion of the key '22' into the AVL tree.

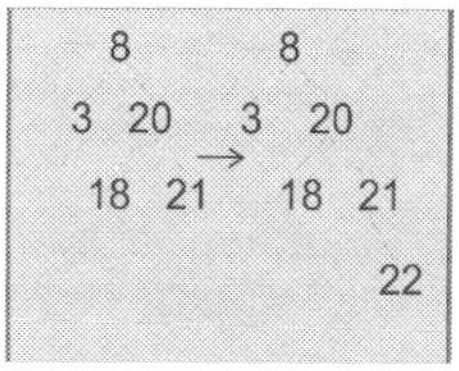

The above insertion unbalances the AVL tree at the node 8. Performing a RR rotation centered at the pivot node 8 balances the tree as shown below.

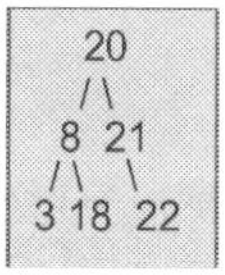

LR rotation

The figure below portrays the state of the AVL tree before and after the insertion of the key '7' in the AVL tree.

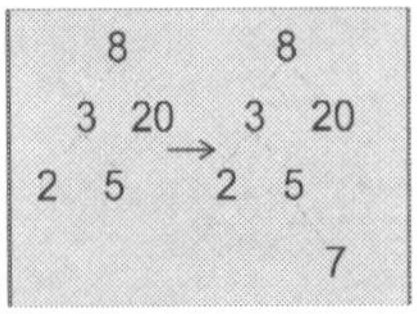

The above insertion unbalances the AVL tree at the node 8. Performing a LR rotation centered at the pivot node 8 balances the tree as shown below.

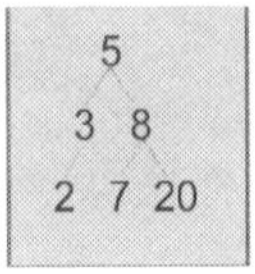

RL rotation

RL rotation in an AVL tree is performed when an insert happens in a way symmetric to the LR rotation as illustrated using the figure below. The figure below portrays the state of the AVL tree before and after the insertion of the key '13' in the AVL tree.

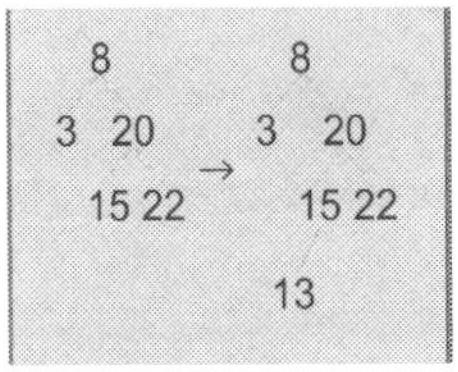

The above insertion unbalances the AVL tree at the node 8. Performing a LR rotation centered at the pivot node 8 balances the tree as shown below.

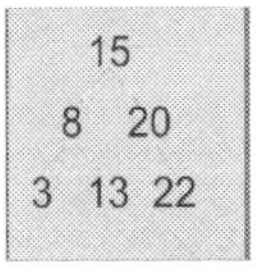

AVL Deletion Algorithm

AVL deletion is performed by initially deleting the node from the AVL tree as per the BST deletion algorithm and following it up with an act of height-balancing of the tree, since the deletion could have unbalanced the tree. The height-balancing is done as explained earlier.

SORTING AND SEARCHING

Q 50. Explain linear search in a sorted array.

Linear search in an array sorted in ascending order for any key is done until an element with a value greater than the key is reached.

The algorithm is better than O (N) since we may not always traverse every element of the array while searching.

Input: Array of sorted integers and its size and the key to be searched.

Output: The location of the key in the array if found otherwise –1.

```
int search(int a[],int key,int sizea)
{
   int i=0,loc=-1;
   while(i<sizea && a[i]<=key)
   {
      if (a[i]==key) loc=i;
      i++;
   }
   return(loc);
}
```

Q 51. Explain the binary search algorithm.

The basic idea of binary search is to compare the value of the element at the center of the sorted array bounded by lower and upper limits with that of the key element, based on which the array to be searched keeps shrinking in its size by half. The key is recursively searched in the resultant shrunken array. The array keeps shrinking until either the key is found or the bounds cross over each other, which happens while searching for a non-existing element.

The algorithm is of O (log N) since the array to be searched gets reduced to half each time.

Input: Array of sorted integers and its size and the key to be searched.

Output: The location of the key in the array if found otherwise –1.

```
int search(int a[],int key,int lower,int upper)
{
   int loc=0,mid=(lower+upper)/2;
```

```
    if (lower>upper) return(-1);
    if (a[mid]==key) return(loc)
    else
    {
        if (a[mid]<key) return(search(a,key,mid+1,upper));
        else return(search(a,key,lower,mid-1));
    }
}
```

52. Explain the selection sort algorithm and state its time complexity.

```
void sort(int *arr,int size)
{
    int i,j,temp;for(i=0;i<size-1;i++)
    {
        for(j=i+1;j<size;j++)
        {
            if (arr[i]>arr[j])
            {
                temp=arr[i];
                arr[i]=arr[j];
                arr[j]=temp;
            }
        }
    }
}
```

Time complexity of the algorithm is O (n^2) where n is the size of the array.

53. Explain the bubble sort algorithm and state its time complexity.

```
void sort(int *arr,int size)
{
    int i,j,temp;
    for(i=0;i<size-1;i++)
    {
```

```
        for(j=0;j<size-i-1;j++)
        {
            if (arr[j]>arr[j+1])
            {
                temp=arr[j];
                arr[j]=arr[j+1];
                arr[j+1]=temp;
            }
        }
    }
}
```

Time complexity of the algorithm is O (n^2) where n is the size of the array.

Q 54. Explain the insertion sort algorithm and state its time complexity.

```
void sort(int *arr,int size)
{
    int i,j,temp;

    for(i=1;i<size;i++)
    {
        for(j=i;j>0 &&arr[j]<arr[j-1];j–)
        {
            if (arr[j]<arr[j-1])
            {
                temp=arr[j];
                arr[j]=arr[j-1];
                arr[j-1]=temp;
            }
        }
    }
}
```

Time complexity of the algorithm is O (n^2) where n is the size of the array.

55. Explain the quick sort algorithm and state its time complexity.

```
void q_sort(int *arr,int lower,int upper)
{
   int i, left = lower, right = upper, pivot, temp;
   if (lower>upper) return;
   pivot = arr[left];
   while (left <= right)
   {
   while ((arr[right] > pivot))
         right–;
   while ((arr[left] < pivot))
         left++;
   if (left > right) break;
         temp = arr[left];
         arr[left] = arr[right];
         arr[right] = temp;
         left++;
         right–;
   }
   q_sort(arr, lower, right);
   q_sort(arr, left, upper);
}
```

The average time complexity of the algorithm is O (N log N) where n is the size of the array and worst case time complexity is $O(N^2)$.

56. Explain the shell sort algorithm and state its time complexity.

```
void shellSort(int numbers[], int array_size)
{
   int i, j, increment, temp;
   increment = array_size/2;
   while (increment > 0)
   {
      for (i=0; i < array_size; i++)
```

```
        {
           j = i;
           temp = numbers[i];
           while ((j >= increment) && (numbers[j-increment] >
           temp))
           {
              numbers[j] = numbers[j - increment];
              j = j - increment;
           }
           numbers[j] = temp;
        }
        if (increment/2 != 0)
           increment = increment/2;
        else if (increment == 1)
           increment = 0;
        else
           increment = 1;
     }
}
```

Time complexity of the algorithm is O (N^2) where n is the size of the array. The shell sort is by far the fastest of the N^2 class of sorting algorithms. It's more than 5 times faster than the bubble sort and a little over twice as fast as the insertion sort, itsclosest competitor. Its average time complexity approaches O(N).

Q 57. State the merge sort principle and its time complexity.

Merge sort algorithm is an external sort algorithm that needs extra memory or storage space. It is used for sorting data in huge files. The algorithm addresses the problem by divide-and-conquer methodology. The data is broken down recursively into smaller chunks until left with 2 data elements where sorting becomes just a comparison of two elements generating a sorted array with two elements. Two such sorted arrays are merged by using the earlier discussed algorithm for merging two sorted arrays. Again two such sorted arrays of four elements are merged again in the same way and so on and so forth until the original array is completely sorted. The time complexity of merge sort is N Log N.

58. Explain the Singly linked list search procedure.

The following code snippet searches for a key in the entire linked list:

Input: Pointer to the head of the linked list and the item to be searched.

Output: Returns the pointer to the node, which contains the key if found, NULL otherwise.

```
link *search(link *head, int item)
{
    link *temp=head;
    while(temp!=NULL)
    {
        if (temp->data==item) return(temp);
        temp=temp->next;
    }
    return(NULL);
}
```

59. Explain the doubly linked list search procedure.

This is not any different from singly linked list search.

Input: Pointer to the head of the linked list and the item to be searched.

Output: Returns the pointer to the node, which contains the key if found, NULL otherwise.

```
dlink *search(dlink *head, int item)
{
    dlink *temp=head;
    while(temp!=NULL)
    {
        if (temp->data==item) return(temp);
        temp=temp->next;
    }
    return(NULL);
}
```

60. Explain a method to sort a singly linked list.

Bubble sort must be used to sort singly linked list.

Input: Pointer to the head of the linked list, which has to be sorted.

Output: Pointer to the head of the sorted linked list.

```
link *sort(link *head, int n)
{
   int i,j,swap;
   link *temp1;
   for(i=0;i<n-1;i++)
   {
   temp1=head;
   for(j=0;j<n-i-1;j++)
   {
      if (temp1->data > temp1->next->data)
      {
         swap=temp1->data;
         temp1->data = temp1->next->data;
         temp1->data=swap;
      }
      temp1=temp1->next;
   }
  }
  return head;
}
```

61. Write an algorithm to derive the lowest common ancestor (LCA) of two nodes in a Binary Search Tree. For example, node 16 is the LCA of nodes 15 and 18. Assume the nodes are present in the tree and are not directly related like say 2, 4, 6 and 12.

Input: Pointer to the head of the Binary Search tree and two integers, a and b.

Output: The integer data stored in the LCA node.

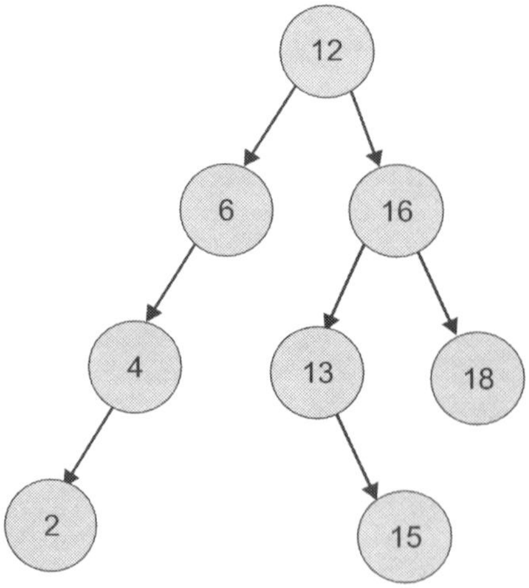


```
int LCA(link *head, int a , int b)
{
    // if we reach NULL node or the node that has a or b then return
failure.
    if ((head == NULL) || (head->data == a) || (head->data == b))
        return -1;
    if ((a <=  head->data) && (b > head->data)) {
        // This is their LCA
        return(head->data);
    }
    if ((b <= head->data) && (a > head->data)) {
        // This is their LCA
        return(head->data);
    }
    if ((a <= head->data) && (b <= head->data)) {
        // LCA is in their left sub-tree
        return(LCA(head->left, a, b));
    }
    if ((a > head->data) && (b > head->data)) {
        // LCA is in their right sub-tree
        return(LCA(head->right, a, b));
    }
}
```

62. Write a simple string pattern matching algorithm.

Input: The text and string pattern that needs to be searched within text.

Output: The first matching index in the string text where the pattern is found. If it is not found then –1 is returned.

```
int is_pattern_found(char *text, char *pattern) {
   int len1, len2, i=0, j, count, start;

   len1 = strlen(text);
   len2 = strlen(pattern);
   // The length of the pattern cannot be larger than the text.
   if (len1 < len2) return(-1);
   while(i<len1) {
       count = 0;
       // Let us start at index i
       start = i;
       for(j=0;j<len2;j++) {
           if (text[start] == pattern[j]) {
               /* We have a match hence expand the window to see if
                * there is a complete match
                */
               start++;
               count++;
           } else {
               break;
           }
       }
       // We have a complete match
       if (count == len2) return(i);
       i++;
   }
   // We have reached the end of text without a complete match.
   return(-1);
}
```

Q 63. Write a program to print the cyclic permutations of an input string. For example, if 'abcd' is input then output should be abcd, bcda, cdab, dabc.

Input: The pointer to the string, which needs to be cyclically rotated with no repeating characters.

Output: The cyclic permutations of the input string.

```
void printCyclic(char *input)
{
        int size, i;
        char *doubleinput, *temp;

        size = strlen(input);
        doubleinput = malloc(size * 2+1); // Allocate one byte extra
         for '\0'
        temp = malloc(size+1);
        if (doubleinput == NULL || temp == NULL) {
          printf("\nmalloc failure");
          return;
       }
        strcat(doubleinput, input);
        strcat(doubleinput, input);
        for(i=0; i<size; i++) {
                    // snprintf comes in handy, but it creates a null
                    terminated string.
                snprintf(temp, size+1, "%s", &doubleinput[i]);
                printf("%s\n", temp);
        }
}
```

64. An array is supposed to contain sorted consecutive integers, but one number is missing in the array. Devise an efficient algorithm to find the missing integer.

An easy but inefficient method would be to linearly keep traversing the sorted array and bail out as soon as you find two numbers out of sequence. But it would perform at order N. Let us devise a better performing algorithm.

Input: A sorted array of consecutive integers with one number missing in the middle, with the array lower and upper bounds.

Output: The missing integer

```
int find_missing(int *arr, int lower, int upper) {
    int mid;
    while(lower<upper) {
        mid=(lower+upper)/2;
        if (arr[mid]==(arr[lower]+mid-lower)) {
            /* Boundary check before dividing the array */
            if ((arr[mid+1] - arr[mid]!=1)) return(arr[mid]+1);
            lower=mid+1;
        } else {
            upper=mid;
        }
    }
    if (lower==upper) return arr[lower-1]+1;
}
```

65. Write the algorithm to free a binary tree.

Let us solve this problem recursively. There are three simple steps in the process as follows:

- Free the left sub-tree.
- Free the right sub-tree.
- Free the current root node.

We have to check if the root node is NULL and terminate the recursion there.

Input: Pointer to the root node.

Output: The tree shall be freed up in its entirety.

```
void free_binary_tree(void *root) {
    if (root) {
        free_binary_root(root->left);
        free_binary_root(root->right);
        free(root);
    }
}
```

SOCKET PROGRAMMING

66. Define Socket.

'Socket' is primarily a concept used in the Transport Layer. It is a mechanism for creating a connection between processes. It is one end of an inter-process communication channel.

It is a programming interface and is bidirectional. Each process has to establish its socket. Two processes can communicate with each other only if their sockets are of the same type and in the same domain.

The socket library function socket() creates a communications end-point or socket and returns a file descriptor with which to access that socket. The socket associates with it a socket address, which consists of a port number and the local host's network address.

67. What are the different socket types?

There are various socket types available as follows:

- Datagram sockets or connectionless sockets, which use User Datagram Protocol (UDP).
- Stream sockets or connection-oriented sockets, which use Transmission Control Protocol (TCP) or Stream Control Transmission Protocol (SCTP).
- Raw sockets (or Raw IP sockets), where the transport layer is bypassed. It is typically available in routers and other network equipment. Internet Control Message Protocol (ICMP), and Open Shortest Path First (OSPF) are two application examples.

68. What are the IP addresses assigned to systems on a private internet?

IP addresses allocation for private networks is defined in RFC 1918. These addresses are not assigned to any organization and do not appear on the internet.

IANA has reserved the following three blocks of IP address space for private networks.

ClassA 10.0.0.0 to 10.255.255.255

Class B 172.16.0.0 to 172.31.255.255

Class C 192.168.0.0 to 192.168.255.255

Class A set of IP addresses are mostly used since it has a large pool of available IP addresses.

69. Define the following socket utility functions: ntohs/ntohl, htons/htonl.

This family of functions converts between network byte order and host byte order. When the two byte orders are different, the endian-ness of the data is changed.

ntohs/ntohl – The function ntohs converts the unsigned short integer from network byte order to host byte order. Similarly, the function ntohl converts the unsigned long integer from network byte order to host byte order.

htons/htonl – The function htons converts the unsigned short integer from host byte order to network byte order. Similarly, the function htonl converts the unsigned long integer from host byte order to network byte order.

70. Define inet_ntoa() , inet_aton() functions.

These routines help in manipulating internet addresses. inet_ntoa() function translates the internet host address given in network byte order to a string in numbers-and-dots notation. inet_aton() function translates the internet host address from standard numbers-and-dots notation into binary data in network byte order.

71. What is the port number used for telnet and ftp applications?

In UNIX the first 1024 ports for both protocols are called 'well known ports'. On UNIX, the configuration file /etc/services lists port numbers against named services. Well-known ports are assigned by IANA. Telnet application is assigned port 23 and ftp is assigned port 20 for data and port 21 for control path. A complete list of these assignments and more information can be found in RFC 1700.

72. Write a sample TCP Client/Server program.

An Iterative server would use the following primary socket calls:

socket() – creates a new socket and returns its descriptor

bind() – Associates a socket with a port and address

listen – establishes queue for connection requests

accept() – accepts a connection request

recv/send() – Receive and/or send data from/to a socket descriptor. The program can do anything else depending on the requirement of the application. A concurrent server would generally use fork() and create a child process at this point.

close() – "one-way" close of a socket descriptor.

The Remote client will use the following sequence of socket calls:

```
socket()
connect()
recv()/send()
close()
```

```
/************************* iter_server.c *************/
/************************* START *************************/

#include <stdio.h>
#include <stdlib.h>
#include <sys/socket.h>
#include <netinet/in.h>
#define SERVERPORT 10000

/* Run with a number of incoming connection as argument */
int main(int argc, char *argv[])
{
  int i, lth, num_of_conn, rc;
  int listen_sockfd, accept_sockfd;
  /* Buffer for data */
  char buffer[200];
```

```
  struct sockaddr_in addr;

  /* If a command line argument was specified, use it to control the
number of incoming connections */
  if(argc >= 2) {
   num_of_conn = atoi(argv[1]);
  } else {
   num_of_conn = 1;
  }

  /* Create an AF_INET stream socket to receive */
  /* incoming connections on */
  listen_sockfd = socket(AF_INET, SOCK_STREAM, 0);
  if(listen_sockfd < 0) {
    perror("Iter_server - socket() error");
    exit(-1);
  }

  /* Bind the socket */
  memset(&addr, 0, sizeof(addr));
  addr.sin_family = AF_INET;
  addr.sin_addr.s_addr = htonl(INADDR_ANY);
  addr.sin_port = htons(SERVERPORT);
      rc   =   bind(listen_sockfd,   (struct   sockaddr   *)&addr,
sizeof(addr));
  if(rc < 0) {
    perror("Iter_server - bind() error");
    close(listen_sockfd);
    exit(-1);
  }

  /* Set the listen backlog */
  rc = listen(listen_sockfd, 5);
  if(rc < 0) {
    perror("Iter_server - listen() error");
```

```
    close(listen_sockfd);
    exit(-1);
  }

  /* Inform the user that the server is ready */
  printf("The Iterative Server is ready!\n");
  /* Go through the below loop once for each connection */
  for(i=0; i < num_of_conn; i++)
  {
    /* Wait for an incoming connection */
    accept_sockfd = accept(listen_sockfd, NULL, NULL);
    if(accept_sockfd < 0)
    {
      perror("Iter_server - accept() error");
      close(listen_sockfd);
      exit(-1);
    }

    /* Receive a message from the client */
    rc = recv(accept_sockfd, buffer, sizeof(buffer), 0);
    if(rc <= 0) {
      perror("Iter_server - recv() error");
      close(listen_sockfd);
      close(accept_sockfd);
      exit(-1);
    }

    /* Echo the data back to the client */
    lth = rc;
    rc = send(accept_sockfd, buffer, lth, 0);
    if(rc <= 0) {
      perror("Iter_server - send() error");
      close(listen_sockfd);
      close(accept_sockfd);
      exit(-1);
```

```
    }

    /* Close the incoming connection */
    close(accept_sockfd);
  }
  /* Close the listen socket */
  close(listen_sockfd);

  return(0);
}

/************************                          iter_server.c
************************/
/************************ END************************/

/************************                          iter_client.c
************************/
/************************ START ************************/

#include <stdio.h>
#include <stdlib.h>
#include <sys/socket.h>
#include <netinet/in.h>
/* Our server port as in the previous program */
#define SERVERPORT 10000

main (int argc, char *argv[])
{
  int lth, rc;
  int sockfd;
  char send_buffer[200];
  char recv_buffer[200];
  struct sockaddr_in addr;

  if(argc !=2) {
```

```
      printf("Usage: %s <Server_name or Server_IP_address>\n",
argv[0]);
    exit (-1);
  }
  /* Create an AF_INET stream socket */
  sockfd = socket(AF_INET, SOCK_STREAM, 0);
  if(sockfd < 0) {
    perror("iter_client - socket() error");
    exit(-1);
  }

  /* Initialize the socket address structure */
  memset(&addr, 0, sizeof(addr));
  addr.sin_family = AF_INET;
  addr.sin_addr.s_addr = htonl(INADDR_ANY);
  addr.sin_port = htons(SERVERPORT);
  /* Connect to the server */
   rc = connect(sockfd, (struct sockaddr *)&addr, sizeof(struct
sockaddr_in));
  if(rc < 0) {
    perror("iter_client - connect() error");
    close(sockfd);
    exit(-1);
  }

  /* Enter data buffer that is to be sent */
  gets(send_buffer);

  /* Send data buffer to the worker job */
  lth = send(sockfd, send_buffer, strlen(send_buffer) + 1, 0);
  if(lth != strlen(send_buffer) + 1)
  {
    perror("iter_client - send() error");
    close(sockfd);
    exit(-1);
```

```
  }

  /* Receive data buffer from the worker job */
  lth = recv(sockfd, recv_buffer, sizeof(recv_buffer), 0);
  if(lth != strlen(send_buffer) + 1)
  {
    perror("iter_client - recv() error");
    close(sockfd);
    exit(-1);
  }

  /* Close the socket */
  close(sockfd);

  return(0);
}

/*************************                              iter_client.c
************************/
/************************* END*************************/
```

73. How can we manipulate socket characteristics?

Socket characteristics can be managed/controlled with functions get/setsockopt, fcntl, ioctl.

74. What is IPSec?

IPSec stands for IP Security. It is a protocol suite for securing IP communications by authenticating and encrypting each IP packet of a data stream. The base specifications are defined in RFC's 1825, 1826 and 1827. It includes protocols for authentication between endpoints at the beginning of the session and negotiation of the cryptographic keys to be used during the session.

THINKER'S CHOICE

75. Explain how, in a singly linked list, you can get to (n-k)th node, where (k<n), in a single traversal using recursion.

76. Explain another procedure to print tree level wise (Hint: use a queue).

77. **Given an array of integers, move all the zeroes to the bottom of the array without using extra storage space.**

78. **Explain some mechanisms to prevent or handle collision in hashing.**

79. **What is the Huffman algorithm and how is the Huffman tree formed?**

80. **What is the traveling salesman problem and how can one solve it?**

81. **What are the various graph shortest path algorithm?**

82. **Explain an algorithm which counts the number of nodes in the input binary tree.**

83. **State the algorithm for BST deletion.**

84. **Discuss a sparse matrix representation, capable of performing matrix operations.**

85. **Explain the TCP handshake mechanism.**

86. **Which IP address will probably be used for an organization having a network of between 1500 and 2000 computers?**

87. **If a person sitting at an Ethernet-connected PC opens a browser and types "http://www.tatamcgrawhill.com/" in the address bar and hits enter. Explain the first packet to appear on the Ethernet and the various events that occur before the page opens on the PC.**

REFERENCES

1. Alfred V. Aho, John E. Hopcroft and Jeffrey Ullman, *Design and Analysis of Computer Algorithms*, Addison Wesley, 1st edition, Pearson Education India.
2. Ellis Horowitz, Sartaj Sahni, *Fundamentals of Data Structures in C*, 2nd edition, Silicon Press.
3. J. P. Tremblay, *An Introduction to Data Structures with Applications*, 2nd edition, Tata Mc-Graw-Hill.
4. Langsam, Augeustein, Tanenbaum, *Data Structures Using C and C++*, 2nd edition, Prentice Hall India.

3

Operating Systems

Introduction

It is necessary for each and every software professional to know at least the elementary concepts of an Operating System (OS). The OS acts as the interface between the application software as well as the hardware. However, for a computer science graduate, an in-depth understanding of OS is a mandatory pre-requisite. This chapter covers the frequently asked interview questions (FAQs) on the OS fundamentals.

GENERAL CONCEPTS

Q 1. What is an operating system?

An operating system (OS) is a collection of software programs. It mainly controls the allocation and usage of hardware resources, such as memory, central processing unit (CPU) time, hard disk space and peripheral devices (like speakers or a mouse). All application programs use the OS to gain access to these hardware resources as and when they are needed. The OS is the first program loaded into the computer as it boots, and it remains in memory at all times thereafter. DOS, OS/2, Win 9x&2000, Unix, HP-UX and Sun-Solaris are some popular operating systems.

In simpler terms, an OS is a master control program that runs the computer. It provides the user interface and routines that let the user load and run software.

Q 2. What are the main services or functions of an operating system?

The main OS services or functions are as follows:

- Process Management
- Memory Management

- Storage/File System Management
- Input/Output Management

3. Name a few operating systems available (commonly encountered).

A few operating systems available commonly encountered are as follows:

- PC–MS/DOS, MS/Windows 3.11, Windows 98, Windows 2000, Windows NT, Windows ME, Windows XP
- UNIX–LINUX, Sun Solaris, AIX, HP/UX
- Apple Mackintosh–OS/X Mobile Operating System–PalmOS, MS Windows Mobile 2003 (Pocket PC 2003)
- Mainframe by IBM–MVS, VM/CMS, MVS/ESA, OS/390
- Embedded processor O/S–device-specific, depending on application, such as printer, digital camera, computer game consoles and intelligent home appliances.

4. What is a kernel?

The part of the OS, which handles all the details of sharing resources and device handling, is the **kernel (core OS)**. The kernel is not something, which can be used directly. The kernel services can be accessed through system calls. A user interface or command line interface (CLI) allows users to log onto the machine and manipulate files, compile programs and execute them using simple commands. Since this is a layer of software that wraps the kernel, it is called a **shell** around the kernel.

5. What is a command interpreter?

Command interpreter is a program that interprets the command input, interactively with the keyboard, or through a command batch file. It is used to enable the user to interact with the OS to trigger the corresponding system programs or to execute some user applications. The command interpreter can be part of the operating system kernel, such as in the case in MS/DOS.

Other names for command interpreter are control card interpreter, command line interpreter, console command processor and shell (UNIX shell).

PROCESS MANAGEMENT

Process Management is an integral part of any operating system. A process uses CPU and memory to accomplish tasks. Multiprocessing support adds to OS complexity. In multiprocessing systems, the OS supports mechanisms of CPU scheduling and inter process communication.

6. What is a Process?

A **process** is a running program, a program under execution. It is an active entity on a machine. A process is also referred to as 'job' on batch systems and 'task' on time-sharing systems. A process has a context and a state as well.

7. What are the basic functions of process management?

The important process management functions of an OS are as follows:

- Creation and deletion of both user and system processes
- Suspension and resumption of processes
- CPU scheduling (and process accounting)
- Process synchronization
- Process communication

8. What is the Process Control Block (PCB)? What information is stored in the PCB?

Process Control Block (PCB) is a structure in the operating system representing a process. It stores important internal data, such as Process ID, Process state, CPU registers content (program counter), memory information, pointers to list of resources, I/O information and accounting information. Process Control blocks are changed during process creation, execution, suspension/resumption or deletion. PCBs are accessed and/or modified by most OS utilities, including those involved with memory, scheduling, performance monitoring and I/O resource access.

9. What is an interrupt?

An **interrupt** is a signal from a device, which typically results in a context switch. Asynchronous events are signaled to the processor via interrupts. An interrupt handler or interrupt service routine is written to handle the interrupts. A list or table giving the starting addresses of each Interrupt Service Routines (ISRs) is maintained in an interrupt vector. Examples of typical interrupts are timer interrupts, disk interrupts, power-off interrupts and traps.

10. What is a zombie process?

Zombies are processes that are dead but have not been removed from the process table. Zombies are created when a parent process terminates without waiting for the child process to complete its execution. The child process after termination exists as a zombie in the system.

11. What is a daemon?

Daemon stands for **Disk and Execution Monitor**. In Unix, the names of daemons conventionally end in "d". Some examples include inetd, httpd, nfsd, sshd, named and lpd. They are background processes, often started immediately after booting and terminate only when the system is shut down.

12. What does context-switching mean?

Associated with each process is a context. It encompasses all the information that completely describes the process's current state of execution (e.g., the contents of the CPU registers, the program counter, the flags, etc.).

Context switching is the process during which the operating system saves the context of the currently running process and restores the context of the next ready process to be run, which is decided by certain scheduling policies. Context switching is an essential feature of a multitasking operating system.

13. What are the different IPC mechanisms?

IPC (Inter Process Communication) provides flexible, efficient message passing and communication mechanisms between processes.

The various IPC mechanisms available are as follows:

- Sockets

  Processes connect using TCP/IP or UDP sockets and exchange data over the sockets.
- Pipes

  A pipe is used for one-way communication of a stream of bytes.
- Shared memory

  Shared memory is when a single block of memory in the address space is shared by two or more processes. If one process makes a change to this memory then it is visible for all the processes accessing the memory.
- Signals

  Signals are one of the oldest inter-process communication methods used by Unix systems. They are used to signal asynchronous events to one or more processes.
- Message Queues

  Message queues allow one or more processes to write messages, which will be read by one or more reading processes.

14. What is a pipe?

A **Pipe** is an IPC mechanism. It can be used for a one-way communication between two related processes. The processes should be related (i.e., one has to be the ancestor of the other). The system called `pipe` is used for this purpose. It takes an argument (of an array of 2 integers) that will be used to save the two file descriptors (one for reading and the other for writing) used to access the pipe.

```
int pipefds[2];
pipe(pipefds);
```

These two file descriptors can be used for block I/O as shown in the following:

```
write(pipefds[1], buffer, SIZE);
read(pipefds[0], buffer, SIZE);
```

A single process would probably not use a pipe. They are used when two processes wish to communicate in a one-way fashion. A process creates a child process using `fork` function call. A pipe opened before the `fork` gets shared between the two processes.

For predictable behavior, one of the processes must close its read end and the other must close its write end. Then it becomes a simple pipeline, which can be used for communicating.

15. What is a Named pipe? What is a FIFO?

One limitation of anonymous pipes (explained earlier) is that only processes 'related' to the process that created the pipe may communicate using them. If we want two unrelated processes to communicate via pipes, we need to use named pipes. A **named pipe** (also called a named FIFO, or just FIFO) is a pipe whose access point is a file kept on the file system. By opening this file for reading, a process gets access to the reading end of the pipe. By opening the file for writing, the process gets access to the writing end of the pipe. If a process opens the file for reading, it is blocked until another process opens the file for writing and vice versa.

A named pipe may be created either via the '`mknod`' or its newer replacement, '`mkfifo`'.

MULTIPROCESSING

16. Define Multiprogramming and Multiprocessing.

Multiprogramming

Several processes (programs) are in memory concurrently and in state of execution. The system switches (process switching) among the programs for efficient processing (CPU usage) and minimal idle time (I/O delays).

Multiprocessing

Several processors are used on a single computer system to increase the processing power of the machine. The co-ordinated processing of programs on such a computer system is **multiprocessing**. It is commonly deployed in network server or client/server applications.

Q 17. Define the difference between pre-emptive and non-pre-emptive scheduling.

Pre-emptive scheduling allows a process to be interrupted in the midst of its execution, taking the CPU away from it and allocating it to another process.

Non-pre-emptive scheduling ensures that a process relinquishes control of the CPU only when it finishes with its current burst of execution.

Non-pre-emptive scheduling is rarely used in a computer, especially in a time-sharing system, because it cannot guarantee that each user gets a share of the CPU at regular intervals. The non-pre-emptiveness allows programs to run indefinitely long. Thus making other processes wait longer or indefinitely.

SYNCHRONIZATION MECHANISMS

Q 18. What is Critical Section?

A **critical section** is a section of code, which only one process (among processes) at a time can be executing. Consider a system consisting of 'n' processes. Each process has a segment of code in which the process may be changing shared variables, writing to a common file, etc. This segment of code is known as a **critical section**. It should be ensured that when one process is executing in its critical section, no other process is allowed to execute in its critical section.

Q 19. What are the different synchronization mechanisms?

There are many ways in which processes and threads can synchronize among themselves. Synchronization is basically controlling access to something that is shared or available across two or more processes or threads. The following mechanisms are available for process/thread synchronization:

- Mutex
- Semaphores
- Monitors
- Condition Variables
- Critical Regions
- Read–Write Locks

20. What is a semaphore?

A **semaphore** is a programming construct available for process synchronization purposes. It is a resource that contains an integer value and allows processes to synchronize by testing and setting this value in a single atomic operation. It assures that when the process that tests the value of a semaphore and sets it to a different value (based on the test), no other process will interfere with the operation.

The two types of operations that can be carried on a semaphore are 'wait' and 'signal'. A set operation first checks if the semaphore's value equals some value. If it does, it decreases its value and returns. If it does not, the operation blocks the calling process until the semaphore's value reaches the desired value. A 'signal' operation increments the value of the semaphore, possibly awakening one or more processes, that are waiting on the semaphore.

21. What is a mutex?

In multithreading, the entire address space is shared across threads. The global variables are accessible and modifiable by any/all threads. These accesses or modifications have to be synchronized to ensure desired behavior by the process.

POSIX provides two thread synchronization primitives—the mutex and the condition variable.

Mutexes are like simple locks protecting access to a shared data resource. A mutex is a mutual exclusion lock. Threads can create and initialize a mutex for later use. Before entering a critical region, the mutex is locked. Any other thread trying to lock the mutex during this period will not be able to lock the mutex and hence will not be able to enter the critical region. The mutex is unlocked after exiting the critical region.

Routines for creating and managing Mutexes:

```
pthread_mutex_init(mutex,attr)
pthread_mutex_destroy(mutex)
pthread_mutex_lock(mutex)
pthread_mutex_trylock(mutex)
pthread_mutex_unlock(mutex)
```

22. What is a condition variable?

Condition variables are synchronization objects that allow threads to wait for certain events (conditions) to occur, i.e., they allow threads to synchronize based upon the actual data value. Condition variables are slightly more complex than mutexes. The rule for using condition variables includes a mutex, a Boolean predicate (true/false expression) and the condition variable itself. The threads that are using condition variables can wait for a condition to occur, or can wake up other threads that are waiting for a condition.

Without condition variables, the thread has to check the condition continuously. This can be very resource consuming. With condition variables, the thread sleeps and waits on the condition variable;

Thread Synchronization APIs for condition variables:

```
// Thread A (waiting thread)
pthread_mutex_lock( &mutex );
while ( !condition )
pthread_cond_wait( &cond, &mutex );
do_something();
pthread_mutex_unlock( &mutex );
// Thread B (Signaling thread)
pthread_mutex_lock( &mutex );
// make condition TRUE
if (cond)
   pthread_cond_signal( &cond );
pthread_mutex_unlock( &mutex );
```

The function `pthread_cond_wait()` atomically releases mutex and causes the 'Thread A' to block on the condition variable 'cond'. Upon successful return, the mutex will again be locked and owned by the 'Thread A'.

Q 23. What are read-write locks?

Read–write locks allow simultaneous read access by many threads while restricting write access to only one thread at a time.

When any thread holds the lock for reading, other threads can also acquire the lock for reading but must wait to acquire the lock for writing. If one thread holds the lock for writing, or is waiting to acquire the lock for writing, other threads must wait to acquire the lock for either reading or writing.

Read–write locks are slower than mutexes, but can improve performance when they protect data that are not frequently written but that are read by many concurrent threads.

24. Define deadlock and the four necessary conditions needed before deadlock and occur.

Deadlock is a condition in which a group of two or more processes are all waiting for a set of resources that are currently taken by other processes within the same group. It is a situation where every process is waiting for an event, which can be triggered only by another process in the group. The processes are hence continuously blocked and cannot proceed further.

The four necessary conditions for deadlock to occur are as follows:

1. At least one resource must be held in a non-sharable mode.
2. A process holding at least one resource is waiting for more resources held by other processes.
3. The resource cannot be preempted.
4. There must be a circular waiting condition for processes.

A deadlock is also a condition in which two or more threads wait for each other to release a shared resource before resuming their execution. Since all threads participating in a deadlock are suspended and, therefore, cannot release the resources they own, no thread can continue, and the entire application hangs.

MEMORY MANAGEMENT

25. What functions constitute the Operating System Memory Management?

The functions are as follows:

- Memory allocation and de-allocation
- Integrity maintenance (what belongs to whom)
- Swapping
- Virtual memory

26. What are the different types of memory?

1. Main memory (Primary memory)

It refers to physical memory that is internal to the computer. It is used for program and data storage during computer operation. The word *main* is used to distinguish it from external mass storage devices, such as disk drives. Another term for main memory is RAM (Random Access Memory).

2. Secondary memory (Backing storage)

It is the slowest and cheapest form of memory. It cannot be processed directly by the CPU. Data must first be copied into primary storage. Secondary memory devices include magnetic disks-like hard drives and floppy disks, optical disks, such as CDs and CDROMs.

3. Cache (Pronounced cash)

Cache is a special high-speed storage mechanism. It can either be a reserved section of main memory or an independent high-speed storage device. It serves as an intermediate temporary storage unit logically positioned between the registers and RAM.

4. Internal processor memory

This comprises a small set of high-speed registers used as a working memory for temporary storage of instructions and data.

Q 27. What is compaction?

As processes are loaded and removed from the memory, the free memory space is broken into small pieces. These pieces are scattered in memory. **Compaction** is the movement of memory to eliminate small free memory partitions. It allows smaller memory partitions to form fewer bigger ones or one large block, thus allowing larger processes to run.

Q 28. Briefly explain the Virtual Memory concept.

Operating systems use a technique of memory management called **virtual memory management**. It simplifies programming to a great extent. The computer is viewed as having a single addressable memory of essentially unlimited size to which each program has unrestricted access. The addresses used by programs are called **logical** or **virtual addresses** and the set of actual addresses used in main memory are the **physical addresses**.

With this technique, operating systems simulate a condition of having more memory (virtual) than is available (physical).

In a virtual memory (VM) system, the program code deals with virtual addresses. When the program is executed, the virtual address is translated by the Memory Management Unit (MMU) to obtain a physical address that is used to access physical memory.

Q 29. What is a Page?

A virtual memory system usually divides main memory into fixed-size contiguous areas called **page frames**. The logical memory used by the program is divided into pieces of the same size called

pages. Pages are often 4 KB or 8 KB in size. This size is determined by the addressing hardware of the machine. Data is read in 'page' units or 'page' bytes at a time. This reduces the amount of physical storage access that is required and speeds up overall system performance.

30. What is demand paging?

In a virtual memory system, **demand paging** is the act of transferring pages between physical memory and backing store (usually disk) as and when they are needed. Processes reside on secondary memory. Whenever a process is executed, its pages are loaded into memory. A page is brought into memory only if the page is required (demanded).

For a process to execute, all the structures for data, text, and soon have to be set up. However, pages are not loaded in memory until they are 'demanded' by a process—hence, the term, demand paging. Demand paging allows the various parts of a process to be brought into physical memory as the process needs them to execute. Only the working set of the process, not the entire process, needs to be in memory at one time. A translation is not established until the actual page is accessed.

When pages need to be paged out from the main memory, different algorithms are used to select those pages that will not be needed soon. LRU (least recently used) is a popular technique.

31. Explain the difference between logical and physical addresses.

Physical addresses are actual addresses used to fetch and store data in main memory while the process is in execution.

Logical addresses are those generated by user programs. Logical addresses are converted to physical addresses by the loader during process loading into physical memory.

32. When does page fault occur?

A page fault occurs when an access to a page takes place that has not yet been brought into the main memory. The operating system verifies the memory access, aborting the program if it is invalid. If the memory access is valid, a free frame is located and I/O (Input/Output) requested to read the required page into the free frame. Upon completion of I/O, the process table and page tables are updated and the instruction is restarted.

33. What is the use of the dirty bit in the page table?

Dirty bit is a bit stored in the page table, which if set, indicates that the page has been modified, and must be written back to backing store before being used as a candidate for page replacement to create a free frame in physical memory.

34. List the factors determining the size of a page.

Page size must be in the powers of 2, varying from 512 to 16,384 bytes/page.

The factors that determine the size of a page include as follows:

- To minimize internal fragmentation—page size should be small
- To minimize I/O times—page size should be large
- The quantity of I/O is reduced for smaller pages as locality is improved
- To minimize the number of page faults—need large pages
- A large page size will keep the page table size small

35. What is thrashing?

Thrashing in a virtual memory system is a high page fault situation, where the system spends most of the time in swapping pages than executing processes. A system that is thrashing can be perceived either as a very slow system or one that has come to a halt. It results in severe performance problems. Thrashing is caused by under-allocation of the minimum number of pages required by a process, forcing it to continuously page fault.

FILE MANAGEMENT

36. What are the basic functions of file Management for an operating system?

File Management functions include

- creation and deletion of files
- creation and deletion of directories
- support of primitives for manipulating files and directories
- mapping of files onto secondary storage
- backup of files on storage media such as disk, tape, etc.

MULTITHREADING

37. What is a thread?

A **thread** is an independent flow of control within a process, composed of a context (which includes a register set and a program counter) and a sequence of instructions to execute.

All processes consist of at least one thread. Multi-threaded processes contain several threads. All threads share the common address space allocated for the process.

38. What is the POSIX standard? What are pthreads?

Portable Operating System Interface for Computer Environments (POSIX) is an interface standard governed by the IEEE and based on UNIX. POSIX is an evolving family of standards that describe a wide spectrum of operating system components ranging from C language and shell interfaces to system administration.

The **Pthread** interfaces are based on a subset of the application programming interfaces (APIs) defined in the POSIX standard. Pthreads is a standardized programming interface to develop portable threaded applications.

39. What are the advantages and disadvantages of using threads?

The advantages and disadvantages of using threads are as follows:

Advantages

- Less system resources required for thread context switching
- Increased throughput of an application
- No special mechanism required for communication between threads
- Program structure more readable and simplified

Disadvantages

- Require synchronization for concurrent read–write access to memory
- Can easily corrupt the address space of its process
- Threads exist only within a single process and are, therefore, not reusable

40. What are the similarities and differences between threads and processes?

The similarities and differences between threads and processes are as follows:

Similarities

1. Threads and processes both have an id, set of registers, state, priority and scheduling policy.
2. Both (kernel threads and processes) have attributes that describe the entity to the Operating System.

3. A thread information block similar to the process information block exists in the system.
4. Threads and child processes share resources with the parent process.
5. The creator, parent process or parent thread can exercise some control over the created threads or child processes.
6. Both can change their attributes or can create new resources.

Differences

1. Threads share the address space of the process that created it; processes have their own address space.
2. Threads have direct access to the data segment of its process; processes have their own copy of the data segment of the parent process.
3. Threads can directly communicate with other threads of its process; processes must use inter-process communication mechanisms (pipes, FIFO's, sockets, etc.).
4. In comparison to threads, processes have considerable overhead from the system perspective. New threads are easily created; new processes require duplication of the parent process.

Q 41. What are the differences between user-level threads and kernel-support threads?

A program using the POSIX pthread APIs creates and manipulates what are called **user-level threads**. A **kernel-support thread** is a kernel-schedulable entity, which may support one or more user threads.

User-levels threads have no kernel support, so they are very inexpensive in terms of resources demand. Creating, destroying, and switching among threads do not cause an interrupt to CPU. The kernel does not do the scheduling of the threads. One thread can block the other threads to access CPU and hence, the whole process might block.

Kernel threads are more expensive (in resources) because system calls are needed to create and destroy them and the kernel must schedule them to share access to CPU. They are more powerful because they are independently scheduled.

COMPILER/LINKER/LOADER

Q 42. What is a compiler?

A **compiler** reads source code and header files, parses the files, conducts optimizations and produces machine understandable object code.

43. What is a linker?

A **linker** produces a single executable file from one or more input object files and libraries. In doing so, it matches external references to global definitions contained in other object files or libraries. By default, the name given to the executable is 'a.out'.

44. What are all the steps for the generation/execution of an executable?

The steps for the generation/execution of an executable are as follows:

- Source and Header Files
- Compilation
- Linking
- Loading

45. What is a Library?

A **Library** is a file containing object code for subroutines and data that can be used by other programs. For example, the standard C library, libc, contains object code for functions that can be used by C, C++ programs to do input, output and other standard operations.

MISCELLANEOUS

46. What are the main differences between operating systems for personal computers and mainframe computers?

A personal computer (PC) performs a large number of applications and also provides a software platform for program development interactively used by a single user. Personal computer operating systems are not concerned with fair use or maximal use of computer facilities. Instead, they try to optimize the usefulness of the computer for individual user, usually at the expense of efficiency.

Mainframe systems are typically used in a data center setup for large organization to handle large number of tasks simultaneously and in a variety of applications. Mainframe operating system needs more complex scheduling and I/O algorithms to keep the various system components highly utilized and operate efficiently. The resource sharing among users is an important factor to be considered as well as maintaining high system throughput, acceptable system response time for interactive users and multiple job streams for job scheduling.

47. What is a Distributed system?

A **Distributed system** is one where distributed processing occurs among several physical processors, which do not share common memory in a networked environment. However, users of the system are not aware of this distribution.

The characteristics of distributed system include resource sharing, load sharing, improved reliability and support for inter-process communications.

48. What are device drivers?

A **device driver** is a software module that resides within the kernel and is the software interface to a hardware device or devices. The purpose of device drivers is to handle requests made by the kernel with regard to a particular type of device. A hardware device is a peripheral, such as a disk controller, tape controller or network controller device. In general, there is one device driver for each type of hardware device. Device drivers can be classified into:

- Block device drivers
- Character device drivers (including terminal drivers)
- Network device drivers and
- Pseudo device drivers

49. What do you mean by 16-bit or 32-bit CPU? What do you mean by MHz?

The bit size of a CPU denotes how many bytes of information it can access from RAM at the same time. For example, a 16-bit CPU can process 2 bytes at a time (1 byte = 8 bits, so 16 bits = 2 bytes), and a 64-bit CPU can process 8 bytes at a time.

Megahertz (MHz) is a measure of a CPU's processing speed, or clock cycle, in millions per second. So, a 32-bit 800-MHz processor can potentially process 4 bytes simultaneously, 800 million times per second.

50. What are system programs?

An OS can be viewed as a collection of functions/processes that allow user programs to execute on hardware and to control and share resources according to requests.

There are two types of system functions:

1. System management functions, such as the functions in the kernel (context switching, interrupt, dispatching, processor scheduling, accounting, memory management, etc.)

2. Functions that support user programs, such as program execution, I/O operations and file manipulation. These functions are accessed from user process through the use of system calls.

THINKER'S CHOICE

Q 51. What is the difference between message queues and semaphores?

Q 52. How is a semaphore different from a mutex?

Q 53. What is the difference between a shared library and an archived library?

Q 54. Why is it necessary to support relocatable code and dynamic loading of code in a multiprogramming system? Suggest instances that relocatable and dynamic loading are being used.

Q 55. Make a study of the Producer–Consumer Problem (Bounded Buffer Problem).

- Pseudo code to represent the problem
- Provide a solution using semaphore
- Provide a solution using monitor
- Provide a solution using inter-process communications (message passing)

Q 56. What resources are used when a thread is created? How do they differ from those used when a process is created?

Q 57. Explain the difference between internal and external fragmentation in memory management. Suggest ways to reduce or solve of both types of fragmentation.

Q 58. What is TLB?

Q 59. What is OS swap space?

Q 60. What is memory mapping?

REFERENCES

1. Andrew S. Tanenbaum, *Modern Operating System*, Prentice Hall.
2. Maurice J. Bach, *Design of the Unix Operating System*, Prentice Hall.
3. Silberschatz, Galvin, Gagne, *Operating System Concepts*, Wiley.

4

Real Time Operating Systems

INTRODUCTION

Real Time Operating System (RTOS) is an OS used in embedded application spaces like automotive, industrial automation, wireless etc. Characteristics of a RTOS is different compared to a normal OS in several aspects. This chapter covers the frequently asked interview questions on RTOS fundamentals.

GENERAL CONCEPTS

Q 1. What is a Real Time System?

A system that has to not only produce correct results but also produce the results within a specified deadline period is a **real time system**.

Q 2. What is hard real time system and soft real time system?

A system that has to meet all the deadlines without fail is called a **hard real time system**. Hard real time systems have stringent requirements and missing a deadline has a catastrophic effect.

Examples Automotive air bag system, antilock brake systems, flight management systems.

A system that can afford to miss a few deadlines without failing the overall system is called a **soft real time system**. Missing a deadline leads to a degraded performance but not to a system failure.

Examples Video conferencing systems, streaming devices.

3. What is a Real Time Operating System (RTOS)?

POSIX Standard defines 'real-time' for operating systems as: "the ability of the operating system to provide a required level of service in a bounded response time".

A *Real* **Time Operating System (RTOS)** is an operating system intended for real time systems. A RTOS is deterministic, provides guaranteed context switching time and lower interrupt latency and typically supports pre-emptive scheduling.

4. Name a few common RTOSes.

VxWorks,

QNX,

Windows CE,

DSP/BIOS,

Nucleus,

RTLinux.

5. Name a few applications where RTOS is used.

RTOS is used in a wide range of applications, such as mobile phones, industrial control, industrial monitoring, automotive control, robotics, audio/video streaming, medical (CT scan, MRI), flight/satellite controllers among many more.

6. How is a RTOS different from GPOS (General Purpose Operating System)?

Real time systems typically serve a specific purpose. The processing power and the memory footprint of real time systems are smaller compared to general purpose computers. A RTOS typically supports priority based scheduling, pre-emptible kernels, faster memory accesses and bounded interrupt latencies. A GPOS typically supports a fair scheduling policy (such as round robin) and offers virtual memory support.

7. Name a few common RTOS scheduling algorithms.

Priority based pre-emptive scheduling, Rate Monotonic scheduling and Earliest Deadline First based scheduling are a few RTOS scheduling algorithms.

8. What is priority inversion?

Consider a system with 3 tasks—T1, T2 and T3 (with Priority of T3 > Priority of T2 > Priority of T1) with the tasks T3 and T1 needing access to the same resource during some operations.

Let us assume the condition where T1 is currently accessing the shared resource. T3 can pre-empt T1 before it finishes access to the shared resource. During its execution, if T3 also needs access to the same resource, it has to wait for T1 to complete the access to the shared resource before it can proceed. T1 must now be allowed to complete the shared resource access and is therefore scheduled to execute. Such a condition where the priorities of the two tasks are effectively inverted is called **priority inversion**.

Once T1 is re-scheduled, it can be pre-empted by the medium priority task T2. Thus, when priority inversion occurs in the system, the medium priority task T2 is capable of further delaying the higher priority task T3.

Priority inversion needs to be avoided in the system to guarantee real time behavior.

9. What is priority inheritance protocol?

Priority inheritance protocol is a mechanism to solve the priority inversion problem.

Consider a system with 3 tasks—T1, T2 and T3 (with Priority of T3 > Priority of T2 > Priority of T1) with the tasks T3 and T1 needing access to the same resource during some operations.

Let us assume the condition where T1 is currently accessing the shared resource. T3 can preempt T1 before it finishes access to the shared resource. During its execution, if T3 also needs access to the same resource, it has to wait for T1 to complete the access to the shared resource before it can proceed and is hence blocked.

In a system supporting priority inheritance, T1 temporarily inherits the priority of the high priority task T3. This prevents a medium priority task T2 from preempting T1. T1 can continue executing until the access to the shared resource is complete. Once the access to the shared resource is complete, T1 resumes its original priority allowing the high priority task T3 to continue execution.

10. What are the drawbacks of priority inheritance protocol?

In some cases, priority inheritance can result in deadlocks in the system.

11. What is priority ceiling protocol?

Priority ceiling protocol is another mechanism to solve the priority inversion problem.

Each shared resource is given a predefined priority called the **priority ceiling**. This priority must be higher than the highest priority of all tasks that need access to the resource.

When a task obtains this shared resource, the task's priority is raised to the priority ceiling of the resource. This ensures that the task cannot be preempted by any other task trying to access the same resource. When the task releases the resource, the task is returned to its original priority level.

12. What are the drawbacks of priority ceiling protocol?

In priority ceiling protocol, the task priority has to be changed every time it acquires or releases any resource. These additional operations take time.

In addition, even if no other task would contend for the resource at the same time, the priority of the task is still changed to the priority ceiling value. This could sometimes result in unnecessarily delaying the execution of medium priority tasks in the system.

13. What is interrupt latency?

The time elapsed between the generation of an interrupt and the start of execution of the corresponding interrupt handler is called **interrupt latency**.

The duration during which the interrupts are turned off in a system add up to the interrupt latency. Also, if the system is processing high priority interrupts, the lower priority interrupts may be queued up adding to the latency as well.

14. What is context switch latency?

The time taken to switch the context and start processing the next program is called **context switch latency**. RTOS typically supports lower context switching latencies.

15. How are memory accesses done in a RTOS?

A RTOS has to support fast memory accesses. RTOS typically supports real addressing mode and virtual addressing mode.

In the real addressing mode, the CPU generates physical addresses. Access to memory does not require any translation. The advantage is that the memory access is quicker. The disadvantage is that it does not provide memory protection between tasks.

In the virtual addressing mode, the CPU generates virtual addresses. Access to memory requires address translation to takes place (using the Memory Management Unit). The advantage of this method is that it supports memory protection between tasks. The disadvantage is that the additional step of address translation leads to increase in memory access time.

16. Explain memory allocation technique used in a RTOS.

Memory allocation has to be fast and free of fragmentation. The allocation techniques are driven by how the heap is organized and managed. A typical approach is to organize the heap into memory pools of fixed number of blocks, each of a fixed size. Applications request for a buffer from a specific pool.

17. Does RTOS support dual mode of operation?

Some types of RTOS support the dual mode of operation. They support the user and the kernel modes of operation. This mechanism helps in protecting the system by inhibiting a user level process to tamper with the kernel (or operating system) data structures.

In the dual mode of operation, a user level process invokes a system call to request an operating system service. The switch between the user space to kernel space and vice versa results in additional latency.

18. Does using a RTOS for an application lead to higher throughput and speed of execution?

Using a RTOS does not necessarily guarantee higher throughput and speed of execution.

The performance of an application depends on a variety of factors including the CPU speed, memory architecture and the overall software design. What an RTOS guarantees is the real time characteristic. The RTOS could sacrifice throughput for being deterministic.

19. What are the key points to be taken care of while designing an application for RTOS?

While designing an application for a RTOS, the user needs to be aware of the following aspects:

Task Partitioning – The system is functionally partitioned into multiple logical tasks. The resource dependencies need to be worked out aptly and the system needs to be free of deadlocks.

Priorities – Critical tasks/interrupts that require faster response times are assigned higher priorities. Non-critical activities need to be de-prioritized.

Interrupt Service Routine (ISR) – ISRs need to be efficient and crisp. Time intensive operations should be avoided in the ISR. In cases that require an elaborate function, the ISR can spawn a task that can handle the time intensive operation. To reduce latencies, interrupts could be re-enabled in the ISR before servicing the current interrupt completely.

Memory Allocation – Avoid dynamic memory allocation in the application. This would free the system from memory leak and fragmentation issues.

Exception Handling – The application needs to handle exceptions. Exception could be generated as a result of timeout, missing a deadline, running out of memory, unknown external event, etc. Real time systems also use watchdogs for monitoring the system state.

20. Does linux support real time?

Linux supports real time through multiple options as follows:

A realtime patch with CONFIG_PREEMPT_RT support is available for the linux kernel that makes much of the standard linux kernel preemptible.

RTLinux product provides a micro kernel that runs the entire linux OS as a fully pre-emptible process.

THINKER'S CHOICE

21. Do all real time applications require a RTOS?

22. What led to the system resets on the Mars Pathfinder in 1997?

23. Provide an example to demonstrate the transitive nature of priority inheritance protocol.

24. Illustrate how priority inheritance can lead to deadlock.

25. What makes code re-entrant?

REFERENCES

1. Abraham Silberschatz, Peter B. Galvin, Greg Gagne, *Operating System Concepts*, Wiley India Pvt. Ltd.
2. C.M. Krishna and Kang G. Shin, *Real Time Systems*, McGraw-Hill.
3. David Simon, *An Embedded Software Primer*, Addison Wesley.
4. Raj Kamal, *Embedded Systems – Architecture, Programming and Design*, Tata McGraw-Hill.

5

C++ Programming

INTRODUCTION

The C++ language has evolved from the C language but has incorporated the features of object orientation for greater programming flexibility and effective design of the problem at hand. Given below is a collection of C++ interview questions and answers.

MOVING FROM C TO C++

Q 1. Mention some of the differences between C++.

- C is a subset of C++.
- C provides action/structure/function oriented programming, whereas C++ provides Object Oriented Programming (OOP) with features, such as Abstraction, Encapsulation, Inheritance and Polymorphism.
- C++ is a strong type checking language compared to C. So many programs that would compile without any warnings or errors on a C compiler might result in many warnings and errors on a C++ compiler.
- C++ supports sophisticated error handling using the Exception Handling Mechanism.

Q 2. What are the advantages of using `cin` and `cout` compared to `scanf (...)` and `print (...)`, respectively?

- Compared to the standard C functions `printf()` and `scanf()`, the usage of the `cin` and `cout` is more type-safe. The format strings, which are used with `printf()` and `scanf()` can define wrong format specifiers for their arguments, for which the compiler (usually) does not warn. In contrast, argument checking with `cin` and `cout` is performed by the compiler.

- In function `scanf()` we need to provide '&' before variable and if we miss this it can cause more damages.
- `cin` and `cout` are stream classes that could be used to receive and print objects, respectively.

3. What is the advantage of using the 'inline' function?

An **`inline`** keyword before a function suggests the compiler to insert the complete body of the function wherever that function is invoked.

Inline expansion is typically used to eliminate the inherent cost involved in calling a function. It is typically used for functions that need quick execution.

4. Can a function be forced as `inline`?

No, `inline` expansion is purely at the hands of the compiler. The compiler can ignore your request if a particular function does not suit for inline expansion. C++ specification does not specify under what condition the compiler will ignore the inline request.

5. Compare inline function with the C macro.

Macro invocations do not perform type checking.

```
#define MULTIPLY(a, b) a * b


inline int mul(int a,int b)
{
    return a*b;
}
    void main()
{
    printf( "%d", MULTIPLY(1+2,3+4));
    printf( "%d", mul(1+2,3+4));
}
```

In the above example, the answer will be 11 and 21. Why?

Because the macro will be expanded as: 1+2*3+4. Since * operator has higher precedence than + operator, the value will be 11 instead of 21. To get the correct answer, the macro should be declared as:

```
#define MULTIPLY(a, b) (a) * (b)
```

This error would not happen with the inline function.

Also,

- Compiler errors within macros are often difficult to track because they refer to the expanded code done by the preprocessor program
- Debugging the inline function is easier than that of macro-expanded code

STRUCTURES AND CLASSES

6. What is the correct way to write a C++ class?

The correct procedure to write a C++ class is, "Implementation of the class should be hidden from its declaration". To do this, always keep class declaration in .h file and class method implementation in one or more .cpp files so that only implementation files could be bundled as a library.

```
File: String.h // interface file

class String
{
   private:
      char *ptr;
   public:
      String(const char *data) ;
      ~String();
   public: // exposed interfaces
      void strcat(const char *data);
};

File: String.cpp // implementation file
String :: String(const char *data)
{
   ptr = new char[strlen[data] +1];
   strcpy(ptr,data);
}
String :: ~String()
{
   delete ptr;
```

```
}
   void String:: strcat(const char *data)
{
   // implementation of strcat method
}
```

Here only the interface file with prototype of 'strcat' would be exposed to the outside world while its implementation file can be bundled and provided as a library file (.lib, .dll, .so and .a). So, whenever there is a change in the implementation of the strcat function, just the library file needs to be replaced instead of the whole application.

7. What are the different Access Specifiers?

Class members can have the following access specifiers:

- **`private`** is the **default** access and private members are accessible only from the member functions of the same class and/or from their friend classes
- **`protected`** members are accessible from member functions of the same class and/or friend classes, and also from members of their **immediate derived** class
- **`public`** members are accessible from anywhere the class is visible

8. How does C++ class differ from a C++ structure?

Structure	Class
Default access is public	Default access is private
Default inheritance type is public	Default is private inheritance

9. When do we need to use forward declaration?

When a class contains a pointer or a reference to another class's instance, forward declaration of the contained class should be adequate to compile the class instead of including the contained class header file. Forward declarations reduce build dependencies, which are normally incurred when header files are included.

```
#include "someclass.h"

// forward declarations
class COtherClass;

class CFooBar
```

```
{
   public:
      CSomeClass m_SomeClass;
      COtherClass *m_pOtherClass;
};
```

In the above example, a forward declaration for the `COtherClassclass` is sufficient to compile the file since CFooBar class contains `COtherClass` pointer. But the header file is required for `CSomeClass` as it is a member instance. Because when the above class is being compiled, the compiler tries to find `size of m_SomeClass` instance, which needs the full class declaration.

KEYWORDS AND OPERATORS

10. Mention the usage of the scope resolution operator.

:: is the scope resolution operator.

A variable can be prefixed by scope resolution operator to signify the global nature of the variable.

```
int x = 10;
void foo()
{
   int x =100;
   cout<<"local Value"<<x;
   cout<<"Global value"<<::x;
}
```

In the above example, **::x** prints 10.

Scope resolution operator is used for the class member function, if the function definition is outside the class declaration.

```
File: Foo.h
class foo
{
int x;
   void print();
};
```

```
File: Foo.C
#include "foo.h"
void foo::print()
{
    cout <<"Hello,I am outside the Class declaration";
}
```

In the above example, **`print`** method in Class foo is implemented outside the class scope. This operator is also used for initializing and accessing the static members of the class.

```
class A
{
    A();
    static int i;
    static foo();
};

int A::i = 0;

void main()
{
    A::i=10;
    A::foo();
}
```

In the above example, class static variable i and static method foo are initialized and accessed using scope resolution operator.

11. What is the `const` keyword? Illustrate its various uses.

const keyword relates to the notion of read-only access.

```
const int i = 1;
```

In the above example, an attempt to change the value of i will cause an error.

const Pointers
With pointers, the real meaning of what actually is constant varies depending on the place of the `const` keyword as explained below.

Pointer to a constant

A **pointer to a constant** is a pointer, which points to data and that data is constant. So you may not alter the data that is present at that location.

```
const char* ptr = "C++"; // pointer to const
char const* ptr = "C++"; // pointer to const
*ptr = 'B'; // wrong. Data (value) cannot be changed
ptr = "Hello"; // Correct. Address can be changed
```

Constant pointer

The address of the pointer is `const.` while the variable may change.

```
char* const ptr = "C++"; // const pointer
*ptr = 'B'; // Correct. Data (value) can be changed
ptr = "Hello"; // Wrong. Address cannot be changed
```

Constant pointer to a constant

It is a combination of the above two concepts. Neither the pointer addresses nor the value can be changed.

```
//constant pointer to a constant
const char* const ptr = "C++";
```

const Reference

A reference may be defined as const, to make it clear that it should not be modified within the given context.

```
void doChange(const int & i)
{
   i= 25 // wrong. the value of i cannot be changed
}
```

const Member Functions

If a member function of a class is defined as const, it cannot change the state of the object. It also improves readability since by looking at the interface prototype we can realize it will not change the object's state. However, it can change the mutable variables.

```
Class A
{
   private :
      int i;
```

```
        mutable int j;
    public:
        void get() const
        {
            i = 20; // Not allowed
            j = 30; // allowed
        }
};
```

const Objects

When an object is declared as const, its member variables cannot be changed. So we can access only const member functions and member variables of that object.

```
Class A
{
    private :
        int i;
        mutable int j;
    public:
        void get() const
        {
            i = 20; // Not allowed
            j = 30; // allowed
        }
void normal()
    {
        cout << "Can't be invoked by const object" ;
    }
};
void main()
{
    const A a;
    a.get(); // allowed
    a.normal(); // not allowed
}
```

12. What is the mutable keyword? When do you use it?

The presence of the **`mutable` keyword** indicates that the data member of a class may be 'safely' changed within a **const member** function. `Mutable` could be used as workaround solution for a design bug.

```
Class A
{
   private:
      int i;
      mutable int j;
   public:
      void get() const
   {
      i = 20; // Not allowed
      j = 30; // allowed
   }
};
```

POINTERS AND REFERENCES

13. Distinguish between a pointer and a reference.

A **reference** should always be initialized at the declaration. There is nothing like a "null reference". However, a **pointer** on the other hand, could point to a null object.

Reassignment of pointers is possible; whereas references always refer to the object, which is once initialized and cannot refer to another variable.

Unlike pointers, references cannot

- refer to themselves
- compare different references
- modify themselves

14. What is the difference between reference and a const pointer?

Operation wise both are same. However, writing a reference variable is easy and elegant. For example,

```
void func1(const char *ptr);
```

is not as elegant as

```
void func1(char& ptr);
```

15. Which is a better option—pass by value or pass by references?

Pass by value is the default argument passing mechanism of both C and C++. When a caller passes by value an argument to a function (known as the *callee*), the latter gets a **copy** of the original argument. This copy remains in scope until the function returns and is destroyed immediately afterwards. Consequently, a function that takes value-arguments cannot change them, because the changes will apply only to local copies, not the actual caller's variables.

Passing by reference combines the benefits of "passing by address" and "passing by value". It is efficient, just like passing by address because the callee does not get a copy of the original value but rather an alias thereof (under the hood, all compilers substitute reference arguments with ordinary pointers). Finally, references are usually safer than ordinary pointers because they are always bound to a valid object—C++ does not have null references so you do not need to check whether a reference argument is null before examining its value or assigning to it.

Passing objects by reference is usually more efficient than passing them by value because no large chunks of memory are being copied and constructor and destructor calls are performed in this case. However, this argument passing mechanism enables a function to modify its argument even if it is not supposed to. To avert this, declare all read-only parameters as const and pass them by reference. This way, the callee will not be able to modify them.

16. What happens if a pointer is deleted twice?

The result of deleting a pointer more than once is **undefined**. A temporary workaround to this bug is assigning a NULL value to a pointer right after it has been deleted. It is guaranteed that a NULL pointer deletion is harmless.

```
String * ps = new String;
//...use ps
if (TrueCondition)
{
   delete ps;
   //safety-guard: further deletions of ps will be harmless
   ps = NULL;
}
```

```
//...many lines of code
//a bug. ps is deleted for the second time. However, it is
//harmless
delete ps;
```

17. What is 'this' pointer?

When a member function is invoked, the **invoking object's pointer** is passed implicitly as an argument. This pointer is called `'this'` pointer.

The `'this'` pointer is a pointer accessible only within the nonstatic member functions of a `class`, `struct`, or `union` type. It points to the object for which the member function is called. Static member functions do not have a `'this'` pointer.

18. How can you return the current involving object from its member function?

```
return (*this);
```

FREE STORE MANAGEMENT

19. Differentiate between new and malloc()'; delete and free().

The use of **`malloc()`** and **`free()`** functions in C++ is not recommended and is even dangerous:

- **`malloc()`** requires the exact number of bytes as an argument, whereas **`new`** calculates the size of the allocated object automatically. By using **`new`**, silly mistakes, such as the following are avoided:

```
//p originally pointed to a int
long * p = malloc(sizeof(int));

long *p = new int; // will not compile
long *p = new long; // will compile
```

- **`malloc()`** does not handle allocation failures, so you have to test the return value of **`malloc()`** on each and every call.

```
// ..........................................
long * p = malloc(sizeof(long));
if(p != NULL)
//...
```

```
long * p1 = malloc(sizeof(long));
if(p1 != NULL)
//...

// ..............................................
```

On the other hand, **new** throws an exception of type `std::bad_alloc` when it fails, so your code may contain only one catch (`std::bad_alloc`) clause to handle such exceptions.

```
try
{
    long *p = new long;
    long *p1 = new long;

}catch (std::bad_alloc a)
{
    //...
}
```

- As opposed to **`new`**, **`malloc()`** does not invoke the object's constructor. It only allocates uninitialized memory. The use of objects allocated this way is undefined and should never occur. Similarly, **`free()`** does not invoke its object's destructor.
- **`new`** and **`delete`** are operators and they can be overloaded; whereas **`malloc()`** and **`free()`** are library functions.

Q 20. What is the difference between delete, delete[], delete 'this' and delete NULL?

- **`delete`** should be called on an object when that object is allocated using **`new`**
- Objects created using **`new []`** must be released using **`delete []`**. It is a mistake to use **`delete`** instead; you may encounter memory leaks or even a program crash
- **`delete this`** is undefined and should not be called
- **`delete NULL`** is safe

```
void f()
{
    string *ps = new string[100];
    ...
```

```
    // wrong
    delete ps;

    //Correct. ensures each member's destructor is called
    delete[] ps;
}
```

21. What is a memory leak? How will you plug these leaks?

```
void leakyFunc()
{
    int *data = new int;
    *data = 20;
}
```

In the above method, the variable **data** is dynamically allocated using **new**. However, it is not de-allocated inside the method. It is memory leak!

These kinds of memory leaks can be avoided using

- **delete** for every **new**
- smart pointers

FUNCTIONS

22. How do you call C functions from C++ and vice versa?

To access a C function from a C++ program, the 'extern' keyword is used.

```
extern "C" void foo();
```

Accessing C++ functions from C is NOT possible

23. Can a function argument have default value?

Function argument can have default value (from right to left).

```
void func(int i, int j, int z = 0); // allowed
//Either j should have default value or i should not.
void func(int i =0, int j, int z = 0); // not allowed.
```

24. What are static members and static functions?

Static members are

- created and initialized only once
- shared among all the class objects.

Static functions are

- similar to the static variables and are associated with the class.
- can only access static variables of a class
- can also be called using the scope resolution operator

```
class Count
{
    static int count;
    public:
        Count(){count++;}
        ~Count(){count—;}
        static void print()
        {
            cout << count;
        }
};
int Count::count=0;

void main()
{
        Count c1,c2,c3;
        c3.print(); // prints 3
        Count::print(); // prints 3
}
```

25. Can a static member function access member variable of an object?

No, because to access the member variable of an object inside its member function, **`this`** pointer is required. Since static member functions are class functions, **`this`** pointer will not be passed as its argument.

Q 26. What is a 'friend' keyword? What are friend functions and classes?

A `friend` is a class or a function prefixed with the '`friend`' keyword that allows access to all of a class's data and member functions. That is, the `friend` has unlimited access to the class's public, protected, and private members.

To declare a class as a `friend` of another class:

```
class X
{
   friend class Y; //Y has access to every member of X
//..
};
```

Though this contradicts the basic tenets of OOP, it is a useful concept and usually friendship is provided to one or two member functions. To avoid indiscriminate access, you can declare individual member functions of B as `friends`. To declare a member function as a friend, simply provide its prototype preceded by the keyword `friend`. For example:

```
class B; // fwd declaration required; A::f() takes B&

struct A
{
   int f(B&);
};
struct B
{
   friend int A::f(B&); // a member function friend
   private:
      int x;
};

int A::f(B& b)
{
   return b.x; // access private member of b
}

int main()
```

```
{
    A a;
    B b;
    a.f(b); // access a private member of b
}
```

CONSTRUCTORS AND DESTRUCTORS

27. What is a constructor?

Constructor is a class method

- provided by a class to **initialize** an object
- that has the same name as its class
- that can have arguments and, thus can be overloaded (Multiple constructors can exist in a class)
- that does not have a return type.

28. What is a default constructor?

Default constructor is a constructor with no arguments or a constructor that provides defaults for all arguments. When a constructor is not explicitly declared in a class, a default constructor is added and is invoked during **object initialization** by the compiler.

29. What is a destructor?

Destructor is a method

- that cleans up or de-initializes each object of a class immediately before the object is destroyed
- that has the same name as the class, prefixed by a tilde, ~,
- that has no arguments and, thus cannot be overloaded
- that does not have a return type.

30. What is the difference between member variables initialization and assignment in a constructor?

Some programmers believe that the proper place for initializing data members is inside a constructor.

```
class Task
{
   private:
      int pid;
      string name;
   public:
      Task(int num, const string & n)
   {
      pid=num;
      name=n;
   }
};
```

The above snippet is incorrect. The constructor assigns, rather than initialize, the members pid and name. This could be a performance overhead as the object is first constructed and only then assigned.

A real initialization of a data member at the time of creation uses a special syntactic constructor with the member initialization list

```
class Task
{
   //..
   public:
      Task(int num, const string & n)  : pid (num), name (n)
      {}
};
```

Q 31. What is a copy constructor?

Copy constructor is

- invoked whenever a class object is to be copied
- a constructor used to make a copy of an object from another object of the same type
- a class constructor that takes a single argument, which is a reference to another object of the same class.

C++ defines four possible forms for a class's copy constructor. For a class called X, a copy constructor can have one of the following forms:

```
X(X&);
X(const X&);
X(volatile X&);
X(const volatile X&);
```

32. Why copy constructor argument accepts only object's reference?

The copy constructor's parameter cannot be "passed by value". Since pass by value invokes the copy constructor again that results in Stack Overflow. Therefore, the following forms are all illegal:

```
X(X); // error, passing by value
X(const X); // ditto
X(X*); // error, only references are allowed
```

33. Can copy constructor accept more than one parameter?

A copy constructor can have only one parameter; additional parameters are allowed only if they have default values. For example:

```
X(const X&, int n=0); // OK, 2nd param has a default value
X(const X&, int n=0, void *p=NULL); // ditto
X(const X&, int n); // Illegal
```

34. How can a constructor return an error condition?

Constructor argument can take a pointer/reference variable that returns error information.

Also an Exception can be thrown from the constructor (which is a not a good option).

35. How can a destructor return an error condition?

Since destructors do not take arguments we cannot use error pointer/reference as an argument. Also, C++ reference guide states, "Exceptions should not be thrown inside destructor" due to stack unwinding problem. We could return error using static variable flag.

```
class A
{
   static int flag;
   A() { };
   ~A()
```

```
    {
        flag =0;
        // do other operations
        flag = 1; // set on error
    }
};
A *a = new A();
// do something on a
delete a;
if(A:: flag == 1)
    cout << "Error in deleting instance" << endl;
```

36. Can I call a destructor directly using an object like the one mentioned below?

```
Obj-> ~destructorName();
```

Yes. But this just de-initializes the object's state rather than release its memory. So the correct approach is always to use **`delete`** operator for de-allocating an object.

INHERITANCE AND POLYMORPHISM

37. What is private, protected and public inheritance?

A simple example will illustrate the different forms of inheritance:

```
class Base;
class Derv_private : private Base;
class Derv_protected : protected Base;
class Derv_public : public Base;
```

In all the three derived classes, no **private** member of **Base** is accessible.

In the case of **private** inheritance **Derv_private**, all the public and protected members in Base become private.

In the case of **protected** inheritance **Derv_protected**, all the public and protected members become protected.

In **Derv_public**, **public** inheritance ensures that public remains public and protected remains protected.

38. In case of inheritance, what is the execution order of constructor and destructor?

Constructor execution is always from Base class to Derived class. Destructor execution is always from Derived class to Base class.

```
class Base
{
   Base()
{
   cout << "I am Base constructor" << endl;
}
~Base()
{
   cout << "I am Base destructor" << endl;
}
};

class Derived : public Base
{
   Derived()
   {
      cout << "I am Derived constructor" << endl;
   }
      ~Derived()
      {
      cout << "I am Derived destructor" << endl;
      }
};
void main()
{
   Derived d;
}
```

In the above example, when object **d** is being constructed, it called Base class constructor first and then executes its own constructor. Also, at the end of main function execution, object d's destructor get executed first and then its base class destructor.

Hence, the output of the above code is:

I am Base constructor

I am Derived constructor

I am Derived destructor

I am Base destructor

39. How do we call a base member function from derived class member function?

To call base class member function from derived class, use scope resolution operator with left operand as Base class name and right operand as base class method to be called.

```
class A
{
    public:
    void a()
    {
        cout << " I am A" << endl;
    }
};

class B : public A
{
    public:
    void a()
    {
        cout << " I am B" << endl;
        A::a();
    }
};
```

```
Prints
I am B
I am A
```

40. Are the following operator overloading methods allowed?

a. void operator +& (int i) // +& is newly user defined operator
b. void operator +(class &obj1, class &obj2)

a. No. Cannot use new operators other than intrinsic operators like *, +,-, etc

b. No. Must use same number of arguments as for built-in types (except `operator()`). For `+ operator` only one argument is allowed as the invoking object is implicitly passed as another argument. However, this statement will work if we declare the method as `friend`.

41. Is it possible to invoke an operator overloading function with the statement like 2+OBj?

Yes. It is possible. Usually, left operand object invokes the operator function and the right operand will be passed as a parameter. In case if both the argument is required to be passed as parameter or if the left operand is not an object (something like 2+obj), then friend operator method should be used.

```
// for 2+obj as 2 can't invoke operator;
friend void operator + (int i, Object &obj);
```

42. Can a function be overloaded based on return types?

Function signature does not depend on the return type. So, overloading cannot be resolved by the return type alone.

43. What are all the operators that cannot be overloaded?

- Direct member access operator.
- De-reference pointer to class member operator .*
- Scope resolution operator ::
- Conditional operator ?:
- Sizeof operator sizeof

44. Where will you use an assignment operator?

(OR)

Differentiate between a Copy Constructor and an Assignment Operator.

Although the copy constructor and assignment operator perform similar operations, they are used in different contexts. The copy constructor is invoked when you initialize an object with another object:

```
string first = "abc";
string second(first); //copy constructor
```

On the other hand, the assignment operator is invoked when an already constructed object is being assigned a new value:

```
string second;
second = first; //assignment operator
```

In the following example, the copy constructor is invoked because **d1** is being initialized rather being assigned.

```
Date Y2Ktest ("01/01/2000");
//although '=' is used, the copy constructor is invoked
Date d1 = Y2Ktest;
```

45. What is shallow and deep copy?

The terms **deep copy** and **shallow copy** refer to the way objects are copied. A **shallow copy** of an object copies all of the member variables. A **deep copy** copies all static as well as dynamically allocated member variables

```
class CopyMethod
{
   char *ptr;
   public:
      CopyMethod()
   {
      ptr = new char[2];
      ptr = 'M';
```

```
    }
    void operator = (CopyMethod &a)
    {
        if(ptr)
            delete ptr;
        ptr = NULL;
        ptr = new char[2];
        strcpy(ptr,a.ptr);
    }
};
void main()
{
    CopyMethod cm1;
    // Default Copy Constructor will do Shallow Copy
    CopyMethod cm2 = cm1;
    // Deep copy using User-Defined assignment operator
    CopyMethod cm3;
    cm3 = cm1;
}
```

In the above example, cm2 object calls default copy constructor, which does memory copy. This means cm2.ptr = cm1.ptr. This is incorrect, as both cm2's and cm1's ptr member points to same memory. This is the problem of **Shallow Copy**. However, if we see the last statement cm3=cm1, it calls the user-defined assignment operator method where we have copied the ptr value properly. This is called **Deep Copy**. So the moral is, if you have a dynamically allocated variable in a class, write your own assignment and copy constructor methods.

46. Can a constructor be overloaded?

Yes. The constructor can be overloaded to pass different arguments to the object at the time of creation.

47. Can a destructor be overloaded?

No. There is no need to overload the destructor as it is called before de-allocating an object.

48. What is the difference between overriding and overloading?

Overloading a method (or function) is the ability for methods of the same name to be re-defined as long as these methods have different signatures (different set of parameters). Method **overriding** is the ability of the inherited class rewriting the virtual method of the base class.

```
class CBase
{
   public:
      CBase ();
      void Func (int param);
      void Func (float param); // overloaded func
      virtual void Func1();
   };
   class CDerived : public CBase
   {
   public:
      CDerived ();
      void Func (char param); // overloaded func
      void Func1(); // overrided func
};
void main ()
{
   CDerived derived;
   int param = 1;

   // Calls Base Class overloaded Func(int) method
   derived.Func (param);
   CBase &base = derived;

   // Calls Derived Class overriden Func1() method
   base.Func1()
}
```

Here is another twist. Suppose you override an overloaded function from the Base class as shown in the below snippet:

```
class CDerived : public CBase
```

```
{
    public:
        CDerived ();
    // overridden the overloaded func
    void Func (float param);
    // overridden func
    void Func1();
};
```

Calling the derived.Func(param) in the **main** method will surprisingly call Derived.Func(float) instead of Base.Func(int). Why?

Because, If you override an overloaded member function (virtual or not), your overriden function hides all overloaded variants of that member function, ***not just the one you overrode.*** To properly override an overloaded member function, you must override all the overloaded variants. In the above code, if you want to override Func (int) then you need to override Func (float) also.

Another workaround is, in CDerived, bring the method overloaded in the CDerived interface by using the C++ statement "using".

```
class CDerived : public CBase
{
    CDerived ();
    using CBase::Func;
    Func (float param);
};
```

With this piece of code the `CBase::Func(int)` is called.

49. How are prefix and postfix operator overloading done?

For primitive types, the C++ language distinguishes between ++x; and x++; as well as between --x; and x--. For objects requiring a distinction between prefix and postfix overloaded operators, the following rule is used:

```
class Integer
{
    private:
        int i;
    //...
```

```
    public:
        void operator++(){++i;} //prefix
        void operator--(){--i;} //prefix
        void operator++(int unused) {i++;} //postfix
        void operator--(int unused){i--;} //postfix
};
```

Postfix operators are declared with a dummy int argument (which is ignored) in order to distinguish them from the prefix operators, which take no arguments:

```
void f()
{
    Integer d, d1;
    ++d; //prefix: first increment d and then assign to d1
    d++; //postfix; first assign, increment d afterwards
}
```

50. What is static and dynamic binding?

The process of connecting the function call to a function implementation is called **binding.** When the binding happens before the execution (by compiler) of the program, it is called **static** or **early binding**. If the binding occurs at run-time, it is called **late** or **dynamic binding**.

51. What is a virtual function? Explain VTABLE with a diagram.

For late binding to happen, there should be a way to identify the type of the object at run-time whose function/method is to be executed. In C++, we have to declare a function as **`virtual`** to achieve late binding.

```
class Base
{
    public:
        Base();
        void static_func();
        virtual void dyn_func();
};
class Derv
{
```

```
    public:
        Derv();
        virtual void dyn_func();
};

void main()
{
    Base b;
        b.static_func();
        Base *b1 = new Derv();
    b1->dyn_func();
}
```

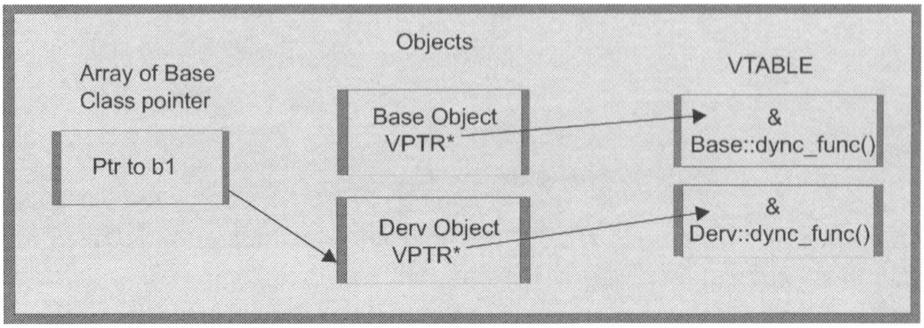

VTABLE Diagram

On compiling this program, compiler replaces `b.static_func()` method call with the starting address of `b.static_func()` method implementation.

When compiler finds the **`virtual`** function, it knows that it should do **late** binding. To accomplish this, the compiler creates a VTABLE for each class that contains virtual functions as shown in the **VTABLE diagram**. The compiler places the addresses of the virtual functions for that particular class in the VTABLE. In each class with virtual functions, it keeps a pointer, called the **vpointer** (abbreviated as VPTR), which points to the VTABLE for that object. So for **`b1->dyn_func()`** method call the compiler quietly inserts code to fetch the VPTR and look up the function address (in this case it finds Derv::dyn_func) in the VTABLE. At runtime, it calls function **Derv::dyn_func**().

52. Can a constructor be declared as virtual?

A constructor cannot be declared **`virtual`** since the constructor invocation model is always from the base class to the derived class.

53. What is a virtual destructor? Why is it needed?

A destructor can be declared `virtual`. **`Virtual`** destructor is mainly useful during inheritance

```
class Base
{
   public:
      Base() { }
      virtual ~Base() { };
};

class Derv
{
   char *ptr;
   public:
      Derv() { ptr = new char[2];}
      ~Derv() { delete ptr; }
};

void main()
{
   Base basePtr = new Derv();
   delete basePtr;
}
```

Use of virtual keyword before ~Base() ensures, it calls first ~Derv() and then ~Base() when delete basePtr statement executed.

An important paradigm of class design is that if a class has one or more virtual functions, it should have a virtual destructor.

54. What is a virtual base class? (a.k.a The classic Diamond problem)

Multiple inheritance is a powerful and useful feature in C++, but it might result in the Diamond problem.

Multiple Inheritance introduces the possibility that a class may have the same (direct or indirect) base class appearing more than once as an ancestor.

For example: The Diamond shape inheritance

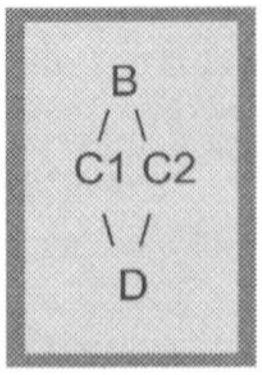

This situation introduces C++ virtual inheritance. When the programmer wants class D to have one B sub-object, B should be a virtual base class; and if two, B should be a normal (non-virtual) base class.

```
class B
class C1 : virtual public B
class C2 : virtual public B
class D: public C1, public C2.
```

55. What is an abstract class?

An abstract class cannot be instantiated, means objects cannot be created for an abstract class.

A class is made **abstract** by declaring one or more of its virtual functions to be pure. A pure virtual function is one with an initializer of = 0 in its declaration.

```
virtual void Func() = 0; // pure virtual functions
```

Note: Initializing to zero is just an indication to the compiler.

56. Why cannot a derived class virtual function be called from a base class constructor?

This is because the TEMPLATES VTABLE will not be fully initialized until the derived constructor executes completely.

TEMPLATES

57. What is the advantage of using templates?

Templates provide a means to write generic functions and classes for different data types. Templates are sometimes called **parameterized types**. Templates can significantly reduce source code size and increase code flexibility without reducing **type safety**.

58. Explain function template.

Function template provides a means to write generic functions for different data types, such as integer, long, float or user-defined objects

```
template <class T>
T GetMaxValue (T a, T b)
{
   T result;
   result = (a>b)? a : b;
   return (result);
}
int main ()
{
int i=5, j=6, k;
   float l=10.1, m=5.2, n;
   k=GetMaxValue<int>(i,j);
   n=GetMaxValue<float>(l,m);
   cout << "Max Integer Value" << k << endl;
   cout << "Max Float Value" << n << endl;
   return 0;
}
```

In the above example, we have used the same function **GetMaxValue** () with arguments of type **int** and **float** having written a single implementation of the function. That is to say, we have written a **function template** and called it with two different type of parameters.

As you can see, within our GetMaxValue () template function the type T can be used to declare new objects:

```
T result;
result is an object of type T, like a and b
```

59. Explain class template.

Class template provides a means to write a generic class for different types so that a class can have members based on generic types that do not need to be defined at the moment of creating the class or whose members use these generic types.

```
template <class T>
class pair
{
   T value1, value2;
   public:
      pair (T first, T second)
      {value1=first; value2=second;}
      T getmax ();
};


template <class T>
T pair<T>::getmax ()
{
            T retval;
            retval = value1>value2? value1 : value2;
            return retval;
}
int main ()
{
   pair <int> myobject (100, 75);
   cout << myobject.getmax();
   return 0;
}
```

In the above class that we defined serves to store two elements of any valid type. For example, if we wanted to declare an object of this class to store two integer values of type `int` with the values **115** and **36** we would write:

```
pair<int> myobject (115, 36);
```

This same class would also serve to create an object to store any other type:

```
pair<float> myfloats (3.1, 2.1);
```

60. Differentiate between a Template and a Macro.

In many ways, templates work like preprocessor macros, replacing the templated variable with the given type. However, there are differences between a macro like this:

```
#define min(x, y) (((x) < (y)) ? (x) : (y))
```

and a template:

```
template<class T> T min (T x, T y){ return ((x < y) ? x : y) }
```

Here are some problems with the macro:

- There is no way for the compiler to verify that the macro parameters are of compatible types. The macro is expanded without any special type checking.
- The `x` and `y` parameters are evaluated twice. For example, if either parameter has a post-incremented variable, the increment is performed two times.
- Because macros are expanded by the preprocessor, compiler error messages will refer to the expanded macro, rather than the macro definition itself. Also, the macro will show up in expanded form during debugging.

61. Differentiate between a template and a void pointer.

Functions that are implemented with **`void`** pointers can be implemented with templates. `void` pointers are used to allow functions to operate on data of an unknown type. When using `void` pointers, the compiler cannot distinguish types, so it cannot perform type checking or type-specific behavior, such as using operator overloading, or constructors and destructors.

With templates, functions and classes can be created that operate on typed data. The type looks abstracted in the template definition. However, at compile time the compiler creates a separate version of the function for each specified type. This enables the compiler to treat class and the function templates as if they act on specific types. Templates can also improve coding clarity, because you do not need to create special cases for complex types, such as structures.

62. What is STL?

Standard Template Library (STL) is a C++ library of container classes (along with algorithms that manipulate the data stored in containers) and iterators (that are used to move through the elements of the container).

Every container in the STL is a template. The purpose of the container classes is to contain their objects. Examples of containers are `list`, `vector`, and `map`.

You can, for example, use a `vector<int>` in much the same way as you would use an ordinary C/C++ array, except that `vector` eliminates the chore of managing dynamic memory allocation by hand.

63. What are the advantages of using on **`iterator`**?

Iterator interfaces (API) are the same for all the containers. For example, a container **`list`** can internally have doubly linked list or singly linked list, but its corresponding iterator interface that is used to access its elements is always the same.

`(iter->next)`

64. What is the difference between a vector and a map?

A **vector** is a sequential container, i.e., all the elements are in a sequence, whereas a **map** is an association container, i.e., all elements are stored in the form of a key-value association pair.

MISCELLANEOUS

65. What is casting?

If a class is derived from a base class containing virtual functions, a pointer to that base class type can be used to call the implementations of the virtual functions residing in the derived class object. Since a derived class completely contains the definitions of all the base classes from which it is derived, it is safe to cast a pointer up the class hierarchy to any of these base classes.

66. What is RTTI?

Run-time type identification (RTTI) mechanism is used to determine the exact type of an object pointer or reference during runtime of a program, i.e., it identifies whether the base class pointer holds the address of a base class object or a subclass object. RTTI is achieved in C++ via the dynamic_cast operator, the typeid operator and the type_info class.

Operator `typeid` retrieves the runtime type information associated with a certain object. `typeid` takes an object or a type name as its argument. Thus, to determine if the dynamic type of object x is of class Y, check whether the expression typeid(x) == typeid(Y) is true:

For example:

```
#include <typeinfo> // needed for typeid

class File
{
```

```
};
class TextFile : public File
{
};
class MediaFile : public File
{
};

class menu
{
   void build(const File * pfile)
   {
      if (typeid(*pfile)==typeid(TextFile))
      {
         add_option("edit");
      }
      else if (typeid(*pfile)==typeid(MediaFile))
      {
         add_option("play");
      }
   }
};
```

In the above example, menu class build member function verifies the pfile pointer's class type using `typeid`.

67. How can you know failure in casting?

bad_cast Exception will be thrown by the C++ runtime.

68. What is the difference between dynamic and static casting?

The `static_cast` operator can be used for operations, such as converting a pointer to a base class to a pointer to a derived class. Such conversions are not always safe.

- In general `static_cast` would be in numeric data type conversions, such as enums to ints or ints to floats.

- static_cast conversions are not as safe as dynamic_cast conversions, because static_cast does no run-time type check, while dynamic_cast does.
- A dynamic_cast to an ambiguous pointer will fail, while a static_cast returns as if nothing were wrong; this can be dangerous.
- Although dynamic_cast conversions are safer, dynamic_cast only works on pointers or references, and the run-time type check is an overhead.

Q 69. What is a namespace?

In C++, **namespace** is used to group all the related classes. For instance, consider these two C++ header files:

```
// something.h
class String { ... };


// somelib.h
class String { ... };
```

With these definitions, it is impossible to use both header files in a single program; the String classes will clash.

A namespace is a declarative region that attaches an additional identifier to any names declared inside it. As long as classes appear in separate namespaces, each name will be unique because of the addition of the namespace identifier. For example:

```
// something.h
namespace SomeThing
{
   class String { ... };
}


// somelib.h
namespace SomeLib
{
   class String { ... };
}
```

Now the class names will not clash because they become SomeThing::String and SomeLib::String, respectively.

In order to use a namespace, the scope resolution operator or **using** keyword is used.

```
namespace myproject
{
   class A
   {
      static int i;
      public:
         static void foo();
};
}
int myproject::A::i=10;
```

or

```
class B
{
   using namespace myproject;
   A::foo();
};
```

70. How would you implement Exception handling in C++?

Exceptions are used to pass information about abnormal runtime conditions and to transfer control to an appropriate handler.

The keywords try, catch, and throw are used in exception handling. **try** defines a block of guarded code, i.e., a sequence of one or more statements that might throw an exception. **catch** defines a catch-block, or a handler, for a particular exception or a set of exceptions. A **throw** statement interrupts the current execution flow and propagates an exception to a matching handler.

Example:

```
class A
{
   public:
      class Except {};
      void foo() { throw Except();}
};
```

```
int main()
{
    A a;
    try
    {
        a.foo();
    }   catch(A::Except)
    {
        cout << "caught Except" << endl;
    }
}
```

71. What is the ellipsis catch handler?

Ellipsis catch handler will catch all the unhandled exceptions.

```
try
{
    throw "Data";
}
catch(...)
{
    cout << "No Exception Handler" ;
}
```

Output in the above example is "No Exception Handler" since there is no matching catch handler for the statement throw "Data".

72. What will happen it a thrown exception is not handled?

If a matching handler (or ellipsis **`catch`** handler) cannot be found for the current exception, the predefined **`terminate`** function is called. (You can also explicitly call `terminate` function in any of your handlers.) The default action of `terminate` function is to call **`abort`** function to stop the program execution. If you want terminate function to call some other function in your program before exiting the application, call the **`set_terminate`** function with the name of the function to be called as its single argument. You can call `set_terminate` at any point in your program. The terminate routine always calls the last function given as an argument to `set_terminate`. For example:

```
#include <eh.h> // For function prototypes
//...
void term_func() { // ... }
int main()
{
   try
   {
      // ...
      set_terminate( term_func );
      // ...
      // No catch handler for this exception
      throw "Out of memory!";
   }
   catch( int )
   {
      cout << "Integer exception raised.";
   }
   return 0;
}
```

The `term_func` function should terminate the program or current thread, ideally by calling exit. If it does not, and instead returns to its caller, `abort` is called.

73. What is the advantage of Exception handling?

Or

What does Stack Unwinding mean?

The real power of C++ exception handling lies in its ability to automatically call destructor functions during **stack unwinding**, for all local objects constructed before the exception was thrown.

The following example demonstrates C++ exception handling using classes with destructor semantics:

```
#include <iostream.h>

void MyFunc( void );
```

```
class CTest
{
   public:
      CTest(){};
      ~CTest(){};
      const char *error() const
      { return "Exception in CTest class."; }
};

class CTester
{
   public:
      CTester();
      ~CTester();
};
CTester::CTester()
{
   cout << "Constructing CTester.\n";
}

CTester::~CTester()
{
   cout << "Destructing CTester.\n";
}
void MyFunc()
{
   CTester D;
   cout<< "In MyFunc(). Throwing CTest exception.\n";
   throw CTest();
}
int main()
{
   cout << "In main.\n";
   try
   {
```

```
        cout << "In try block, calling MyFunc().\n";
        MyFunc();
    }
    catch( CTest E )
    {
        cout << "In catch handler.\n";
        cout << "Caught CTest exception type: ";
        cout << E. error () << "\n";
    }
    catch( char *str )
    {
    cout << "Caught other exception:"<<str<< "\n";
    }
cout << "Back in main. Execution resumés here.\n";
    return 0;
}
```

This is the output from the preceding example:

```
In main.
In try block, calling MyFunc().
Constructing CTester.
In MyFunc(). Throwing CTest exception.
Destructing CTester.
In catch handler.
Caught CTest exception type: Exception in CTest class.
Back in main. Execution resumés here.
```

Note that in this example, the exception parameter (the argument to the catch clause) is declared in both **catch** handlers:

```
catch( CTest E )
// ...
catch( char *str )
// ...
```

The above statements need not to be declared; in many cases, it may be sufficient to notify the handler that a particular type of exception has occurred. However, if the exception object is not declared in the exception-declaration, access will not be there to that object in the **catch** handler clause.

A throw-expression with no operand re-throws the exception currently being handled. Such an expression should appear only in a **catch** handler or in a function called from within a **catch** handler. The re-thrown exception object is the original exception object (not a copy).

For example:

```
try {
    throw CSomeException();
}
catch(...) { // Handles all exceptions
    // ...
    throw;     // Pass exception to some other handler
}
```

PROBLEMS AND SOLUTIONS

74. Will this code compile?

```
class A
{
    public:
        void func1(A *a)
        {
            this = a;
        }
};
```

Answer

No. Because, the 'this' pointer is non-modifiable, so assignment to this pointer is not allowed.

75. In the following program, what is the difference between the two statements?

this->a = a; and b = a;?

```
class A
{
    int a;
```

```
    int b;
    public:
        void set(int a)
        {
            this->a = a;
            b = a;
        }
};
```

Answer

In the first statement, to differentiate the local variable `'a'` and the member variable `'a'` for the compiler, **`this`** keyword is used for the member variable. Also, for the second the member variable `'b'` has **`this`** implicitly it is not necessary to write explicitly.

76. Write a string class.

```
class String
{
    public:
        String(const char *str = 0);
        String(const String& s);
        String& operator=(const String& s);
        ~String();
    private:
        char *value;
};
//String Constructor
String::String(const char *str)
{
    value = NULL; // for safety
    if (str)
    {
        value = new char[strlen(str) + 1];
        strcpy(value,str);
    }
```

```
    else
    {
        value = new char[1];
        *value = '\0';
    }
}
//String destructor
String::~String()
{
    if (value)
    {
        delete value;
    }
    value = NULL; // for safety
}

//String assignment operator
String& String::operator=(const String& s)
{
    if (this == &s)
        return *this;
    delete [] value;

    value = new char[strlen(s.value) + 1];
    strcpy(value, s.value);
return *this;
}
```

77. Let us say in your C++ code (in a list of files), there are lots of "cout" statements. Now you need to log only five statements out of that to verify a fix, however, you do not have time to comment all the cout.

There might be many options to do this, in that, we chose the one that is explained here

Use **cerr** instead of **cout** for those five statements. In the command line, while executing type

```
*.exe >> logFileName
```

This logs only the five **cerr** statements.

78. Consider class 'A' with a method given below:

```
void add(float i, float f); //function

A obj; // A's object
```

Will this statement obj.add (2,3); work?

Answer

Yes. Always best match is used, i.e., to add integers 2 and 3, if method `add(int i,int j)` is not available then `add(float j, float j)` will be called.

79. Debug the code below:

```
struct test
{
   int t;
   char a[20];
   virtual void func() { cout << t<< "Hello"; };
};

void main()
{
   test *t = new test;
   memset(t,0,sizeof(t));
   t->func();
}
```

Answer

When memset is called on the VTABLE ptr for the `func()` will be set to NULL. So, when `t->func()` is executed the program will crash.

80. Will this code compile?

```
class B;

class A
{
   B b;
};

class B
{
};
```

Answer

No. Because when class A is being compiled, it tries to find `sizeof` class B to allocate instance `b`. Forward declaration did not help here.

81. Will this code compile?

```
//File: A.h

#include "B.h"

class A
{
   B b;
};
//File: B.h
#include "A.h"

class B
```

```
{
    A a;
};
```

Answer

No. Because when file `A.h` is being compiled, it tries include file `B.h`, which in turn tries to include `A.h` ends in compiler error stating recursive #include inclusion.

82. Consider a class A with two methods given below:

```
A& operator + (A & obj1)
A& operator * (A & obj2)
```

Say instances `s1,s2` and `s3` are created for class A. What is the value of `s1+s2*s3`?

Answer

Obey same precedence rules as for built-in types. So * operator has more priority than + operator. Hence, `s2*s3` will be executed first and then result will be added to `s1`.

83. Implement the friend function in the given class.

```
class A
{
    friend operator<< (ostream &, const A &);
    private:
    int a;
};

int main (int, char*[])

{
    A a;
    cout << a << endl;
    return 0;
}
```

Answer

Use the following code:

```
ostream & operator<< (ostream & o, const A &a)
{
    o << "A::a = " << a.a;
    return o;
}
```

84. Fix the bug in this snippet.

```
class A
{
    int x;
    void int(int x)
{
    x = x;
}
};
```

Answer

Statement x=x assigns the local method variable x to itself. To assign the local method value x to class member variable x, re-write statement as this->x = x;

85. Fix the bug in this code.

```
class A
{
    public:
        int i;
};
void main()
{
    A *a = new A();
    a->i= 20;
    free(a);
}
```

Answer

Object allocated with new got de-allocated using `free()`, which is an incorrect approach. Because `free()` function does not know how to de-allocate objects. Always use `new` with `delete` operator and `malloc` with free function.

86. Give one C++ language problem you face when we use multiple inheritance (apart from diamond case).

Let us assume class **derv** gets derived from **base1** and **base2** classes, respectively as given below. The classes base1 and base 2 have virtual functions that are implemented/overridden in the derv class.

```
class base1
{
   public:
      virtual void temp1();
};

class base2
{
   public:
      virtual void temp2();
};
class derv : public base1, public base2
{
   virtual void temp1() {};
   virtual void temp2() {};
};

base1 *b1;
base2 *b2;

b1 = new derv;
b1->temp1(); // allowed
b1->temp2(); // error

b2 = new derv;
```

```
b2->temp2(); // allowed
b2->temp1(); //error
```

Answer

The derv class object could be assigned either to **base1** or **base2** class pointer/reference. This confusion exists due to multiple-inheritance.

87. Look at this code snippet.

```
1) class A
   {
   };
   A a;
2) class B
   {
      virtual int func() {};
   };
   B b;
```

What are the size of objects, a and b?

Answer

Empty object size is always 1. Hence, size of the object a is 1.

If a class has one or more virtual function then a VPTR (virtual table pointer) will be inserted into the object created for that class. So the size of the object b is 4 (addr of VPTR).

88. Can you implement a Class using a 'C' structure?

In free terms, we could say a class is a collection of related member variables and member functions. To simulate a Class using C structure, use variables and function pointers.

```
struct ClassType
{
   int var1;
   int var2;
   void (*funcPtr1) ();
   }ClassType;
```

However, remember that we cannot specify **Access level** (private, public and protected) for the C structures as possible in the C++ class.

THINKER'S CHOICE

Q 89. How do you pass an object of a C++ class to/ from a C function?

Q 90. Can an exception be thrown from a destructor?

Q 91. Why cannot the scope resolution operator be overloaded?

Q 92. lo To the String class in Q/6 add the operator+ method.

Q 93. How do you set up a class so that it cannot be inherited?

Q 94. How do you open a stream in binary mode?

Q 95. What is Object Serialization?

Q 96. When do you use container classes rather than arrays?

Q 97. Overload 'new' and 'delete' operator to allocate and de-allocate memory.

Q 98. Write an implementation for dynamic array.

Q 99. What is a Smart Pointer?

Q 100. What is Object Slicing?

REFERENCES

1. Bjarne Stroustrup, *The C++ Programming Language*, 3rd edition, Addison-Wesley.
2. Bruce Eckel , *Thinking in C++*, 2nd edition, Prentice Hall.
3. Scott Meyers, *Effective C++*, 3rd edition, Addison-Wesley.
4. Scott Meyers, *More Effective C++*, Professional Computing Series, Addison-Wesley.

6

Java

INTRODUCTION

Java is a modern object oriented language, which has been designed keeping the Internet in mind. Java has mitigated or eliminated many problematic areas found in C++. This chapter covers the interview questions on various aspects of the Java language and concepts like J2EE.

BASICS

1. Describe a Java source file.

- A Java source file must have '.java' extension.
- It should have at-least one top-level, public class definition and any number of non-public class definitions. The file name (without the extension) should match the public class name.

File: PublicClass.java

```
public class PublicClass {
    ...
}
class Non-PublicClass {
    ...
}
```

2. What is the Bytecode?

Each Java program is converted into one or more class files. The content of the class file is a set of instructions called **bytecode** to be executed by Java Virtual Machine (JVM). JVM is an interpreter for bytecode. Java introduces bytecode to create Platform (hardware) independent program.

3. Why does the main method need a static identifier?

The main method needs a static identifier because static methods and members do not need an instance of their class to invoke them and main is the first method, which is invoked.

4. Will the program compile, if the main method does not have static identifier?

It will compile. But the program cannot be executed.

5. Which is the default parent class for a Java class?

`java.lang.Object.` By default (implicit), all the Java classes extend this class unless they have their own parent class. Also, the **`package java.lang`** is imported into all Java files by default.

6. How are Java objects passed to a method?

In Java, both the primitive types and objects will be **passed by value**. During object passing, the object's reference will be copied.

7. What are native methods?

Native methods are methods implemented in another programming language, such as C. The Java Native Interface (JNI) is the API to invoke these native methods from a Java class.

8. What are the main differences between an applet and application?

Applets are useful for creating dynamic and interactive web applications. An applet runs under the control of a browser, whereas an application runs as a stand-alone application on the desktop.

An applet is subjected to tougher security restrictions in terms of file and network access, whereas an application can easily access the file system and network.

9. What is the order of declaring class, package and import statements within a Java file?

The order should be package, import statements and then class definition.

10. Which keywords are reserved?

'goto' and 'const' are the 2 reserved keywords in Java.

11. How are 'this and 'super' keyword used?

'this' keyword is used to refer to the current object instance. 'super' keyword is used to refer to the variables and methods of the superclass of the current object instance.

12. Can a variable be an unsigned integer?

No. In Java all the data types are signed numeric numbers.

13. Can a private method be static?

Yes.

14. What are the various bit wise operators?

a & b	Bit wise AND
a | b	Bit wise OR
a ^ b	Bit wise exclusive or (XOR)
~a	Complement
a<<n	Left shift
a>>n	Right shift
a>>>n	Unsigned right shift

The complement unary operator (~) toggles each bit in its operand, i.e., 0 to 1 and 1 to 0.

The left shift infix operator (<<) shifts the bits in the operand n places to the left filling in the bits on the right with zero.

The right shift infix operator (>>) operates in a similar manner but moving bits to the right and filling in the left side with the most significant bit. Thus, given the binary number:

1000 (decimal value is 8), assuming a 4 bit architecture, 1000 >> 2 would produce 1110 (decimal value is 14).

The >>> operator when applied to the above number:

1000 >>> 2 will produce 0010 (decimal value is 2), i.e., the operator fills in the left hand side with zero bits instead of the most significant bit.

15. What is the use of 'Instanceof' operator?

The `instanceof` operator verifies whether its first operand is an instance of its second.

```
op1 instanceof op2.
```

`op1` must be the name of an object and `op2` must be the name of a class/interface/array type.

An object is considered to be an instance of a class if that object directly or indirectly descends from that class.

```
class A {
}
   class B extends A{
}

A a = new B();

if(a instanceof A) {
   System.out.println("Instance of A");
}
if(a instanceof B) {
   System.out.println("Instance of B");
}
```

In the above example, the output will be

Instance of A
Instance of B

16. Mention the access modifiers for a class, method, and variables.

Public

A class that is declared as **public** has global scope and an instance of this class can be created from anywhere within or outside of the class, i.e., by other classes in the same package as well as classes in other packages. Only one non-inner class in any file can be defined with the **public** keyword. The **public** modifier can be used for variables, methods and classes.

Protected

A **protected** variable is visible within the same class, same package and in subclasses in other packages. Any class in the same directory is considered to be in the default package, and thus protected classes will be visible. This can be used for Methods, Variables and Inner classes.

Default

A variable defined with no access modifier is said to have **default visibility**. Default visibility means a variable/method can be seen within the class and from elsewhere within the same package, but not from other packages.

Private

Private variables are only visible from within the same class. This means they are NOT visible within sub classes. This allows a variable to be insulated from being modified by any methods except those in the current class.

This can only be used for Methods, Variables and Inner classes.

17. What is the widening conversion and narrowing conversion?

A widening conversion happens when we try to cast an object of lesser size to an object of larger size, e.g., : int to long.

A narrowing conversion is when we try to cast an object of larger size to an object of lesser size, e.g., long to int.

18. How can you create Java API documentation?

Using the **javadoc** tool parses the declarations and documentation comments in a set of Java source files and produces a corresponding set of HTML pages describing (by default) the public and protected classes, nested classes (but not anonymous inner classes), interfaces, constructors, methods and fields. You can use it to generate the API (Application Programming Interface) documentation or the implementation documentation for a set of source files.

19. What are `jar`, `war` and `ear` files?

JAR: It is a Java archive file used to package classes, property files, etc., as a single file. To create a jar file use the **jar** command. This is similar to the zip file in windows.

For example, to create a jar file with all class files under the current directory:

```
jar -cvf jarfilename.jar *.class
```

WAR: It is a web archive file used to package a web application, i.e., classes, JSPs, property files, etc., as a single file.

EAR: It is an enterprise archive file. This format is used to package EJB, JSP, Servlets, Property files, etc. This is used to package an entire enterprise application. It can consist of multiple WAR files.

Note: Each WAR and EAR will have its own deployment descriptor. The descriptor is a XML based file.

20. Differentiate Java from C++.

- Java does not support pointers.
- Java does not provide the operator overloading option for programmers though it internally use it for string concatenation.
- Java does not support multiple **class** inheritance. However, it supports multiple inheritance using **interface**.
- Java does not support global variables, global functions, typedef, structures or unions.
- Java uses **final** keyword to avoid a class or method to be overridden. Using final with variable is somewhat similar to using **const** in C++.

JVM AND GARBAGE COLLECTION

21. How many JVMs can run on a single machine?

No limitation. A JVM is just like any other process.

22. What is the Just-In-Time (JIT) Compiler?

The Java interpreter on any platform will interpret the compiled bytecode into instructions understandable by the particular hardware. However, the Java Virtual Machine handles one bytecode instruction at a time. The Java Just-In-Time compiler compiles the bytecode into the particular machine code (as though the program had been compiled initially on that platform). Once the code has been (re-)compiled by the JIT compiler, it will usually run more quickly in that system.

23. What is the use of 'classpath' environment variable?

Classpath is the list of directories through which the JVM will search to find a class. It is different from the OS environment variable PATH.

Note: Classpath that a JVM has to use can be specified using the classpath option as follows: If this is not specified then the value specified for the environment variable is taken.

```
C:> Java -classpath classpath1;classpath2 MyClass.java
```

24. Can Java code be retrieved from byte-code?

Yes, class files can be decompiled using utilities like JAD. This takes the class file as an input and generates a Java file. This is especially useful when you are confused as to which version of Java file was used to generate the class file, in a multi-user environment.

25. What is a garbage collector?

When an object is no longer required (when its reference count is 0), its memory needs to be cleaned up and freed. This is what the garbage collector does. **Garbage Collector** is a thread running as part of the JVM process. This thread scans program for objects that will never be accessed again and release their resources back to the system. The basic garbage collector uses mark and sweep algorithm. This algorithm marks all the unused (whose reference count is 0) variables and sweeps them.

26. Can the garbage collector be forced to run?

No. Calling the `System.gc()` method only suggests that the JVM expend effort toward recycling unused objects in order to make the memory they currently occupy available for reuse. When control returns from the method call, the JVM has made a best effort to reclaim space from all discarded objects. This does not guarantee that the garbage collector is called.

The call `System.gc()` is effectively equivalent to the call:

```
Runtime.getRuntime().gc()
```

STRINGS

27. What is the difference between
1. `String s1= new String ("abc");`
2. `String s2="abc";?`

"abc" is known as a string literal. In order to store the string literals, a **string pool** will be created by the JVM. When a string literal is found in a class, it will be added to the string pool. However, if the same literal already exists in the pool, then it uses the existing one in the pool, as string object is **immutable** (cannot be modified).

In the first case, a new memory space is allocated in the heap on account of the "new" and also allocated in the pool on account of the literal "abc".

In the second case, when the statement is being compiled, a pointer to the string literal "abc" is stored in s2. However, if the same string had not been present, then it would have created a new instance in the pool and stored the reference.

28. What happens when intern(). method on a string object is invoked?

Interned strings avoid duplicate strings. There is only one copy of each String that has been interned, no matter how many references point to it. The process of converting duplicated strings to shared ones is called interning. You can compare interned Strings with simple == (which compares references) instead of **equals()** method, which compares the characters of the String one by one. Also, when `intern()` method is invoked, a reference to the String is added to the String pool. This is the reason why you can compare the reference using ==. because both the variables hold the some reference.

29. What is the difference between a String and StringBuffer class?

String class is immutable, i.e., it cannot be modified once declared.

StringBuffer class is not immutable and Strings can be appended to the original String. It is more efficient than using String when the string value could be changed.

For example,

```
String str= "abc" ;
str=str+"def";
```

This creates a brand new String and puts the pointer in str.

```
StringBuffer strBuff="abc";
StrBuff.append("def");
```

This appends to the same String and is more efficient.

30. What is the use of StringTokenizer class?

The StringTokenizer class allows an application to break a string into tokens. The StringTokenizer methods do not distinguish among identifiers, numbers and quoted strings, nor do they recognize and skip comments.

The set of delimiters (the characters that separate tokens) may be specified either at creation time or on a per-token basis.

```
StringTokenizer st = new StringTokenizer("we are Testing");
while (st.hasMoreTokens()) {
System.out.println(st.nextToken());
}
```

```
prints the following output:

we are Testing
```

THREADS

Q 31. Mention the two ways to create a thread.

The first method of creating a thread is to simply extend from the Thread class. This should be done only if the class does not ever need to be extended from another class.

```
import java.lang.*;
public class Count extends Thread
{

    public void run()
    {
        ....
    }
}
```

The above example creates a new class Count that extends the Thread class and overrides the `Thread.run()` method. The run() method is where all the work of the Count class thread is done. The same class can be created by implementing the interface Runnable.

```
import java.lang.*;
public class Count implements Runnable
{
    Thread T;
    public void run()
    {
        ....
    }
}
```

Here, the abstract run() method is defined in the Runnable interface and is being implemented. Note that we have an instance of the Thread class as a variable of the Count class. The only difference between the two methods is that by implementing Runnable, there is greater flexibility in the creation of the class Count. In the above example, the opportunity still exists to extend the

Count class, if needed. The majority of classes created that need to be run as a thread will implement Runnable since they probably are extending some other functionality from another class.

An interface only provides a design upon which classes should be implemented. In the case of the Runnable interface, it forces the definition of only the run() method.

32. What does Thread.start() do?

The start method creates the system resources necessary to run the thread and schedules the thread to run. After the start method has returned, the thread is actually in the Runnable state. When a thread gets the CPU time, it will be executed.

33. How is a thread prioritized?

Execution of multiple threads on a single CPU, in some order, is called **scheduling**. The Java runtime supports a very simple, deterministic scheduling algorithm known as **fixed priority scheduling**. This algorithm schedules threads based on their priority relative to other runnable threads.

When a Java thread is created, it inherits its priority from the thread that created it. You can also modify a thread's priority at any time after its creation using the setPriority() method. Thread priorities are integers ranging between MIN_PRIORITY (1) and MAX_PRIORITY (10) (constants defined in the Thread class). The value 5 is the default priority. The higher the integer, the higher the priority. At any given time, when multiple threads are ready to be executed, the runtime system chooses the runnable thread with the highest priority for execution. Only when that thread stops, yields or becomes not runnable for some reason will a lower priority thread start executing. If two threads of the same priority are waiting for the CPU, the scheduler chooses one of them to run in a round-robin fashion. The chosen thread will run until one of the following conditions is true:

- A higher priority thread becomes runnable.
- It yields, or its run method exits.
- On systems that support time-slicing, its time allotment has expired.

Then the second thread is given a chance to run, and so on, until the interpreter exits.

The Java runtime system's thread scheduling algorithm is also preemptive. If at any time a thread with a higher priority than all other runnable threads becomes runnable, the runtime system chooses the new higher priority thread for execution. The new higher priority thread is said to preempt the other threads.

34. What is the difference between yielding and sleeping in threads?

When a thread invokes its `yield()` method, it returns to the ready state. When a thread invokes its `sleep()` method, it returns to the waiting state.

35. What is the difference between pre-emptive scheduling and time slicing?

Under pre-emptive scheduling, the highest priority thread executes until it enters the waiting or dead states or a higher priority thread comes into existence. Under time slicing, a thread executes for a predefined slice of time and then re-enters the pool of ready threads. The scheduler then determines which thread should execute next, based on priority and other factors.

36. What are synchronized methods and synchronized statements?

Synchronized methods are methods that are used to control access to an object. A thread only executes a synchronized method after it has acquired the lock for the method's object or class. Synchronized statements are similar to synchronized methods. A synchronized statement can only be executed after a thread has acquired the lock for the object or class referenced in the synchronized statement. This means that no other thread can access the object till the current thread releases the object. This is used to make code thread safe and prevent dirty reads.

37. When do you use synchronized statements?

Synchronized statements are good to use when

- ➢ it is sufficient to synchronize only a part of the method

```
void method()
{
    // some statement
    Synchronized(this)
    {
        this.a = 20;
    }
    //some statement
}
```

- ➢ if a class whose object to be locked is part of a third party jar file

```
void method()
{
    // some statement
    Synchronized(thirdPartyObject)
    {
```

```
        thirdPartyObject.a = 20;
    }
    //some statement
}
```

38. How can a dead thread be restarted?

A dead thread cannot be restarted.

39. What invokes a `thread's run()` method?

After a thread is started, via its `start()` method or that of the Thread class, the JVM scheduler invokes the thread's `run()` method once the turn comes for the thread to run.

40. When do threads go out of runnable state?

A thread becomes Not Runnable when one of these events occurs

- its sleep method is invoked.
- the thread calls the wait method to wait for a specific condition to be satisfied.
- the thread is blocking on I/O.

41. What is a monitor?

A *monitor* is a lock on an object, which allows only one thread to access/modify the contents of that object.

42. How do you make code thread safe?

The keyword **synchronized** is used to temporarily lock an object to have exclusive access to it. It marks a block of code or an entire method as **critical section**. Only one thread can execute it at any point in time. Other threads will wait for their turn to use the critical section.

When **an instance** method is synchronized, the synchronized code can be run by many threads on different objects simultaneously, since the locking is on the object. For a synchronized class method, the locking is on the class object, which thus limits to only one thread executing that code.

43. What does `Thread.wait()`. Do?

`Thread.wait()` and `Thread.notify()` methods are used for inter-thread communication. `Thread.wait()` makes the thread go to sleep until some other thread wakes it up using `Thread.notify()` method.

The wait method is defined in the object class. Since all classes in Java extend object by default, it is available in all classes.

44. What is a daemon thread?

Daemon threads are sometimes called "service" threads that normally run at a low priority and provide a basic service to a program or programs when activity on a machine is reduced.

The garbage collector thread is an example of a daemon thread. This thread, provided by the JVM, will scan programs for variables that will never be accessed again and free up their resources back to the system. A thread can set the daemon flag by passing a true Boolean value to the setDaemon() method. If a false Boolean value is passed, the thread will become a user thread. However, this must occur before the thread has been started.

The JVM scheduler's basic rule is if there are only **Daemon threads** running, the Java Virtual Machine (JVM) will exit.

45. What is the difference between `notify().` and `notifyall()`?

`notify():` This can be called only from within **synchronized** method/block. It wakes up a single thread, which is waiting on the objects lock. If there is more than one thread waiting, the choice is arbitrary, i.e., there is no way to specify, which waiting thread should be awakened.

`notifyAll():` wakes up all the waiting threads. The JVM scheduler will then decide, which thread will run.

COLLECTIONS

46. What is the difference between ArrayList and Vector?

ArrayList	Vector
Methods are not synchronized; therefore, they are not thread safe. Hence, more efficient and faster.	Methods are synchronized. Any method that touches the Vector's contents is thread safe.
ArrayList increases its array size by 50 percent when it gets filled.	A Vector defaults to doubling the size of its array, when it gets filled.

47. Which collection sorts data?

TreeMap is a collection class that sorts data.

The Java API reference states:

It is an implementation of the SortedMap interface. This class guarantees that the map will be in ascending key order, sorted according to the **natural order** for the key's class (see Comparable), or by the comparator provided at creation time, depending on which constructor is used.

48. What is the difference between Hashtable and HashMap?

Hashtable	HashMap
Methods are synchronized. Any method that touches the Hashtable's contents is thread safe.	Methods are not synchronized; therefore, they are not thread safe. Hence, it is more efficient and faster.
Does not permit null key or null value.	Permits null key and null value.

49. What is the difference between Enumeration and Iterator interface?

Iterators differ from enumerations in two ways:

- allows the caller to remove elements from the underlying collection during the iteration.
- method names have been improved.

EXCEPTION HANDLING

50. What is the order of execution of try catch finally? What happens if an exception occurs in the finally block?

```
try {
   statements;
}
catch (exceptionType1 identifier1)
{
   // one or multiple statements;
}
catch (exceptionType2 identifier2)
{
   //statements;
}
...
}
finally {
```

```
// one or none statements;
}
```

- Every try block must have either one catch clause or a finally clause
- We can have multiple catch clauses but only one finally clause
- The statements within the **try** block are executed until an exception is thrown or it completes successfully
- We get a compiler-error if the code included in the **try** statement will never throw one of the caught checked exceptions
- If an exception is thrown, each **catch** clause is inspected in turn for a type to which the exception can be assigned
- The catch blocks must be ordered from most specific to least specific.Ex: `catch(Exception e)` should come last after all the other Exceptions like `catch(IOException e)`
- When a match is found, the exception object is assigned to the identifier and the catch statements are executed a catch clause may throw another exception
- If a **finally** clause is included, it's statements are executed after all other try-catch processing is complete
- The finally clause executes whether or not an exception is thrown or a break or continue are encountered
- If a **catch** clause invokes **System. exit ()** the finally clause WILL NOT execute.

Q 51. What are checked and unchecked Exceptions?

Checked exceptions

- represent invalid conditions in areas outside the immediate control of the program (invalid user input, database problems, network outages, absent files)
- are subclasses of `Exception`
- methods are **obliged** to establish a policy for all checked exceptions thrown by its implementation (either pass the checked exception further up the stack, or handle it somehow)

Unchecked exceptions

- represent defects in the program (often invalid arguments passed to a non-private method)
- are subclasses of `RuntimeException`, and are usually implemented using `IllegalArgumentException`, `NullPointerException`, or `IllegalStateException`

➢ methods are **not** obliged to establish a policy for the unchecked exceptions thrown by its implementation (and they almost always do not do so).

52. What is the Throwable class?

The **Throwable class** is the superclass of all errors and exceptions in the Java language. Only objects that are instances of this class (or one of its subclasses) are thrown by the Java Virtual Machine or can be thrown by the Java throw statement. Similarly, only this class or one of its subclasses can be the argument type in a catch clause.

53. How do you write a custom exception?

Custom exceptions can be written by extending the java.lang.Exception class. The toString () method should be overridden to print an appropriate error message.

54. What happens if an exception is not caught?

An uncaught exception results in the uncaughtException() method of the thread's ThreadGroup being invoked, which eventually results in the termination of the program in which it is thrown.

55. What is printed when printStackTrace () method is invoked?

The Java API ref explains the functionality of the method as follows:

```
public void printStackTrace()
```

Prints this throwable and its backtrace to the standard error stream. This method prints a stack trace for this `Throwable` object on the error output stream that is the value of the field System.err. The first line of output contains the result of the `toString()` method for this object. Remaining lines represent data previously recorded by the method `fillInStackTrace()`. The format of this information depends on the implementation, but the following example may be regarded as typical:

```
java.lang.NullPointerException
   at MyClass.mash(MyClass.java:9)
   at MyClass.crunch(MyClass.java:6)
   at MyClass.main(MyClass.java:3)
```

This example was produced by running the program:

```
class MyClass {
   public static void main(String[] args) {
```

```
        crunch(null);
    }
    static void crunch(int[] a) {
        mash(a);
    }
    static void mash(int[] b) {
        System.out.println(b[0]);
    }
}
```

56. What are the characteristics of `Final`, `Finally` and `Finalize` keywords?

`Final`

- When a variable is marked as final, then the compiler could perform various optimizations knowing that its value cannot change.
- Class member variables can be declared as final without a value assigned to it. This forces all its constructors to initialize the blank final variables.
- When a static variable declared as final, it is similar to constant variable of C.
- When a class declared as final, it cannot be sub-classed.
- If an object or array (array in Java is an object) is declared as final, it does not stop you from changing the fields in the object or elements of the array. It just stops you from pointing that variable to a different object or array. If you want to protect the object, you must make it **immutable**.
- When a method declared as final, it cannot be overridden.

`Finally`

The keyword **`finally`** is used in Exception handling. The finally block is placed after a try-catch block. The code contained in the finally block would get executed under following conditions:

- If exception is thrown in try block
- If exception is not thrown in try block
- If exception is thrown in Catch block

➢ We usually close resources or clean up variables inside the finally block. See the example below:

```
class X {
   Void dbUpdate() {
   Connection connection = new Connection(...);
   try {
      doSomeUpdates(); // using connection instance
   }catch ( DatabaseException e ) {
      System.out.println( "The error is"+e.toString() );
      throw e;
}
   finally {
      connection.close(); // always executed
   }
}
```

In this example connection instance is getting closed inside the **`finally`** as it is safer approach.

`Finalize`

The finalize method is used for garbage collection. You can put clean up code in the finalize block. When an object is about to be garbage collected, its finalize method will run. However, we cannot be sure that, during machine shutdown, the finalizers will be called. So you cannot depend on them. The prototype of finalize method is:

```
protected void finalize() throws Throwable {...}
```

CONSTRUCTORS

57. What is the use of 'super' keyword inside a constructor?

The super keyword is used to invoke the constructor of the parent class. This is invoked by default when the constructor of any class is called, i.e., a call to the default constructor of parent class is inserted at the beginning of the constructor of child class and it gets executed first and then the execution continues with the child class constructor.

58. Can a constructor be private?

Yes, it can be private. We use this feature in Singleton pattern to prevent anyone from instantiating the class directly. Instead an instance can be got by invoking a static method on the class.

59. How are `this()` and `super()` method used with constructors?

`this()` method within a constructor is used to invoke another constructor in the same class. `super()` method within a constructor is used to invoke its immediate superclass constructor.

OVERLOADING AND OVERRIDING

60. Does Java support Operator Overloading?

Java does not allow the programmer to perform operator overloading. However, Java internally supports operator overloading for performing String concatenation using + operator.

61. When overloaded methods and variables are in child classes, which version of the method gets called?

Let us take an example:

```
class A{
    public int a=10;
    public void someMethod(){
        System.out.println("In the class A");
    }
}
class B extends A {
    public int a=20;
    public void someMethod(){
        System.out.println("In the class B");
    }
}

A objA=new A();
System.out.println(ObjA.a);
System.out.println(ObjA.someMethod());

ObjA=new B();
System.out.println(ObjA.a);
System.out.println(ObjA.someMethod());
```

```
This will print
10
In the class A
20
In the class B
```

This shows that the member variable, which is displayed, will be based on the type of the object variable and the method, which is invoked, is based on the type of the object held in the object variable.

Q 62. What is the overloading and overriding?

Polymorphism refers to the ability of a method to behave differently based on the kind of input. There are two ways in which polymorphism is implemented in Java.

- Overloading
- Overriding

Overloading methods

Overloaded methods have the same name, but different parameter lists and returns types and appears in the same class or subclass. The decision as to which method should be called is taken at runtime, based on the parameter list. This is known as **late-binding.**

An example of an overloaded method is **`abs()`** in the **`java.lang.Math`** class.

```
public static double abs(double a)
public static float abs(float a)
public static int abs(int a)
public static long abs(long a)
```

Overriding methods

In overriding, we **re-define** a method that is inherited from a superclass.

- Overridden methods can only exist in subclasses. They have the exact same name and method signature.
- The **access modifier** for the overriding method may not be more restrictive than the access modifier of the superclass method.
- Private methods are not inherited so we can have any access modifier in subclass.
- The **throws** clause of the overriding method may only include exceptions that are thrown by the superclass method, including it's subclasses.

63. Compare an Interface and an Abstract class.

- Neither Interface nor Abstract classes can be instantiated.
- Direct multiple inheritance cannot be done in Java, like in C++. We have interfaces to take care of this problem. A class can implement any number of interfaces, but can extend only one class.
- An interface has all public members and no implementation. An abstract class is a class, which may have the usual flavors of class members (private, protected, etc.), but has some abstract methods.
- Use interface as much as possible and only use an abstract class in the case where you want to provide some (but not all, of course) implementation.

64. Can you instantiate an abstract class?

No we cannot instantiate an abstract class.

To declare that your class is an abstract class, use the keyword abstract before the class keyword in your class declaration:

```
abstract public class Number {
    . . .
}

class Integer extends Number {
}
```

If you attempt to create instance for the abstract class Number, the compiler displays an error and refuses to compile your program.

65. Can an abstract class be final?

An abstract class cannot be declared as final. The purpose of having an abstract class is that child classes can extend its functionality.

STREAMS

66. What is the Object Serialization?

Serialization refers to the process of writing the contents of an object to a file and re-creating the object from the file at a future date.

67. What is the use of 'transient' keyword?

On Object Serialization, if any of the object's members need not be serialized, they should be declared as **`transient`**.

68. Compare Byte Streams and Character Streams.

Byte Streams	Character Streams
java.io.InputStream and java.io.OutputStream are the base Byte Stream classes. These are 8-bit streams.	java.io.Reader and java.io.Writer are the base character streams. These are 16-bit Unicode character streams. These are available since JDK1.1.
The method names end with a suffix InputStream or OutputStream.	The method names end with a suffix Reader or Writer.
They are less efficient.	They are more efficient.

INTERFACE AND INNER CLASS

69. What are the types of variables can be there in an Interface?

An interface is like a class but with a few restrictions.

- All its variables must be static final, i.e., constants.
- A class can inherit multiple interfaces.
- All methods in an interface are implicitly declared public and abstract.
- All variables in an interface must be constants. They are implicitly declared public static final.

70. What is an inner class?

Class present inside a class is called **inner class.** Inner classes increase the complexity of code and should be used only if absolutely necessary. Inner classes are used to implement adapters in AWT program.

```
class A{
   int a;
   public void doSomething(){
   }

   //Inner class
```

```
    class B {
        public void doAnotherThing(){
        // can access the instance variables of the parent
        a=20;
        }
    }
}
```

71. What are anonymous classes?

An inner class can be declared without naming it. Here is yet another version of the now-tired `Stack` class, in this case using an **anonymous class** for its enumerator:

```
public class Stack {
    private Vector items;
    ...//code for Stack's methods and constructors not shown...
    public Enumeration enumerator() {
        return new Enumeration() {
            int currentItem = items.size() - 1;
            public Boolean hasMoreElements() {
                return (currentItem >= 0);
            }
            public Object nextElement() {
            if (!hasMoreElements())
                throw new NoSuchElementException();
            else
                return items.elementAt(currentItem–);
            }
        }
    }
}
```

Anonymous classes can make code difficult to read. You should limit their use to those classes that are very small (no more than a method or two) and whose use is well-understood (like the AWT event-handling adapter classes).

DATABASE SUPPORT

72. What are the various types of JDBC drivers?

The Sun Java developer Forum describes the types of JDBC drivers as follows:

JDBC technology drivers fit into one of four categories:

Type 1 A *JDBC-ODBC bridge* provides JDBC API access via one or more ODBC drivers. Note that some ODBC native code and in many cases native database client code must be loaded on each client machine that uses this type of driver. Hence, this kind of driver is generally most appropriate when automatic installation and downloading of a Java technology application is not important.

Type 2 A *native-API partly Java technology-enabled driver* converts JDBC calls into calls on the client API for Oracle, Sybase, Informix, DB2, or other DBMS. Note that, like the bridge driver, this style of driver requires that some binary code be loaded on each client machine.

Type 3 A *net-protocol fully Java technology-enabled driver* translates JDBC API calls into a DBMS-independent net protocol, which is then translated to a DBMS protocol by a server. This net server middleware is able to connect all of its Java technology-based clients to many different databases. The specific protocol used depends on the vendor. In general, this is the most flexible JDBC API alternative. It is likely that all vendors of this solution will provide products suitable for Intranet use. In order for these products to also support Internet access they must handle the additional requirements for security, access through firewalls, etc., that the Web imposes. Several vendors are adding JDBC technology-based drivers to their existing database middleware products.

Type 4 A *native-protocol fully Java driver* converts JDBC technology calls into the network protocol used by DBMSs directly. This allows a direct call from the client machine to the DBMS server and is a practical solution for Intranet access. Since many of these protocols are proprietary the database vendors themselves will be the primary source for this style of driver. Several database vendors have these in progress. This is the most preferred driver because it improves portability.

73. What does Class.forName () do?

The following is the definition given in the API reference:

```
public static Class forName(String className)
                        throws ClassNotFoundException
```

Returns the Class object associated with the class or interface with the given string name. Invoking this method is equivalent to:

```
Class.forName(className, true, currentLoader)
```

where currentLoader denotes the defining class loader of the current class.

For example, the following code fragment returns the runtime Class descriptor for the class named java.lang.Thread:

```
Class t = Class.forName("java.lang.Thread")
```

A call to forName ("X") causes the class named X to be initialized.

Parameters

className—the fully qualified name of the desired class.

Returns

The Class object for the class with the specified name.

Throws

LinkageError—if the linkage fails
ExceptionInInitializerError—if the initialization provoked by this method fails
ClassNotFoundException—if the class cannot be located.

74. What is the URL used to connect using type 4 driver? What does it mean?

```
jdbc:oracle:thin:@machine_name:port_number:instance_name
```

where

- machine name can be the name or the IP address of the machine on which the Database instance is running.
- port is the port on which the DB is listening, usually 1521 for oracle.
- instance name is that particular Database instance you want to connect to. There can be more than one instance on the same machine.

75. Can the resultset be used after closing the connection?

No. The resultset becomes invalid once the connection is closed.

76. Can a connection object be serialized and used from another machine?

No, a connection object cannot be serialized and used from another machine. This is because the connection is created for the current machine IP address.

77. How do you get hold of the column names fetched in a resultset?

To retrieve information about the resultset, which is fetched, use the method `con.getMetaData()`. It returns a MetaData Object using which the various properties of the resultset can be fetched.

78. What does the connection pooling mean?

Connection pooling is a technique to allow multiple clients to share a cached set of connection objects that provide access to a database resource. Various application server vendors implement pooling in different ways.

79. What does setAutoCommit (true) do?

A transaction is one or more SQL statements that form a logical unit of work. Within a transaction, all SQL statements must succeed or fail as one logical entity. Changes are made to the database only if all statements in the transaction succeed and a COMMIT is issued. If one or more statements fail, we must issue a ROLLBACK to undo the changes. This ensures the integrity and security of data in the database.

By setting AutoCommit to false, we prevent the connection from committing the changes unless the commit method is called in the program. We can commit or rollback in the code based on whether all the statements within the transaction succeed.

80. Can a resultset be updated?

Yes, we can update the database values from the resultset.

81. What are the various types of statements? What are the advantages and disadvantages of them?

There are three types of statements, these are interfaces and every vendor has his/her own implementation. The API ref states that

```
public interface Statement
```

The object used for executing a static SQL statement and returning the results it produces.

By default, only one ResultSet object per Statement object can be open at the same time. Therefore, if the reading of one ResultSet object is interleaved with the reading of another, each must have been generated by different Statement objects. All execution methods in the Statement interface implicitly close a statement's current ResultSet object if an open one exists.

```
public interface PreparedStatement extends Statement
```

PreparedStatement objects represents precompiled SQL statements. A SQL statement is precompiled and stored in a PreparedStatement object. This object can then be used to efficiently execute this statement multiple times.

Note: The setter methods (`setShort`, `setString` and so on) for setting IN parameter values must specify types that are compatible with the defined SQL type of the input parameter. For instance, if the IN parameter has SQL type `INTEGER`, then the method `setInt` should be used.

If arbitrary parameter type conversions are required, the method `setObject` should be used with a target SQL type.

In the following example of setting a parameter, `con` represents an active connection:

```
PreparedStatement pstmt = con.prepareStatement(
"UPDATE EMPLOYEES SET SAL = ? WHERE EMPID = ?"
);
pstmt.setBigDecimal(1, 153833.00)
pstmt.setInt(2, 110592)
```

```
public interface CallableStatement extends PreparedStatement
```

The interface used to execute SQL stored procedures. The JDBC API provides a stored procedure SQL escape syntax that allows stored procedures to be called in a standard way for all RDBMSs. This escape syntax has one form that includes a result parameter and one that does not. If used, the result parameter must be registered as an OUT parameter. The other parameters can be used for input, output or both. Parameters are referred to sequentially, by number, with the first parameter being 1.

```
{?= call <procedure-name>[<arg1>,<arg2>, ...]}
   {call <procedure-name>[<arg1>,<arg2>, ...]}
```

IN parameter values are set using the set methods inherited from PreparedStatement. The type of all OUT parameters must be registered prior to executing the stored procedure; their values are retrieved after execution via the get methods provided here.

A CallableStatement can return one ResultSet object or multiple ResultSet objects. Multiple ResultSet objects are handled using operations inherited from Statement.

For maximum portability, a call's ResultSet objects and update counts should be processed prior to getting the values of output parameters.

82. How to call a stored procedure from JDBC?

Given below is a sample piece of code demonstrating how we can invoke a stored procedure using CallableStatement.

```
CallableStatement cstmt = con.prepareCall(
                          "{call getTestData(?, ?)}");
cstmt.registerOutParameter(1, java.sql.Types.TINYINT);
cstmt.registerOutParameter(2, java.sql.Types.DECIMAL, 3);
cstmt.executeQuery();
byte x = cstmt.getByte(1);
java.math.BigDecimal n = cstmt.getBigDecimal(2, 3);
```

SERVLETS

83. Why is HTTP called a stateless protocol?

HTTP is called a **stateless protocol** since every request is independent of the previous request. The server does not keep track of whether the same user is making repeated requests.

84. What is the order in which the life cycle methods are called in a Servlet/ HttpServlet and which ones can be overridden?

- `init()`—Called only once during the initialization of the Servlet.
- `destroy()`—Called only once when Servlet instance is about to be destroyed.
- `service()`—Do not override this method.
- `doGet()`, `doPost()`, `doPut()`, `doDelete()`, `doOptions`, `doTrace()`.—These methods are called according to the type of HTTP request received. Override them to generate your own response.
- `log()`—Writes messages to the Servlet's log files.
- `getLastModified()`—Override this method to return your Servlet's last modified date.
- `getServletInfo()`—Override this method to provide a String of general info about your Servlet such author, version, copyright, etc.
- `getServletName()`—Override this method to return name of the Servlet.

- `getInitParameter()`, `getInitParameterNames()`—First one returns value of given initialization parameter, second one returns an Enumeration object containing names of all initialization parameters provided.

85. What is the difference between GET and POST requests?

The HTML specifications technically define the difference between `"GET"` and `"POST"` so that the former means that form data is to be encoded (by a browser) into a URL while the latter means that the form data is to appear within a message body. We might say that **`"GET"`** is basically for *just getting (retrieving) data* whereas `"POST"` may involve anything, like storing or updating data, ordering a product or sending E-mail.

86. What is the difference between ServletContext and HttpSession?

The interface ServletContext defines a set of methods that a servlet uses to communicate with its servlet container, for example, to get the MIME type of a file, dispatch requests or write to a log file.

There is one context per "web application" per Java Virtual Machine the context can be used as a location to share global information.

The interface HttpSession provides a way to identify a user across more than one page request or visit to a Web site and to store information about that user.

The servlet container uses this interface to create a session between an HTTP client and an HTTP server. The session persists for a specified time period, across more than one connection or page request from the user. This time period can be set either in a property file or in the code. A session usually corresponds to one user, who may click on various links, thus hitting the website multiple times. The server can maintain a session in many ways, such as using cookies or rewriting URLs.

This interface allows servlets to

- view and manipulate information about a session, such as the session identifier, creation time and last accessed time.
- bind objects to sessions, allowing user information to persist across multiple user connections.

87. What is the difference between forward() and sendRedirect() methods?

Forward

It finds the Servlet on the local server, and calls its service (request, response) method, passing the same request and response that was used by the current page.

The parameters stored in the request object are available to the called request, when we forward a request. The users will not see a change in the url in their address bar.

Redirect

It sends a response to the client with a meta-refresh that makes the client send a new request to the page specified. We can also make requests to pages other than those on the local server as well. The parameters stored in the request object are lost when we redirect. The url in the address bar will change. The objects shared in session and application scope are available only if the new page is within the some context. They will not be available if it is in a different context.

88. Are variables declared at the class level in a servlet thread safe?

There is only one copy of the instance variables per instance of the servlet and all of the threads share this copy. In the case of the multithreaded model, multiple threads may access an instance variable simultaneously, which makes it unsafe. In the case of the single-threaded model, only one thread executes the methods of a servlet instance at a time. Therefore, an instance variable is thread-safe for the single-threaded model.

By wrapping non-thread-safe code in a synchronized code block, you force the requesting thread to acquire the instance lock in order to gain access to the code block.

Example

```
synchronized (this) {
count++;
}
```

89. How many instances of a servlet are created?

Only one instance of a servlet gets created. This instance is accessed by all the requests hitting the server.

90. How do you make a servlet Single threaded and how many instances are created?

A Servlet can be made thread safe by implementing `SingleThreadModel` interface. The number of instances created depends on what Servlet container decides to do. It may just create one instance, it might create more.

91. What is the argument of init() method? What does Interface ServletConfig contain?

An object of type ServletConfig is passed. ServletConfig is an interface.

A servlet configuration object is used by a servlet container to pass information to a servlet during initialization. Some of the methods available are as follows:

```
getServletName()

getServletContext() etc.
```

92. What are the exceptions thrown by service method?

The Exceptions thrown are `ServletException` and `IOException`.

`ServletException` is thrown to report any problems encountered in the servlet engine trying to service the HTTP request, whereas an `IOException` can be thrown when using the `PrintWriter` object to stream web resources back to the client browser.

93. What happens if the service method in HttpServlet is overridden?

If we override the service method in an HttpServlet, we have to take care of calling the default service method. In some cases, it does make sense to override the service() method. For example, when you have a lot of Servlets that need to perform the same checks (for example, is the session authenticated) before processing the request. Rather than having to copy the logic into each Servlet you write, you can develop a common base class that extends HttpServlet. The logic inside the service method is effectively:

```
service(...) {
   common processing logic....
   super.service(...);
}
```

Another option is to write the logic in a helper method and call it at the beginning of both the doGet and doPost methods.

94. How do you keep track of the sessions created in a servlet container?

The session can be tracked using the following two objects:

HttpSessionListener

Implementations of this interface are notified of changes to the list of active sessions in a web application. To receive notification events, the implementation class must be configured in the deployment descriptor for the web application.

HttpSessionEvent

This is the class representing event notifications for changes to sessions within a web application.

95. What are the methods available in HttpSessionListener?

sessionCreated and sessionDestroyed are the two methods available. An HttpSessionEvent object is passed to these methods by the container when a new session is created or when an existing session is destroyed.

96. How does an object know when it is put in session?

HttpSessionBindingListener

This causes an object to be notified when it is bound to or unbound from a session. The object is notified by an HttpSessionBindingEvent object.

- The method valueBound(HttpSessionBindingEvent event) Notifies the object that it is being bound to a session and identifies the session.
- The method valueUnbound(HttpSessionBindingEvent event) Notifies the object that it is being unbound from a session and identifies the session.

HttpSessionBindingEvent

It has methods like getName, which Returns the name with which the object is bound to or unbound from the session.getSession, which Returns the session to or from which the object is bound or unbound.

97. How do you set the session time out for a session? How do you make it infinite?

The method setMaxInactiveInterval in HttpSession can be used to set the timeout

```
public void setMaxInactiveInterval(int interval)
```

interval, specifies the time, in seconds, between client requests before the servlet container will invalidate this session. A negative time indicates the session should never timeout.

This can also be set in the configuration files of the application server.

The value set in the code takes precedence over what is specified in the config file.

98. How do you do session management?

Since HTTP is a stateless protocol, we use a variety of methods to maintain information of the history of actions performed during a session. There are four ways in which we can do session management.

- Cookies
- URL Rewriting
- Hidden Fields
- HttpSession

Cookies

A **`cookie`** is a piece of information stored on the client machine by the browser. Cookies are widely used by various server-side programming techniques for the purpose of implementing session tracking. The cookie is a text file, which is stored on the client machine. These cookies are sent to the server whenever a user makes a request to the same server from which the cookies were created. The Java API provides us various classes and methods designed to allow us to use cookies in servlets.

The constructor sets the name and value of a cookie when the **`Cookie`** object is instantiated. The **`setValue()`** method can be used to assign a new value to the cookie after it is instantiated.

The various places where a cookie can be used are as follows:

- Storing user preferences
- Shopping cart applications, etc.

A cookie has a name, a single value, and optional attributes, such as a comment, path and domain qualifiers, a maximum age, and a version number. Some Web browsers have bugs in how they handle the optional attributes, so use them sparingly to improve the interoperability of your servlets.

The servlet sends cookies to the browser by using the `HttpServletResponse.addCookie(javax.servlet.http.Cookie)` method, which adds fields to HTTP response headers to send cookies to the browser, one at a time. The browser is expected to support 20 cookies for each Web server, 300 cookies total, and may limit cookie size to 4 KB each.

URL rewriting

In this method, the data is appended to the URL over successive requests. In addition to the current data, the values of the previous data with which the user invoked the servlet are retrieved from the incoming URL and appended to the new URL. In other words, the parameter values for each successive URL that is generated match those of the previous URL. In addition, new parameter values are added, which represent the current data.

Hidden Fields

In html, we have a type of field called HIDDEN. This type of field is not visible on the browser but gets passed to the application server. Every time the client makes a request to the server, a HTML form is created and sent back to the client. Hidden fields are added to the form each time it is created. The hidden fields contain the data from the previous request that would be required by the future requests. Using this approach, the historical data is saved by embedding it in the new HTML form that is returned to the client. Thus, the historical data need not be saved in a database or in the server's file system. This method is not recommended. But its advantages are that, it places no special requirements on the server software and is compatible with all browsers that support HTML forms.

This approach has been used by CGI programmers (i.e., Pro*C, Pro Cobol, etc.) is reliable, and is easy to implement.

HttpSession

The HttpSession object is created and maintained by the application server. We can get hold of the session object using request.getSession(true). Where request is of type HttpServletRequest. Once we have a handle on this object we can store data in this object and this is shared between the various requests coming from the same user in one session ie from one browser window. Sessions are used to maintain state and user identity across multiple page requests. The session persists for a specified time period. This can be set using setMaxInactiveInterval(int interval). The manner in which the session is maintained varies from one server to the other. The Java documentation states:

"A session can be maintained either by using cookies or by URL rewriting." We can add and retrieve object from a session using the following methods:

```
void setAttribute(java.lang.String name,java.lang.Objectvalue) ;
java.lang.Object getAttribute(java.lang.String name) ;
```

EJB

99. Illustrate State Diagrams/Lifecycle of Entity, Session Beans.

Stateless Session Beans

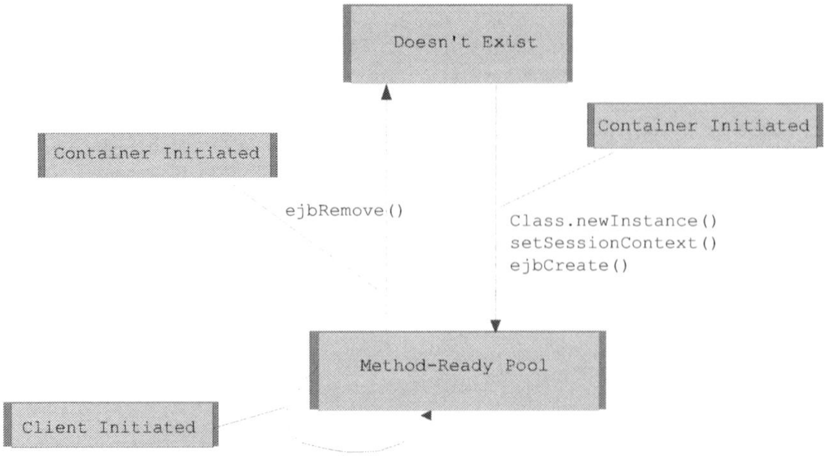

Life Cycle State Diagram of the Entity Bean

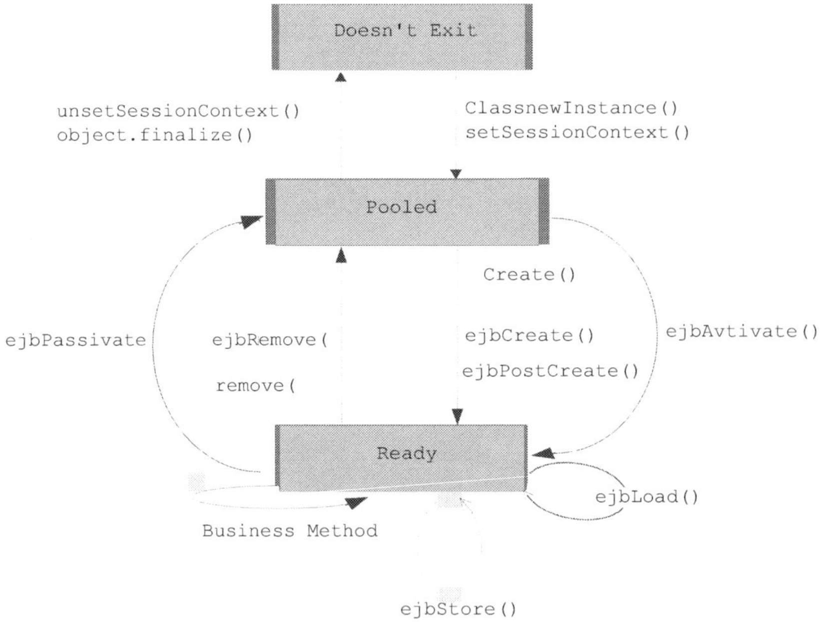

Stateful Session Beans

EJB 1.1 stateful session bean life cycle

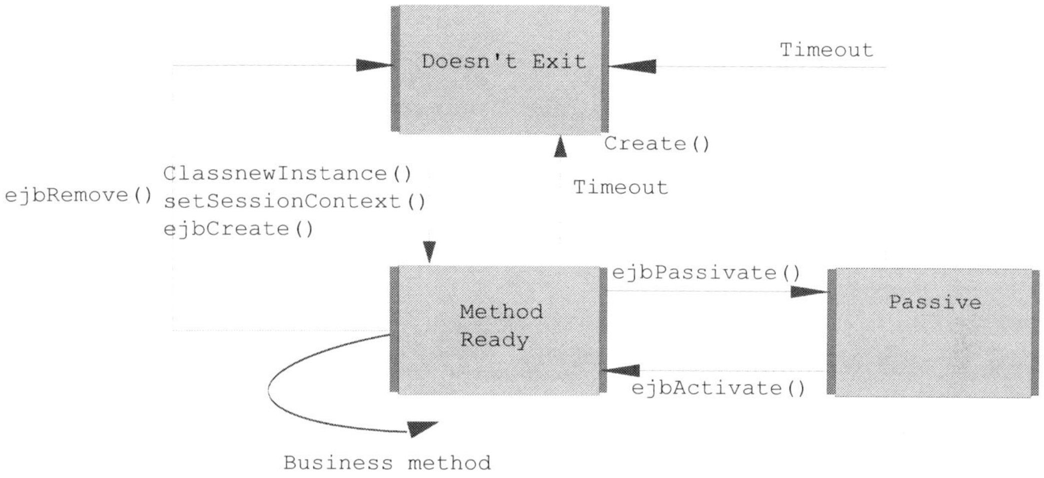

EJB1.0 life cycle state diagram of the stateful session bean life cycle

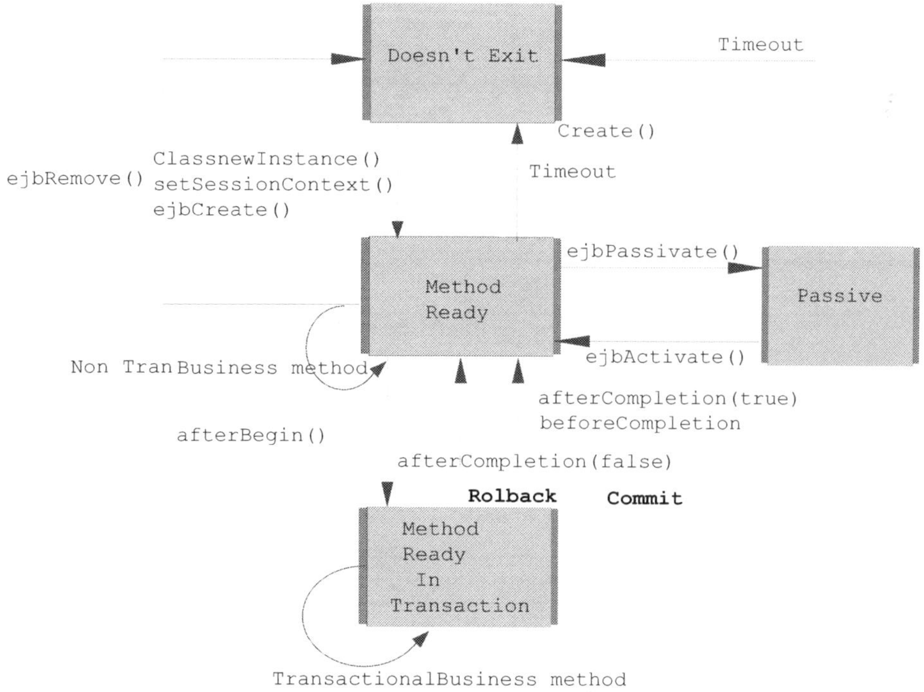

EJB 1.1 life cycle of a stateful session bean with session synchronization interface

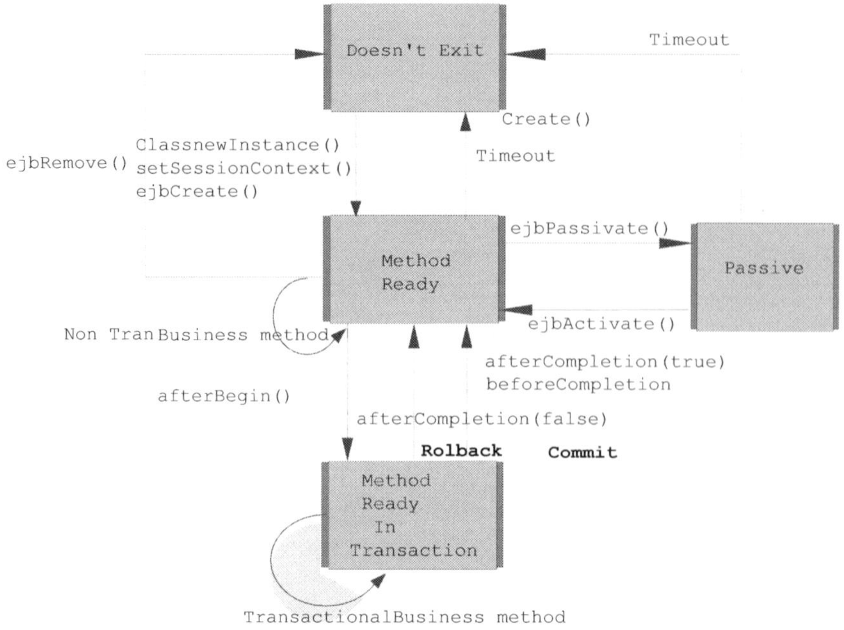

EJB 1.0 life cycle of the stateful session bean with session synchronization interface

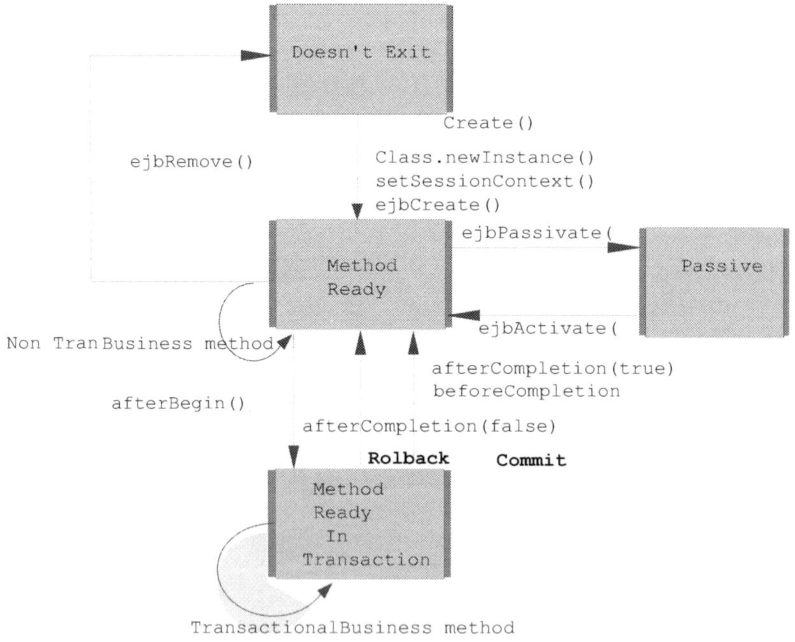

100. What are isolation levels? Mention the various levels of isolation.

Isolation level can be defined as:

The degree to which operations on data by a certain transaction are affected by concurrent transactions, i.e., the other transactions running at the same time. Also, the degree to which operations on data by a transaction can affect data in concurrent transactions.

The various levels of Isolation are as follows:

Dirty

A dirty read will occur when the first transaction reads uncommitted changes made by a second transaction. If the second transaction is rolled back, the data read by the first transaction would be invalid because the rollback reverses the changes. The first transaction will not be aware that the data it has read has become invalid.

Transaction Attribute	EJB 1.1 Text Value	EJB 1.0 Constant
Not Supported	NotSupported	TX_NOT_SUPPORTED
Supports	Supports	TX_SUPPORTS
Required	Required	TX_REQUIRED
Requires New	RequiresNew	TX_REQUIRES_NEW
Mandatory	Mandatory	TX_MANDATORY
Never (1.1)	Never	
Bean Managed (1.0)		TX_BEAN_MANAGED

Repeatable

A repeatable read occurs when the data read is guaranteed to look the same if read again during the same transaction. Repeatable reads can be guaranteed in one of two ways: either the data read is locked against changes or the data read is a snapshot that does not reflect changes. If the data is locked, then it cannot be changed by any other transaction until the current transaction ends. If the data is a snapshot, then other transactions can change the data, but these changes will not be seen by this transaction if the read is repeated.

Phantom Reads

Phantom reads occur when new records inserted into the database are detectable by transactions that started prior to the insert. Queries will include records added by other transactions after their transaction has started.

101. What are Heuristic decisions?

Transactions are usually controlled by a transaction manager across multiple databases and servers. This transaction manager uses a protocol called two-phase commit (2-PC) to manage transactions. 2-PC is a protocol for managing transactions that commit updates in two stages. The transaction manager controls the transaction, based on the results of a poll against the resources (databases and other servers), it decides whether all the updates should be committed or rolled back. A Heuristic decision is when one of the resources makes a decision to commit or roll back by itself, without permission from the transaction manager. Once a Heuristic decision has been made, the atomicity of the transaction is lost and possible data integrity errors can occur.

102. What are the various transaction types will be there in EJB?

The following table summarizes the various transaction attributes:

Not Supported

This attribute means that when a method on a bean with this transaction attribute is called, the transaction gets suspended until the method is completed. This means that the transaction scope is not propagated to the Not Supportedbean or any of the method calls it makes. Once the method in the Not Supported bean is done, the original transaction resumes its execution.

Supports

Invoking a bean with this attribute will include it in the current transaction scope, i.e., if the bean or client that invokes the Supportsbean is part of a transaction scope, the Supports bean and all beans accessed by that bean become part of the original transaction. However, the Supports bean does not have to be part of a transaction and can interact with clients and beans that are not included in a transaction scope.

Required

When a bean's transaction attribute is set as required, it means that the bean method must be invoked within the scope of a transaction. If the calling client or bean is part of a transaction, the Requiredbean is automatically included in its original transaction scope. However, if the calling client or bean is not involved in a transaction, the Required bean starts its own new transaction. The new transaction's scope covers only the Required bean and all beans accessed by that bean. Once the method invoked on the Required bean is done, the new transaction's scope ends.

Requires New

When a bean's transaction attribute is set as Requires New, it means that a new transaction is always started. Regardless of whether the calling client or bean is part of a transaction, a method with the Requires New attribute begins a new transaction when invoked. If the calling client is already involved in a transaction, that transaction is suspended until the Requires New bean's method call returns. The new transaction's scope only covers the Requires New bean and all the beans accessed by that bean. Once the method invoked on the Requires New bean is done, the new transaction's scope ends and the original transaction resumes.

Mandatory

When a bean's transaction attribute is set to Mandatory, it means that the bean method must always be made part of the transaction scope of the calling client. If the calling client or bean is not part of a transaction, the invocation will fail, throwing a javax.transaction.TransactionRequiredException.

Never (EJB 1.1 only)

When a bean's transaction attribute is set to never it, means that the bean method must never be invoked within the scope of a transaction. If the calling client or bean is part of a transaction, the Never bean will throw a RemoteException. If, however, the calling client or bean is not involved in a transaction, the Never bean will execute normally without a transaction.

Bean Managed (EJB 1.0 only)

When a bean's transaction attribute set to Bean Managed it, means that the bean or method does not have its transactional context implicitly managed by the EJB server. Instead, the developer can use the Java Transaction API (JTA) to explicitly manage transactions.

103. What is meant by Re-entrant?

The re-entrant element in deployment descriptor of on EJB declares that the bean either allows loopbacks (re-entrant invocations) or not. This element can have one of two values: True or False. True means that the bean allows loopbacks; False means that the bean throws an exception if a loopback occurs. Beans are non re-entrant by default.

When a bean is declared as re-entrant then it means that a method that is downstream in the sequence of method calls will call back the bean. This is not advisable.

104. How do you commit transactions over multiple databases?

A protocol called 2 phase commit is used. This will commit the transaction only after updates have gone through on all the different database instances.

JSP

105. How is a JSP processed?

A JSP is converted into a Servlet by the application server and then the request is serviced. Once compiled, the Servlet object created from the JSP remains in memory just like any other Servlet. When a change is made to the JSP then the servlet object get re-created. This could vary depending on the server.

106. What is an 'include'? Mention the types of 'includes'.

We can use the <jsp:include> element to include either a static or dynamic resource in a JSP page. If the resource is static, its content is included in the calling JSP page as it is. If the resource is dynamic, it acts on a request and sends back a result that is included in the JSP page. When the include action is finished, the JSP container continues processing the remainder of the JSP page.

If the included resource is dynamic, we can use a <jsp:param> clause to pass the name and value of a parameter to the resource. As an example, we can pass the string userId and a value to a login form that is coded in a JSP page.

107. How do you use Tag Libraries in a JSP?

A tag library is a set of actions that encapsulate functionality. These tags are then used within JSP pages. This helps us to reuse common functionality like connecting to a database.

```
<%@ taglib prefix="sql" uri="http://java.sun.com/jstl/sql" %>
```

For JSP pages that do not have a default database, <sql:setDataSource> can prepare a database for use.

The code below shows how to create a data source.

```
<sql:setDataSource
   var="example"
   driver="oracle.jdbc.driver.OracleDriver"

url="jdbc:oracle:thin:@<OracleServerName>:1521:<OracleInsta
nceName>"
   user="scott"
   password="tiger"
/>
```

108. How is exception handling done in JSP?

You can specify error page in the 'page' directive. Then if any exception is thrown, the control will be transferred to that error page where you can display a useful message to the user about what happened and also inform your sysadmin about this exception depending, obviously, on how important it may be.

```
<%@ page errorPage="ExceptionHandler.jsp" %>
<%@ page isErrorPage="true" import="java.io.*" %>
```

109. What are the implicit objects in JSP?

There are nine implicit objects that are available in a JSP:

- **Application** is the broadest context state available. It is equivalent to ServletContext. It allows the JSP page's servlet and any Web components contained in the same application to share information.
- **Config** allows initialization data to be passed to a JSP page's servlet. This is equivalent to ServletConfig object passed to init method in Servlet.
- **Exception** houses exception data to be accessed only by designated JSP "error pages".
- **Out** provides access to the servlet's output stream.
- **Page** is the instance of the JSP page's servlet processing the current request. Not typically used by JSP page authors.
- **PageContext** is the context for the JSP page itself. It provides a single API to manage the various scoped attributes. This API is used extensively when implementing JSP custom tag handlers.
- **Request** provides access to HTTP request data, as well as providing a context for associating request-specific data.
- **Response** enables direct access to the HTTPServletResponse object and is rarely used by JSP authors.
- **Session** is perhaps the most commonly used of the state management contexts. This is useful in staring a user's information when he accesses the web application over several requests.

110. How do you prevent caching of the page?

You can use Microsoft Internet Information Server (IIS) to easily mark highly volatile or sensitive pages using the following script at the extreme beginning of the specific Active Server Pages (ASP) pages:

```
<% Response.CacheControl = "no-cache" %>
<% Response.AddHeader "Pragma", "no-cache" %>
<% Response.Expires = -1 %>
```

111. What are the various 'scopes' in a JSP?

The various scopes in a JSP are as follows:

- PageScope
- RequestScope
- SessionScope
- ApplicationScope

PROBLEMS AND SOLUTIONS

112. Will this compile?

```
import java.util.*;
import java.sql.*;

class Test {
   Date d = new Date ( 2005, 01. 01);
   System.out.println(d.toString());
}
```

Answer

No. Since both until and Date packages has Date class, Compiler does not know which class to use.

113. Will this code compile?

```
for (int i=0,int j=0;i<10;i++){}
```

Answer

No. The above code will throw a compile time exception. We cannot declare more than one variable in a 'for' loop. It is possible to initialize more than one variable but we can declare only one variable. The right statement is

```
for (int i=0, j=0;i<10;i++){}
```

114. Will this compile?

```
class Test {
      public static void main(String a[]) {
      boolean i = 1;
      System.out.println(i);
   }
}
```

Answer

No. Since Boolean data type value must only be true or false.

115. What will be printed if this code is run with the following command line?

```
java myprog good morning
public class myprog{
   public static void main(String argv[])
   {
      System.out.println(argv[2]);
   }
}
   1. myprog
   2. good
   3. morning
   4. exception raised:java.lang.ArrayIndexOutOfBoundsException:2
```

Answer

4. Exception raised:java.lang.ArrayIndexOutOfBoundsException: 2

Unlike C/C++, Java does not start the parameter count with the program name. It does, however, start from zero. So in this case zero starts with good, morning would be 1 and there is no parameter 2; so an exception is raised.

116. Which of the following statements is true?

1. Methods cannot be overridden to be more private.
2. Static methods cannot be overloaded.

3. Private methods cannot be overloaded.
4. An overloaded method cannot throw exceptions not checked in the base class.

Answer

1. Methods cannot be overridden to be more private.

Static methods cannot be overridden but they can be overloaded. There is no logic or reason why private methods should not be overloaded. Option 4 is a jumbled up version of the limitations of exceptions for overridden methods.

117. What will happen if the following code is compiled and executed?

```
class Base {}
class Sub extends Base {}
class Sub2 extends Base {}
public class CEx{
   public static void main(String argv[]){
      Base b=new Base();
      Sub s=(Sub) b;
   }
}
   1. Compile and run without error
   2. Compile time Exception
   3. Runtime Exception
```

Answer

3. Runtime Exception

Without the cast to sub you would get a compile time error. The cast tells the compiler that you really mean to do this and the actual type of b does not get resolved until runtime. Casting down the object hierarchy is a problem, as the compiler cannot be sure what has been implemented in descendent classes. Casting up is not a problem because sub classes will have the features of the base classes.

118. Which of the following methods can be legally inserted in place of the comment //Method here?

```
Class Base{
```

```
    public void amethod(int i) { }
}
public class Scope extends Base{
    public static void main(String argv[]){
    }
    //Method Here
}
```

1. `void amethod(int i) throws Exception {}`
2. `void amethod(long i)throws Exception {}`
3. `void amethod(long i){}`
4. `public void amethod(int i) throws Exception {}`

Answer

2,3

Options 1 and 4 will not compile as they attempt to throw Exceptions not declared in the base class. Because options 2 and 3 take a parameter of type long they represent overloading not overriding and there are no such limitations on overloaded methods.

119. What modifiers would be legal at XX in the below code?

```
public class MyClass1 {
public static void main(String argv[]){ }
/*Modifier at XX */ class MyInner {}
}
```

1. `public`
2. `private`
3. `static`
4. `friend`

Answer

1,2,3

public, private, static are all legal access modifiers for this inner class.

120. You need to create a class that will store unique object elements. You do not need to sort these elements but they must be unique. What interface might be most suitable to meet this need?

1. `Set`
2. `List`
3. `Map`
4. `Vector`

Answer

1. `Set`

The Set interface ensures that its elements are unique, but does not order the elements. In reality, you probably would not create your own class using the Set interface. You would be more likely to use one of the JDK classes than use the Set interface, such as HashSet or TreeSet.

THINKER'S CHOICE

121. What is the difference between AWT and Swing components?

122. What is the component and container?

123. What is the difference between panel and frame class?

124. What is the Model View Control architecture? Explain it with JTable as an example.

125. Mention the usage of Flow, Border, Grid, Card and GridBag-Layout.

126. What is the difference between Java 1.0 and Java 1.2 event model?

127. Which one is right to use: Observer/Observable or Event Delegation Model?

128. Why wrapper classes are required for primitive data types?

129. What is meant by Abstract Interface?

130. **What is the RMI?**

131. **Explain object serialization mechanism.**

132. **In Socket programming, when to use ServerSocket or DatagramSocket?**

133. **How can you get the IP address of a machine from its hostname?**

134. **How do you perform a hostname lookup for an IP address?**

135. **How can you find out the current IP address for my machine?**

136. **Why cannot an applet connect via sockets, or bind to a local port?**

137. **Why does C/C++ give better run-time performance than Java?**

138. **What is a null interface?**

139. **What is the class loader?**

140. **Mention some feature incorporated in current Java SDK.**

141. **How do you do applet-servlet communication?**

REFERENCES

1. Bruce Eckel, *Thinking in Java,* 4th Edition, Prentice Hall (2006).
2. Cay S. Horstmann, *Core Java: Advanced Features*, Sun Microsystems Press (2005).
3. Hans Bergsten, *Java Server Pages*, 3rd Edition, O'Reilly Publication.
4. Herbert Schildt, *The Complete Reference—Java*, 7th Edition, Tata McGraw-Hill.
5. Jason Hunter, *Java Servlet Programming*, 2nd Edition, O'Reily Publication.

7

Database

INTRODUCTION

Any enterprise software application invariably has a Database. Understanding the data storage mechanism is very essential for a software professional. This chapter provides interview questions and answers on database management system.

DBMS CONCEPT

Q 1. What is an RDBMS?

MSDN documentation states, "RDBMS stands for Relational Database Management System. Basically, it is a way to store the information in a database, creating relationships among different, related data in order to enable the user to query many different factors and receive the widest range of data from a single query. Simply put, it is a system that organizes data into related rows and columns".

Q 2. What is SQL?

SQL stands for Structured Query Language. SQL

- allows access to a database
- can insert/update/delete records in a database
- can retrieve data from a database

Q 3. What are the different kinds of database management systems (DBMS)?

DBMS consists following kinds of databases:

- Hierarchical
- Network

- Relational
- Object
- Object-Relational

In all this, Relational is the most widely used database.

Q 4. What are the feature of a relational database?

The relational model makes no presumptions about the interrelationships between data elements. Relationships are represented by one table, containing key data extracted from another table. Relations are dynamic and determined as needed.

In a relational database, everything is stored in TABLES. Tables contain columns and rows. In formal relational theory, tables are known as **relations;** hence, these came to be known as relational databases. Creation of these tables and their columns is done using SQL. Similarly storage and retrieval of data is also done using SQL.

Q 5. What are data types?

When a column on a table is being created, we need to say what type of data is to be stored in it. Such column type definitions are known as **data types.** Common data types that can be stored and manipulated are NUMBER, CHAR or DATE. But many RDBMS also provide the ability to store newer types, such as TEXT and IMAGE.

Q 6. What is an Entity-Relationship (E-R) diagram?

One of the best methods in designing the database is to draw an image of the tables with the relationship between them. This graphical representation of database tables is called an **Entity-Relationship** or an **E-R diagram.**

Q 7. What is referential integrity?

Referential Integrity prevents users or applications from entering inconsistent data into a table. Referential integrity rules are applied when a relationship is created between two tables. Different RDBMSs have different referential integrity rules. These rules help in maintaining the integrity of the data.

For example, if we are dealing with 'order' table and multiple items contained in an order, it is possible for us to set referential integrity rule in such a way that all items.

8. What is a primary key?

Primary key is used to uniquely identify a row of data in a table. This can be a single column of a table or a combination of more than one column, in which case it is known as composite key.

9. What is a foreign key?

A key column in a table that identifies records in a different table is called a **foreign key**.

For example, we have an 'order' table and an 'item' table. In the item table, let us say that our primary key is the combination of 'order_id' and 'item_number'. In this case, the 'order_id', which is the primary key of the 'order' table is a foreign key in the 'item' table.

10. What is an alternate key in a table?

In a database table, apart from primary key column(s), other column, may need to be a key. These are known as alternate key. This column value may or may not be unique.

For example, if we have a student table, the table contains columns student_num, first_name, last_name, etc. We have assigned each student_num as the primary key. The student's last name would be an alternate key.

11. What is normalization?

Normalization is the process of efficiently organizing data in a database. This includes creating tables and establishing relationships between those tables according to normalization rules designed to make the database more flexible by eliminating two factors: redundancy and inconsistent dependency.

Redundant data wastes disk space and creates maintenance problems. If data that exists in more than one place must be changed, the data must be changed in exactly the same way in all locations. For example, a customer address change is much easier to implement if that data is stored only in the Customer's table and nowhere else in the database.

Inconsistent dependencies can make data difficult to access; the path to find the data may be missing or broken. While, it is intuitive to look in the Customer's table for the address of a particular customer, it may not make sense to look there for the salary of the employee who calls on that customer. The employee's salary is related to, or dependent on, the employee and thus should be moved to the Employees' table.

There are a few rules for database normalization. Each rule is called a **normal form**. If the first rule is observed, the database is said to be in "first normal form." If the first three rules are observed, the database is considered to be in "third normal form." Although other levels of normalization are possible, third normal form is considered the highest level necessary for most applications.

12. Explain the First Normal Form.

First Normal Form states

- eliminate duplicative columns from the same table.
- create a separate table for each set of related data and identify each set of related data with a primary key.

Do not use multiple fields in a single table to store similar data. For example, to track an inventory item that may come from two possible sources, an inventory record may contain fields for Supplier Code 1 and Supplier Code 2.

But what happens when you add a third Supplier? Adding a field is not the answer; it requires program and table schema modifications and does not smoothly accommodate a dynamic number of vendors. Instead, place all supplier information in a separate table called SupplierDetails, then link inventory to Supplier with an item number key, or supplier to inventory with a supplier id key.

13. Explain the Second Normal Form.

Second Normal Form states

- create separate tables for sets of values that apply to multiple records.
- create relationships between these new tables and their predecessors through the use of foreign keys.

Records should not depend on anything other than a table's primary key. For example, consider a customer's address in an accounting system. The address is needed by the Customer's table, but also by the other tables like Orders, Invoices and Accounts tables. Instead of storing the customer's address as a separate entry in each of these tables, store it in one place, either in the Customer's table or in a separate Addresse's table.

14. Explain the Third Normal Form.

Third Normal Form states

- eliminate fields that do not depend on the primary key.

➢ values in a record that are not part of that record's key do not belong in the table. In general, any time the contents of a group of fields may apply to more than a single record in the table, consider placing those fields in a separate table.

For example, in an Employee Recruitment table, a candidate's university name and address may be included. But you need a complete list of universities for group mailings. If university information is stored in the Candidates' table, there is no way to list universities with no current candidates. Create a separate Universities' table and link it to the Candidates' table with a university code key.

15. Considering the given unnormalized table, try to normalize it to various normalized forms.

Unnormalized table

Student No	Advisor	Adv-Room	Class 1	Class 2
1	Rajesh	123	10–12	13–12
2	Manish	342	98–11	34–01

First Normal Form: Eliminating duplicate column(s)

Since one student has several classes, these classes should be listed in a separate table. Fields Class1, Class2, & Class3 in the above record are indications of design trouble.

Another way to look at this problem: with a one-to-many relationship, do not put the one side and the many side in the same table. Instead, create another table in first normal form by eliminating the repeating columns (Class#), as shown below:

Student No	Advisor	Adv-Room	Class No
1	Rajesh	123	10–12
1	Rajesh	123	13–12
2	Manish	342	98–11
2	Manish	342	34–01

Second Normal Form: Eliminating Redundant Data

Note there is multiple Class number values for each Student number value in the above table. Class number is not functionally dependent on Student number (primary key), so this relationship is not in second normal form.

The following two tables demonstrate second normal form:

Student:

Number	Advisor	Adv-Room
1	Rajesh	123
2	Manish	342

Registration:

Student Number	Class Number
1	10–12
1	13–12
2	98–11
2	34–01

Third Normal Form: Eliminate Data Not Dependent On the Key

In the last example, Adv-Room (the advisor's office number) is functionally dependent on the Advisor attribute. However, it is not dependent on Student Number. The solution is to move that attribute from the Students table to the Faculty table, as shown below:

Student:

Student Number	Adv Name
1	Rajesh
2	Manish

Registration:

Student Number	Class Number
1	10–12
1	13–12
2	98–11
2	34–01

Faculty:

Adv Name	Adv Room
Rajesh	123
Manish	342

16. What is an index, and how is it used to improve performance?

Index is an ordering of the records in a database according to the values in a particular field or fields. Indexes are used to gain fast access to specific (more frequently required) information in a database table. For example, the name column of the employee table. If we were looking for a specific employee by his/her name, the index would help us to get that information faster than if we had to search all the rows in the table.

The index provides pointers to the data values stored in specified columns of the table, and then orders those pointers according to the sort order we specify. The database uses the index much as we use an index in a book—it searches the index to find a particular value and then follows the pointer to the row containing that value.

As a general rule, the index should be created on a table only if the data in the indexed columns will be queried frequently. Indexes take up disk space and slow the adding, deleting and updating of rows.

Columns should generally be indexed when

- the column is a primary or foreign key
- the column is sorted
- joins will be used on the column
- user's will search for values in that column

17. What are the types of indexes, and if separate indexes are created on each column of a table, what are the advantages and disadvantages of this approach?

Indexes are of two types:

- Clustered indexes
- Non-clustered indexes

When you create a *clustered index* on a table, all the rows in the table are stored in the order of the clustered index key. So, there can be *only one clustered index per table. Non-clustered indexes* have their own storage separate from the table data storage. Non-clustered indexes are stored as B-tree structures (so do clustered indexes), with the leaf level nodes having the index key and its row locater. The row located could be the Row ID or the Clustered index key, depending upon the absence or presence of clustered index on the table.

If you create an index on each column of a table, it improves the query performance, as the query optimizer can choose from all the existing indexes to come up with an efficient execution plan. At the same time, data modification operations (such as INSERT, UPDATE, DELETE) will become slow, as every time data changes in the table, all the indexes need to be updated. Another disadvantage is that, indexes need disk space, the more indexes you have, more disk space is used.

18. What is SQL Data Manipulation Language (DML)?

SQL (Structured Query Language) is syntax for executing queries and updating, inserting and deleting records.

These query and update commands together form the Data Manipulation Language (DML) part of SQL:

- SELECT—extracts data from a database table
- UPDATE—updates data in a database table
- DELETE—deletes data from a database table
- INSERT INTO—inserts new data into a database table

19. What is SQL Data Definition Language (DDL)?

The Data Definition Language (DDL) part of SQL provides syntax for creating or deleting database tables. We can also define indexes (keys), specify links between tables and impose constraints between database tables.

- CREATE TABLE—creates a new database table
- ALTER TABLE—alters (changes) a database table
- DROP TABLE—deletes a database table
- CREATE INDEX—creates an index (search key)
- DROP INDEX—deletes an index

20. What is de-normalization?

De-normalization is the reverse process of normalization. It is the controlled introduction of redundancy in to the database design. It helps to improve the query performance as the number of joins could be reduced. This is used in data ware housing /OLAP systems.

21. What is a transaction and ACID properties?

The term ACID stands for **Atomic**, **Consistent**, **Isolated** and **Durable**. These properties ensure predictable behavior, reinforcing the role of transactions as all-or-none propositions designed to reduce the management load when there are many variables.

Atomic: A transaction is a unit of work in which a series of operations occur between the BEGIN TRANSACTION and END TRANSACTION statements of an application. A transaction executes exactly once and is atomic—either all of the work is done or none of it.

Consistent: States that only valid data will be written to the database. If, for some reason, a transaction is executed that violates the database's consistency rules, the entire transaction will be rolled back and the database will be restored to a state consistent with those rules

Isolated: A transaction is a unit of isolation that allows multiple transactions to occur at the same time without impacting each other's execution. Isolation requires that each transaction appear to be the only transaction manipulating the data store even.

Durable: A transaction is also a unit of recovery. If a transaction commits, the system guarantees that its updates will persist even if the computer crashes immediately after the commit. Durability is ensured through the use of database backups and transaction logs that facilitate the restoration of committed transactions in spite of any subsequent software or hardware failures.

22. What is the difference between DELETE TABLE and TRUNCATE TABLE command?

DELETE TABLE is a logged operation, so the deletion of each row gets logged in the transaction log, which makes it slow. **TRUNCATE TABLE** also deletes all the rows in a table, but it will not log the deletion of each row, instead it logs the de-allocation of the data pages of the table, which makes it faster.

23. What are constraints? What are the different types of constraints?

Constraints enable the database system to enforce the integrity of the database automatically, without needing to create triggers, rule or defaults.

Types of constraints: NOT NULL, CHECK, UNIQUE, PRIMARY KEY, FOREIGN KEY

For example, NOT NULL constraint on a column prevents the value of it be as NULL.

24. What are cursors? What are the different types of cursors?

A **cursor** is like a virtual table, with rows and columns specified by the query. A cursor also has a notion of a current row, which is essentially a pointer to a row in the virtual table.

Types of cursors: Static, Dynamic, Forward-only, Keyset-driven.

25. What are the disadvantages of cursors? How can avoid cursors?

Each time you fetch a row from the cursor, it results in a network roundtrip, whereas a normal SELECT query makes only one roundtrip, however large the result-set is. Cursors are also costly because they require more resources and temporary storage (results in more IO operations). Further, there are restrictions on the SELECT statements that can be used with some types of cursors.

Most of the times, set based operations can be used instead of cursors. Here is an example.

You have to give a flat hike to your employees using the following criteria:

```
Salary between 30,000 and 40,000—5000 hike
Salary between 40,000 and 55,000—7000 hike
Salary between 55,000 and 65,000—9000 hike
```

In this situation, many developers tend to use a cursor, determine each employee's salary and update his salary according to the above formula. But the same can be achieved by multiple update statements or can be combined in a single UPDATE statement as shown below:

```
UPDATE tbl_emp SET salary =
CASE WHEN salary BETWEEN 30,000 AND 40,000 THEN salary + 5000
WHEN salary BETWEEN 40,000 AND 55,000 THEN salary + 7000
WHEN salary BETWEEN 55,000 AND 65,000 THEN salary + 10,000
END
```

Another situation in which developers tend to use cursors is as follows:

You need to call a stored procedure when a column in a particular row meets certain conditions. You do not have to use cursors for this. This can be achieved using WHILE loop, as long as there is a unique key to identify each row.

26. What is a join and explain different types of joins.

Joins are used in queries to explain how different tables are related. Joins also let you select data from a table depending upon data from another table.

Types of joins: INNER JOIN, OUTER JOIN, CROSS JOIN. OUTER JOIN are further classified as LEFT OUTER JOIN, RIGHT OUTER JOIN and FULL OUTER JOIN.

27. What is a self-join? Explain it with an example.

Self-join is just like any other join, except that two instances of the same table will be joined in the query.

Here is an example: An employee's table, which contains rows for normal employees as well as managers. So, to find out the managers of all the employees, you need a self-join.

```
CREATE TABLE emp
(
empid int,
```

```
mgrid int,
empname char(10)
)

INSERT emp SELECT 1,2,'Vyas'
INSERT emp SELECT 2,3,'Mohan'
INSERT emp SELECT 3,NULL,'Shobha'
INSERT emp SELECT 4,2,'Shridhar'
INSERT emp SELECT 5,2,'Sourabh'

SELECT t1.empname [Employee], t2.empname [Manager]
FROM emp t1, emp t2
WHERE t1.mgrid = t2.empid
```

Here's an advanced query using a LEFT OUTER JOIN that even returns the employees without managers (super bosses).

```
SELECT t1.empname [Employee], COALESCE(t2.empname, 'No manager')
[Manager]

FROM emp t1

LEFT OUTER JOIN

emp t2

ON

t1.mgrid = t2.empid
```

28. How do you implement one-to-one, one-to-many and many-to-many relationships while designing tables?

One-to-One relationship can be implemented as a single table and rarely as two tables with primary and foreign key relationships.

One-to-Many relationships are implemented by splitting the data into two tables with primary key and foreign key relationships.

Many-to-Many relationships are implemented using a junction table with the keys from both the tables forming the composite primary key of the junction table.

29. What is the difference between a primary key and a unique key?

Both primary key and unique key enforce uniqueness of the column on which they are defined. But by default, a primary key creates a clustered index on the column, where are unique creates a non-clustered index by default. Also, primary key does not allow NULL value, but unique key allows NULL value, but only one.

A default is a value that will be used by a column, if no value is supplied to that column while inserting data. IDENTITY columns and TIMESTAMP columns cannot have defaults.

30. What does lock escalation mean?

Lock escalation is the process of converting a lot of low level locks (like row locks, page locks) into higher-level locks (like table locks). Every lock is a memory structure so too many locks occupy more memory.

31. What are triggers? How do you invoke a trigger on demand?

Triggers are special kind of stored procedures that get executed automatically when an INSERT, UPDATE or DELETE operation takes place on a table.

Triggers cannot be invoked on demand. They get triggered only when an associated action (like INSERT, UPDATE and DELETE) happens on the table on which they are defined.

Triggers can be used to extend the referential integrity checks also, but wherever possible, constraints should be used for this purpose, instead of triggers, as constraints are much faster.

32. What is a Stored Procedure? What are the advantages?

A **Stored Procedure** is a set of pre-compiled T-SQL statements, which can be executed whenever required.

These are similar to procedures in any other programming language and hence can accept input parameters, return output parameters and even can return status values advantages of using stored procedures are as follows:

- Increased modularized programming
- Faster execution as they are pre-compiled
- Reduce the network traffic by sending the call to the stored procedure, instead of sending the hundreds of T-SQL lines, which is embedded in the stored procedure

33. What is the difference between Stored Procedure and a Trigger?

Trigger is a special type of stored procedure that is cannot be called directly by a user. At the time of creating the trigger, it is defined to be executed when a specific type of data modification (like Insert, Update or Delete) is made against a specific table or column.

34. What are the different types of parameters available in Stored Procedure?

Parameters are used as the way to communicate to and from a stored procedure. A stored procedure can have

- Input parameters allow the caller to pass the value to the stored procedure. Output parameters allow the stored procedure to pass the value to the caller. Interestingly, these parameters act as InOut parameters. Values can also be sent to the stored procedures using the Output parameters.
- In addition to the Input and Output parameters, every stored procedure returns an integer value to the caller. This can be used to indicate the caller about the success or failure status. If this is not set inside, the procedure the return code will be 0 (zero).

PROBLEMS AND SOLUTIONS

35. CREATE INDEX myIndex ON myTable(myColumn). What type of Index will get created after executing the above statement? Why?

Non-clustered index. Because, by default, a clustered index gets created on the primary key, unless specified otherwise.

36. How do you get the distinct rows in atable/resultset?

By using the DISTINCT keyword, this can be achieved. The following example selects the distinct names from the employee table.

```
SELECT DISTINCT lname FROM employee
```

37. How do you get the distinct rows without using the keyword DISTINCT?

By using the GROUP BY keyword, this can be achieved. The following example selects the distinct names in the employee table, without using the DISTINCT keyword.

```
SELECT lname FROM employee GROUP BY lname
```

38. How can you get the duplicated rows from the table listed below using a single query?

Table 1 ***Duplicated rows from the table using a single query***

Field1	Field2	Field3	Field4	Field5
1	2	3	4	5
2	4	5	6	7
2	4	5	6	7
3	4	3	2	1
1	2	3	4	5

```
SELECT Field1, Field2, Field3, Field4, Field5 FROM Table1GROUP BY
Field1, Field2, Field3, Field4, Field5 HAVING COUNT
(1) > 1
```

39. How can you get the total number of records in a table?

By using the COUNT () function, this can be achieved. The following example gives the count of employees in the organization.

```
SELECT COUNT (1) AS EmpCount FROM employee
```

40. How can you swap values between two rows in a table using single SQL Statement?

A straight forward way of doing this is:

```
UPDATE table SET column = -1 WHERE column = @id1
UPDATE table SET column = @id1 WHERE column = @id2
UPDATE table SET column = @id2 WHERE column = -1
```

But, as the requirement is to do this in a single SQL statement, the solution is:

```
UPDATE table SET column =
(CASE WHEN column = @id1 THEN @id2 WHERE column IN (@id1, @id2)
```

41. How can you insert values in multiple rows using one Insert Statement?

```
INSERT INTO table
```

```
select ('Value1','Fernando')
  UNION ALL
select ('Value2','Carlos')
  UNION ALL
select ('Value3','Vincent')
```

THINKER'S CHOICE

42. Which of the following statements contains an error?

```
SELECT * FROM emp WHERE empid = 493945;
SELECT empid FROM emp WHERE empid= 493945;
SELECT empid FROM emp;
SELECT empid WHERE empid = 56949 AND lastname = 'SMITH';
```

The default character for specifying runtime variables in SELECT statements is

- **Ellipses**
- **Quotation marks**
- **Asterisk**
- **Ampersand**

43. What will happen when a Rollback statement is executed inside a Trigger?

44. What is RAID? What are the different types of RAID configurations?

REFERENCES

1. *MSDN*—Documentation from Microsoft Developer Network.

8

Data Networks

INTRODUCTION

Internet is a network of networks. The Internet is used for information (data) exchange electronically. Knowledge of networking is essential for graduates who would like to be part of telecom domain companies and those like to be a Network Administrator. This chapter provides the basic networking questions and answers.

INTERNETWORKING BASICS

Q 1. What is a Network element?

Elements that are part of a network are generally referred to as a network element, host, node or device.

Q 2. What is Local Area Network (LAN)

A **LAN** supplies networking capability to a group of computers in close proximity to each other such as within an office building, a school or a home. A LAN is useful for sharing resources like files, printers, games or other applications.

Q 3. What is Wide Area Network (WAN)?

A **WAN** spans a large geographic area, such as a state, province or country. WANs often connect multiple smaller networks, such as local area networks (LANs).

Q 4. What is the difference between internet and intranet?

One of the major differences between internet and intranet is that the internet is an open, public space, while an intranet is designed to be a private space. An intranet may be accessible from the

Internet, but as a rule it is protected by a password and accessible only to employees or other authorized users.

5. What does the word 'protocol' mean?

When two devices in a network want to communicate, they should know a common language for communication. This common language that provides rules and regulations for their communication is known as **protocol.** In a data network, communication means exchange of messages between any two machines.

6. What is a reference model?

A **reference model** is a conceptual blueprint of how communication should take place between two dissimilar network elements in a given network. All the processes required for this effective communication are logically grouped into layers. A reference model hides the details of network hardware and permits disparate network elements to communicate, independent of their physical connection.

Examples for reference models include:

- Open System Interconnection (OSI) by International Organization for Standardization (ISO)
- Department of Defense (DoD)

7. Explain the layers in the OSI reference model.

OSI reference model has seven layers as shown in Figure 8.1.

Host A		Host B
Application	Data	Application
Presentation	Data	Presentation
Session	Data	Session
Transport	Segments	Transport
Network	Packets	Network
Data Link	Frames	Data Link
Physical	Bits	Physical

Figure 8.1 *OSI Model*

Application layer

This layer will mainly be used by the application program. The main functionality of this layer is to identify the application program requested communication partner and establish the communication channel with it. For example, if the Internet explorer application needs to upload a file to a FTP server, it connects to the FTP server via the FTP protocol

Examples: Telnet, HTTP, FTP, SNMP, SMTP

Presentation layer

The main functionality of this layer is to encode/decode the application layer specific data format into generic data format and vice versa. For example If an application needs to transfer the integer value 1, at the presentation layer the value 1 will be converted to a generic value using encoding schemes like BER (Basic Encoding Rule).

Examples: Tiff, JPEG, MPEG

Session layer

The main functionality of this layer is to set up, manage and then clean up sessions established between the presentation layer entities. Also, it ensures dialogue communication between devices by offering three different modes: simplex, half-duplex and full-duplex.

Examples: Network File Systems (NFS), Structured Query Language (SQL), Remote Procedure Call (RPC)

Transport layer

This layer segments and re-assembles data into a data stream. This layer supports connection-oriented and connectionless transport layer protocol service.

The main functionality of connection oriented transport protocol is to provide reliable, end-to-end data transport services by establishing logical connection between sending and receiving hosts.

Example: Transport Control Protocol (TCP)

The main functionality of connectionless transport protocol is to provide unreliable, end-to-end data transport services.

Example: User Datagram Protocol (UDP)

Network layer

The main functionality of this layer is to manage device addressing, to track the location of the devices on the network and to determine the best way to move data, which means that this layer must transport traffic between devices that are not locally attached. Routers operate at this layer.

Example: Internet Protocol (IP), IPX

Data link layer

The main functionality of this layer is to ensure that messages are delivered to the proper device on a LAN using hardware addresses and translates messages from the Network Layer into bits (data frames) for the physical layer to transmit.

Data link layer is sub-divided into two sub-layers:

- Logical Link Control (LLC)—the upper sub-layer hides underlying network types (Ethernet, token ring, etc) from the network layers (IPX, TCP/IP).
- Medium Access Control (MAC)—the lower sub-layer controls and communicates directly with the physical network media through the network interface card. This layer converts data frame into bits and vice versa.

Switches and bridges operate at this layer.

Examples: Ethernet, FDDI, 802.11 Wi-Fi, Frame relay, PPP, HDLC, ATM

Physical layer

The main functionality of this layer is to send and receive bits to and from the physical carrier (wire). Also, this layer defines things like pin outs, electrical characteristics, modulation and encoding of data bits on carrier signals

8. Compare OSI with DoD (TCP/IP) Model.

OSI		TCP/IP
Application	Data	Application
Presentation		
Session		
Transport	Segments	Transport
Network	Packets	Network
Data Link	Frames/Bits	Physical
Physical		

Figure 8.2 *OSI vs. TCP/IP reference model*

9. What is data encapsulation?

Each layer within the OSI model is primarily responsible for communicating with a peer layer on another machine. In other words, when two clients communicate, one layer, such as the Transport Layer, on one client is primarily responsible for communicating with the exact same layer, in this case the Transport Layer, on the other client (See Figure 8.2).

This communication between peers is done in Protocol Data Units (PDU). The actual name for the PDU changes from layer to layer. For instance, as Figure 8.2 shows, the Transport layers communicate via Segments.

Even though this communication logically takes place between peers, each layer is actually dependent upon the layers below it for the actual delivery. Each layer passes it is PDU to the layer below it. The underlying layer then adds a header, creating its own PDU. In this manner, the data payload for lower layers is the PDU of the layer immediately above. This process of taking one PDU and enveloping it within another is called data encapsulation.

The following diagram depicts the 5 step encapsulation process:

Step1: (Application—Transport Layer)

Data

Step 2: (Transport—Network Layer)

Segment Header	Data

Step 3: (Network to Data Link Layer)

Network Header	Segment Header	Data

Step 4: (Data Link to Physical Layer)

Frame Header	Network Header	Segment Header	Data

Step 5: (Physical Layer to Wire)

10001110000110000111100001110101010

10. What does the word 'throughput' mean?

In computer technology, **throughput** is the amount of work that a computer can do in a given time period.

11. What is the difference between baud and bit rate?

Bit rate is a measure of the number of bits ('0' or '1') transmitted per unit of time. If we transmit 2400 bits of '1' and '0' per sec then Bit rate is 2400 bps (Bits per sec).

The **baud rate** is a measure of the number of symbols (characters) transmitted per unit of time. Each symbol will normally consist of a number of bits, so the baud rate will only be the same as the bit rate when there is one bit per symbol.

12. What is BER?

BER is Basic Encoding Rule. An encoding standard for converting application data into machine independent information transmitted across the network. BER is widely used to encode (Abstract Syntax Notation) ASN.1 data types.

13. What is tunneling?

Tunneling results in the original packet/data frame being hidden inside a new packet/data frame. Tunneling happens in the same layer whereas encapsulation happens between layers.

NETWORK TECHNOLOGY

14. What is Ethernet technology?

Ethernet technology is a high speed (10Mbps), packet switching, broadcast bus technology. It is bus because all the stations share a single ether channel; it is broadcast because all the stations receive every single transmitted signal.

15. What is the use of Network interface card (NIC)?

A **network interface card** is used to connect a computer to an Ethernet network.

16. Explain Ethernet access scheme.

Ethernet access scheme uses Carrier Sense Multiple Access with Collision Detection (CSMA/CD) concept.

In a network, when any host wants to transmit data, before transmission, it checks the carrier (ether wire) for the presence of digital signal. If no signal is sensed, then it transmits the data. This is CSMA. However, there may be chances for two hosts to sense the carrier is free and both tries to send data. In this case, the signal jam (collision) happens. To avoid this, any transmitting host will constantly monitor the carrier. This is CD.

Note: If station detects the collision, it waits for the random period of time before attempting to transmit again. This random period is implemented using **back-off algorithm**.

17. What is token ring technology?

This is a type of network in which all the devices are arranged (schematically) in a circle. A token, which is a special bit pattern, travels around the circular network.

Whenever a device wishes to send its frame

- it waits for the token, temporarily stops forwarding other devices frame
- as soon as it receives the token, it initiates transmission of its frame; passes the token back to the network; starts forwarding other devices frames

When a device receives the token, it sends only one packet before passing the token. If there is no one to receive the transmitted frame, it circulates back to the source station, where it is removed.

ETHERNET NETWORKING CONCEPTS

18. What is Broadcast domain?

When a device in the Ethernet LAN transmits a packet, all other devices in the LAN will receive it as Ethernet follows broadcast technology. However, only the device for which the packet is intended will accept and forward it to the upper layer while others just discard the packet. Thus, Ethernet LAN forms a broadcast domain. Usually, broadcast domains will be connected/separated using routers (See Figure 8.5).

19. What is network segmentation? What is Collision domain?

When two network devices transmit simultaneously, packet collision occurs. Such a condition would arise if too many devices were on one network. To avoid this, it is good idea to segregate a network into multiple network segments. Segmenting a LAN can extend the existing network, and reduce congestion. Each segment is considered as collision domains. Usually, collision domains will be connected/separated using bridges or switches (See Figure 8.4).

20. Briefly explain the functionality of a hub.

A **hub** is a multi-port repeater. It receives electrical signal, amplifies it and re-transmits to all the active ports without looking into the data packet. A hub operates on Physical layer of the OSI model. A hub is also known as concentrators. As illustrated in the Figure 8.3 hub does not break collision or broadcast domain.

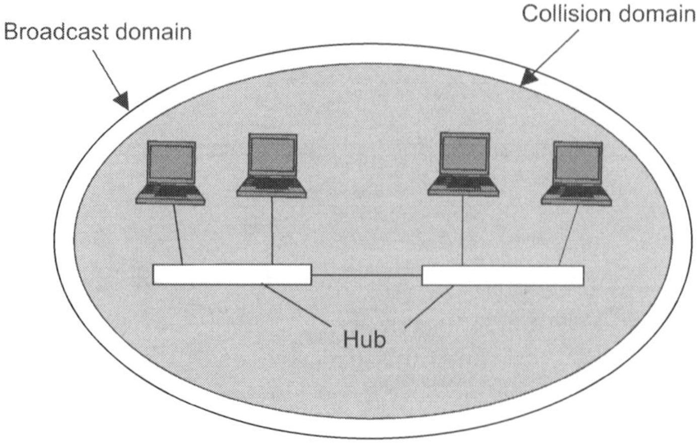

Figure 8.3 *Hub network design*

21. Briefly explain the functionality of a bridge and switch.

Bridge and switch read the destination MAC address from each received data frame; refer the database; if the MAC addresses port is present then it forwards the frame to the corresponding port or else floods the frame to all the ports. Bridge and switch operate on **Data-link layer** of the OSI model.

Some of the major difference between a bridge and a switch are as follows:

- A switch supports more ports than a bridge
- Bridges switch using software whereas Switches switch using hardware (Integrated circuits – ASIC)
- In Switches each individual port could be configured for different data rate.

As illustrated in the Figure 8.4 Bridge/Switch controls collision but not broadcast domain.

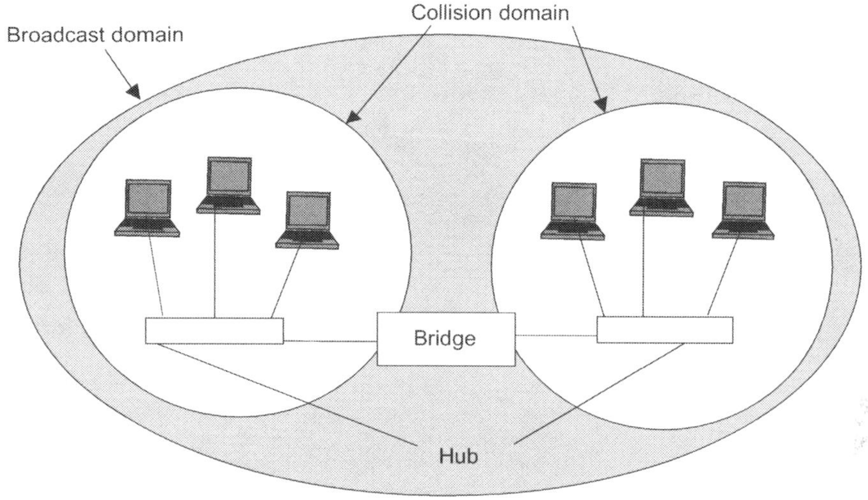

Figure 8.4 *Bridge and Switch network design*

22. Briefly explain the functionality of a Router.

Routers interconnect multiple (sub-) networks and route information between these networks by choosing an optimal path ("route") to the destination. Router operates on Network layer of the OSI model.

As illustrated in Figure 8.5, Router controls collision and broadcast domains.

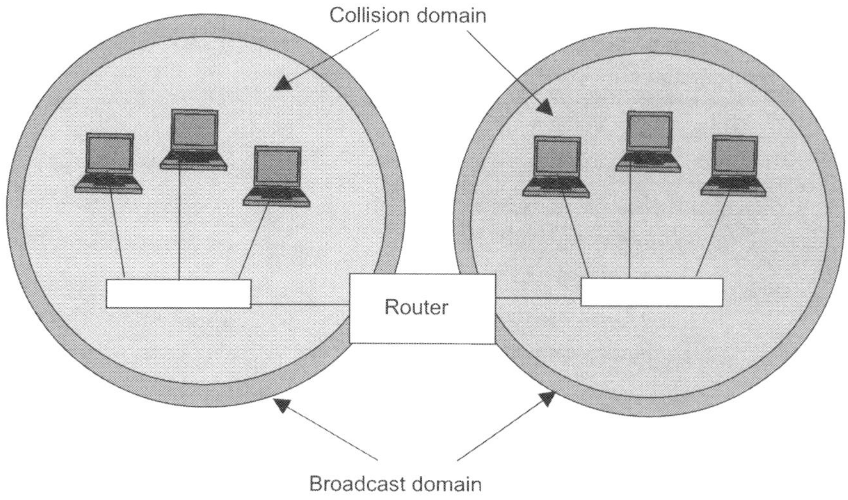

Figure 8.5 *Router network design*

23. Briefly explain the functionality of a Gateway.

A **gateway** is a device that interconnects network that supports different protocols. They usually operate on Transport layer and above it. For example, gateway could be used to interconnect an IPX and TCP/IP network.

DATA LINK LAYER

24. What is an MAC address?

An **MAC address** is a number (typically written as twelve hexadecimal digits, 0 through 9 and A through F, or as six hexadecimal numbers separated by periods or colons, i.e., 0080003012ef, 0:80:0:3:12: ef) which uniquely identifies a device that has an Ethernet interface.

The first half of a MAC address contains the ID number of the adapter manufacturer. These IDs are regulated by an Internet standards body. The second half of a MAC address represents the serial number assigned to the adapter by the manufacturer. For example:

00:A0:C9:14:12:30

The prefix "00:A0:C9" – indicates the manufacturer is Intel Corporation.

25. What is the need for spanning-Tree protocol?

Spanning-Tree Protocol is a data-link management protocol that provides path redundancy while preventing undesirable loops in the network. For an Ethernet network to function properly, only one active path can exist between two stations. Multiple active paths between stations cause loops in the network. If a loop exists in the network topology, the potential exists for duplication of messages.

In the below example, to have network uptime of 24 hours, 7 days, two switches are used between device A and device B. If any one of the switches become down, the other one will take control over to transfer data between A and B. Let us say a broadcast frame is delivered by device A. Switch-1 receives the frame via its port-1 and transmits the frame via its port-2. Since the redundancy is enabled in this network, the frame will also be received by Switch-2 via its port-1. Switch-2 re-transmits the frame via its port-2 which will again reach Switch-1 via its port-2. This will lead to a looping. To avoid this looping, spanning tree protocol is developed.

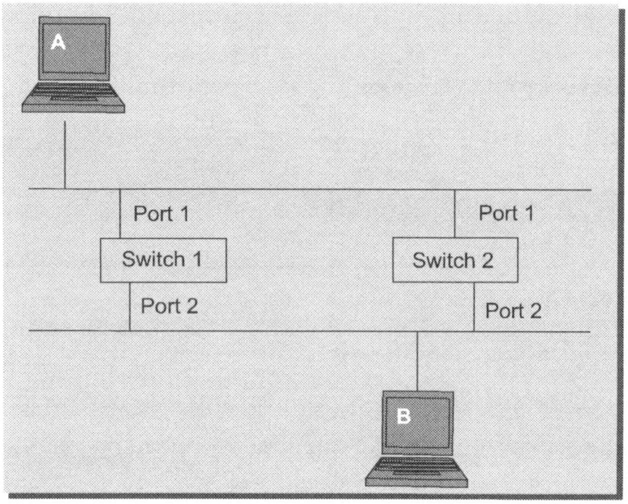

26. What is the use of ATM technology?

ATM is Asynchronous Transfer Mode. It is designed for the high-speed transfer of voice, video, and data using cell relay technology. The basic unit of information used by ATM is a fixed-size cell consisting of 53 octets, or bytes. The first 5 bytes contain header information, while the remaining 48 bytes contain the data, or payload.

27. What are the advantages of ATM technology over Ethernet technology?

The advantages of ATM technology over Ethernet technology are as follows:

- ATM uses special hardware designed high-speed switches (ASIC) between host and the other ATM switches.
- ATM uses optical fiber connections whose transmission rate is much faster (more 100Mbps) than copper cables (10Mbps).
- Because the ATM switch does not have to detect the size of a unit of data (since it is fixed to 53 octets), switching can be performed efficiently.
- The small size of the cell also makes it well suited for the transfer of real-time data, such as voice and video.

28. What is the use of VPN technology?

VPN is Virtual Private Network. A VPN is used to connect remote users to the private intranet or an intranet to other intranet via the public network (internet). Prior to VPN technology, enterprises (companies) used leased/dedicated lines to have a secure connection between their two remote intranets or between users and the private network. These leased lines are costly. VPN uses virtual connections (a secure tunnel) routed through the Internet from the company's private network to the remote site.

29. Explain wireless networking in brief.

Wireless networks utilize radio waves and/or microwaves to create communication channels between network elements.

A wireless network offers advantages and disadvantages compared to a wired network.

- Advantages of wireless include mobility and elimination of cumbersome cables.
- Disadvantages of wireless include the potential for radio interference due to weather, other wireless devices or obstructions like walls.

Popular wireless local area networking (WLAN) products conform to the 802.11 Wi-Fi (Wireless Fidelity) standards.

Mostly, Wireless Network devices operate at data link layer (layer 2).

IP LAYER

30. What is an IP address?

An **IP address** is an address used to uniquely identify a device on an IP based network. The address is made up of 32 binary bits which is divisible into a network portion and host portion. The 32 binary bits are broken into four octets (1 octet = 8 bits). Each octet is converted to decimal and separated by a period (dot). For this reason, an IP address is said to be expressed in dotted decimal format (e.g., 172.16.81.100). The value in each octet ranges from 0 to 255 decimal, or 00000000 – 11111111 binary.

31. What is static and dynamic IP address? Which is better to use?

Each network element in a network will be assigned with unique IP address. This IP can be a static or dynamic one.

- Static IP address—is usually configured by the administrator/user manually. Once this is assigned that IP address cannot be reused by any other device in the same network.
- Dynamic IP address—will be provided to each device by DHCP server at the time of their TCP/IP stack initialization.

Both the static and dynamic IP address has its advantages and disadvantages.

Dynamic IP address system allows your machine (say laptop) to move to a different subnet and gets its IP for that subnet from the DHCP server. However, the problem is, if your machine has a name to IP address mapping in the DNS server then when a new IP comes the DNS server entry, it needs to be manually updated which is not required for static IP.

32. What are public and private IP addresses? What ranges are reserved for private IP addresses?

InterNIC has reserved certain IP addresses as private addresses for use with internal Web sites or intranets. These addresses are not routable on the public Internet, but are meant for devices that reside behind a router or other Network Address Translation (NAT) device or proxy server. Private IP addresses are used either to hide systems from the public Internet or to provide an additional range of addresses to organizations that do not have sufficient public IP addresses to distribute on their network.

IPv4 private address:

- Class A – 10.0.0.0 – 10.255.255.255
- Class B – 172.16.0.0 – 172.31.255.255
- Class C – 192.168.0.0 – 192.168.255.255

IPv6 private address:

- Site local addresses are similar to RF1918 addresses (10.0.0.x, 192.168.2.x).
- Site local prefixes begin with fecx, fedx, feex and fefx (fecx is most commonly used).

33. What is Network Address Translation (NAT)?

With the explosion of the Internet and the increase in home networks and enterprise networks, the number of available IP addresses is simply not enough. The obvious solution is to redesign the address format to allow for more possible addresses. This is being developed (called IPv6), but will take several years to implement because it requires modification of the entire infrastructure of the Internet.

Another solution is to use Network Address Translation (NAT). NAT allows a single device, such as a router, to act as an agent between the Internet (or "public network") and a local (or "private") network. This means that only a single, unique IP address is required to represent an entire group of computers.

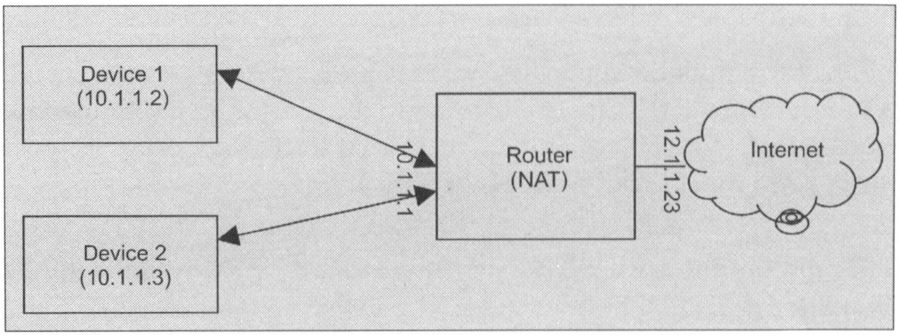

In the above example, if the Device-1 (10.1.1.2) sends out a packet to the router (10.1.1.1) aimed at 13.1.1.34, then the IP packet contains the source IP has 10.1.1.2 and source port has say 1080, together with the destination port (say 1078) and IP address (13.1.1.34).

When it arrives at the router, the router will de-encapsulate the packet and rewrite the source IP as its IP (12.1.1.23); source port (say 1109) and the newly allocated for this IP and sends out the packet onto the Internet.

The router will also add an entry into a table it keeps, which maps the internal address (10.1.1.2) and source port number your machine (1080) generated against the port number (1109) it allocated to this session. Therefore, when the machine 13.1.1.34 sends a reply packet to the router, the router can quickly read the map table and replace the destination IP and destination port in the packet with the Device-1 IP address and port information.

34. Compare MAC addresses with IP addresses.

MAC addressing works at the data link layer (layer 2), IP addressing functions at the network layer (layer 3). The MAC address generally remains fixed and follows the network device, but the IP address changes (Dynamic IP) as the device moves from one network to another.

35. What is Address Resolution Protocol (ARP)?

ARP maps an IP address to its corresponding physical network address. It is a low-level protocol (at layer 2 in the OSI model) usually implemented in the device drivers of network elements operating system. ARP is most commonly seen on Ethernet networks, but ARP has also been implemented for ATM, Token Ring, and other physical networks.

When an IP packet arrives at a router, the router needs to map the destination IP address to the appropriate MAC address so that it can be delivered over Ethernet. Some IP-to-MAC address mappings are maintained in an ARP cache, but if the given IP address does not appear there, the router will send an ARP request that is broadcast on the local network. The host with the given

IP address sends an ARP reply to the router, which in turn delivers the packet (and updates its cache).

36. What is Reverse Address Resolution Protocol (RARP)?

Reverse Address Resolution Protocol (RARP) is the reverse of ARP. It is a mechanism to map MAC addresses to IP addresses. It is used (mainly by disk-less workstations upon boot-up) to find out their IP addresses from a BOOTP server. The BOOTP server contains all of the boot-up configuration files that the workstation needs to boot-up.

On NICs (network interface cards) of every network device, there is an empty DIP socket that is used for holding a Boot PROM. The Boot PROM holds a special software program that tells the workstation (upon powering up) to go and find a BOOTP server.

One of the first tasks of the workstation is to find out its IP address. The MAC layer address is burnt into the NIC, and is already known. A RARP broadcast datagram is sent out that asks: "Does any BOOTP server know what my IP address is?" The BOOTP server will reply with: "Here's the IP address that belongs to your MAC address".

Once the IP address is known, then the rest of the configuration files can be downloaded (for the disk-less workstation to boot up).

Note: RARP uses the same PDU header as ARP.

37. What is TTL? Why is it required?

TTL is Time To Live. TTL will be used to avoid packet looping in a network. Every IP packet will be delivered with a TTL value. When a router decodes an IP packet, it decrements TTL value by 1. If the value, after decrement becomes zero, the packet will be discarded and an error message will be sent back to the source.

38. What is MTU?

MTU is Maximum Transfer Unit. It specifies the largest amount of data that can be transferred across a given physical network. If the receiving network MTU is less than the sender, then fragmentation is required.

39. What is Network Byte Order?

Network device could send data in little-endian (LSB-MSB) or big-endian (MSBLSB) format. To create an independent data transmission format, TCP/IP standard specifies, that data in network should always be in Big-endian format.

C language API's used for Network Byte Order to machine byte order and vice versa are htonl(), htonls(), ntohl(), ntohs()

40. What is Internet Control Message Protocol (ICMP)?

ICMP messages are delivered in IP packets, are used to report network errors, network congestion, etc., mentioned as follows:

- Reports network errors—such as a host or entire portion of the network being unreachable, due to some type of failure. For example "Destination host is temporarily out of service" or "Destination address is not valid" errors are indicated to the source using Destination Unreachable ICMP message.
- Reports network congestion—When a router begins buffering too many packets, due to an inability to transmit them as fast as they are being received, it will generate ICMP Source Quench messages saying "rate of packet transmission to be slowed".
- Assist Troubleshooting—ICMP supports an Echo function, which just sends a packet on a round–trip between two hosts. Ping, a common network management tool, is based on this feature. Ping will transmit a series of packets, measuring average round-trip times and computing loss percentages.
- Announce Timeouts—If an IP packet's TTL (Time To Live) field drops to zero, the router discarding the packet will often generate an ICMP response packet announcing this information. Traceroute is a program that prints the path to destination from a source by sending a sequence of datagram with TTL set to 1, 2, ... and so on and uses ICMP Time Exceeded messages that come back to find the routers along the path.

41. What is Internet Protocol (IP)?

IP defines the unreliable, connectionless delivery of datagram. IP is the Internet's most basic protocol.

IP provides several services. Some of them are mentioned as follows:

- ***Addressing***: IP headers contain 32-bit addresses which identify the sending and receiving hosts. These addresses are used by intermediate routers to select a network path for the packet.
- ***Fragmentation***: IP packets may be split, or fragmented, into smaller packets. This permits a large packet to travel across a network which can only handle smaller packets. Once a packet is fragmented, it will be considered as a individual packet with its own IP header.
- ***Packet timeouts***: Each IP packet contains a Time-To-Live (TTL) field, that is decremented every time routers process the datagram (IP packet). If TTL reaches zero, the packet is discarded, preventing packets from looping forever and flooding a network.

➢ ***Options***: IP provides several optional features, allowing a packet's sender to set requirements on the path it takes through the network (source routing), trace the route a packet takes (record route) and label packets with security features.

42. Explain the classes of IP address.

IP address are classified into Class A, Class B, Class C, Class D and Class E as shown in Figure 8.6.

The class of an IP address can be determined from the five high-order bits. Figure 8.6 shows the significance in the five high order bits and the range of addresses that fall into each class.

In a Class A address, the first octet is the network portion, octets 2, 3 and 4 (the next 24 bits) are for the network manager to divide into subnets and hosts as he/she sees fit. Class A addresses are used for networks that have more than 65,536 hosts (actually, up to 16777214 hosts!).

Loopback—The IP address 127.0.0.1 is used as the loopback address. This means that it is used by the host computer to send a message back to itself. It is commonly used for troubleshooting and network testing.

In a Class B address, the first two octets are the network portion, octets 3 and 4 (16 bits) are for local subnets and hosts. Class B addresses is used for networks that have between 256 and 65,534 hosts.

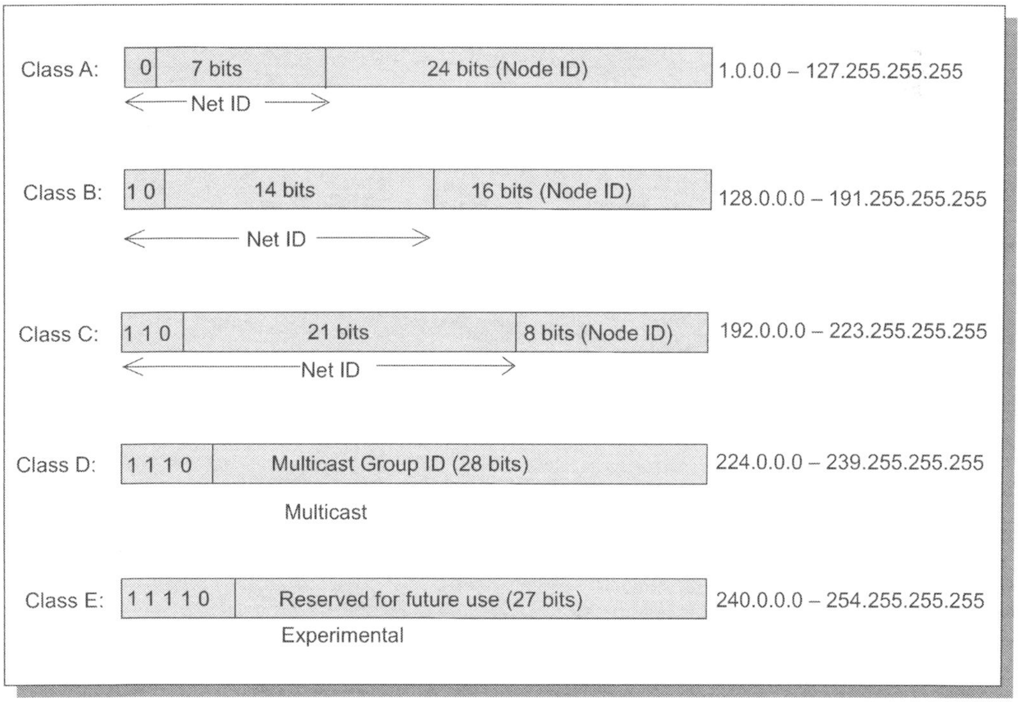

Figure 8.6 *Various IP address range*

In a Class C address, the first three octets are the network portion, octet 4 (8 bits) is for local subnets and hosts—perfect for networks with less than 254 hosts.

Class D is mainly for multicast group and Class E is reserved for future use.

Q 43. What do broadcast, unicast and multicast mean?

Broadcast

Data-link layer: The destination MAC address specifies that the data frame should be delivered to all hosts in the network. The broadcast IP address will always be FF.FF.FF.FF.FF.FF

IP layer: The destination IP address specifies that the packet should be delivered to all hosts in the network. The broadcast IP address will always be 255.255.255.255

Unicast

The destination IP address specifies that the packet should be delivered to specific host in the network.

Multicast

The destination IP address specifies that the packet should be delivered to set of hosts in the same network or different networks.

Q 44. Explain Network Mask.

A *network mask* helps you know which portion of the address identifies the network and which portion of the address identifies the node on a given IP address. Network Mask is mainly useful when a network is divided logically into sub-networks. Class A, B and C networks have default masks, also known as natural masks, as shown as follows:

Class A: 255.0.0.0

Class B: 255.255.0.0

Class C: 255.255.255.0

An IP address on a Class A network that has not been sub netted would have an address/mask pair similar to: 12.20.9.1 255.0.0.0. To see how the mask helps you identify the network and node parts of the address, convert the address and mask to binary numbers.

12.20.9.1 = 00001100.00010100.00001001.00000001

255.0.0.0 = 11111111.00000000.00000000.00000000

Once you have the address and the mask represented in binary, then identifying the network and host ID is easier. Any address bits which have corresponding mask bits set to 1 represent the network ID. Any address bits that have corresponding mask bits set to 0 represent the node ID.

```
12.20.9.1 = 00001100 . 00010100.00001001.00000001
255.0.0.0 = 11111111 . 00000000.00000000.00000000
            ----------------------------------------------
                  Netid | Hostid

Netid = 00001000 = 12

Hostid = 00010100.00001111.00000001 = 20.9.1
```

45. Explain Subnetting.

Subnetting allows you to create multiple logical networks that exist within a single Class A, B or C network. If you do not subnet, you will only be able to use one network from your Class A, B or C network, which is unrealistic.

Each network must have a unique network ID. If you break a major network (Class A, B or C) into smaller sub networks, it allows you to create a network of interconnecting sub networks. This network would then have a unique network/sub network ID. Any device, or gateway, connecting *n* networks/sub networks has *n* distinct IP addresses, one for each network / sub network that it interconnects.

To subnet a network, extend the natural mask using some of the bits from the host ID portion of the address to create a sub network ID. For example, given a Class C network of 204.12.8.0, which has a natural mask of 255.255.255.0, you can create subnets in this manner:

```
204.12.8.0        =    11001100.00001100.00001000. 00000000

255.255.255.224   =    11111111.11111111.11111111. 11100000
                       -------------------------------|sub|------
```

By extending the mask to be 255.255.255.224, you have taken three bits (indicated by "sub") from the original host portion of the address and used them to make subnets. With these three bits, it is possible to create eight subnets. With the remaining five host ID bits, each subnet can have up to 32 host addresses, 30 of which can actually be assigned to a device *since host ids of all zeros or all ones are not allowed.* So, with this in mind, these subnets have been created.

204.12.8.0 255.255.255.224 host address range 1 to 30

204.12.8.32 255.255.255.224 host address range 33 to 62

204.12.8.64 255.255.255.224 host address range 65 to 94

204.12.8.96 255.255.255.224 host address range 97 to 126

204.12.8.128 255.255.255.224 host address range 129 to 158

204.12.8.160 255.255.255.224 host address range 161 to 190

204.12.8.192 255.255.255.224 host address range 193 to 222

204.12.8.224 255.255.255.224 host address range 225 to 254

This mask can be denoted in two ways. First, since you are using three bits more than the actual Class C mask, you can denote these addresses as having a 3-bit subnet mask. Or, secondly, the mask of 255.255.255.224 can also be denoted as /27 as there are 27 bits that are set in the mask. By second method, one of these networks can be described with the notation prefix/length. For example, 204.15.5.32/27 denotes the network 204.15.5.32 255.255.255.224.

46. Write out the IPv6 datagram format.

Base Header (40 octet)	Extn. Header 1 (N octet)	Extn. Header 2 (N octet)	…	Extn. Header M (N octet)	**Data**

47. How IPv6 addresses will be represented?

As the Dotted notation used in IPv4 is difficult to read 128 bits, IPv6 uses "Colon Hexadecimal Notation" to represent IP address. For example, an IPv6 number will be represented as follows:

FE05:0:0:12:0:0:0: FD

This can also be written as FE05::: 12:::FD by compressing zeroes.

48. Compare IPv6 with IPv4.

- Larger Addresses—IPv6 uses 128 bit instead of 32 bit.
- Flexible Header format—Unlike IPv4 where datagram header size is fixed, IPv6 allows optional headers.

- Control information—IPv6 allows user to have control information as part of datagram.
- Resource Allocation—unlike IPv4, IPv6 supports resource pre-allocation by which it guarantees real-time video.

Q 49. What does 'Routing' mean?

Routing refers to the process of identifying a shortest network path to send packets.

Q 50. What is the use of Routing protocol? Mention any two routing protocols.

Routing protocols are used to propagate routing information between any two routers in an autonomous system.

Routing Information Protocol (RIP) and Open Shortest Path First (OSPF) are the examples of routing protocols.

TCP LAYER

Q 51. What is Transmission Control Protocol (TCP)?

The **Transmission Control Protocol** (TCP) is responsible for reliable, end-to-end delivery (segments of information) of a given piece of data. A segment is the term that is used to describe the data that is transmitted and received at the Transport level of the OSI model (i.e., where TCP resides).

The reliable, end-to-end delivery of data is accomplished by the following:

- Connection-oriented service: Segments are acknowledged to the source when received by the destination. A sliding window is used to enable unacknowledged segments on the "wire" in order to speed up transmission rates.
- Sequencing of segments: Data is broken up into segments that are numbered (sequenced) when transmitted. The destination TCP layer keeps track of the received segments and places them in the proper order (re-sequences).
- Requesting retransmission of lost data: If a segment is lost in transmission (missing sequence number), the destination will timeout and request that all segments starting at the lost segment are retransmitted.
- Error checking: Segments are checked for data integrity when received using a 32-bit CRC check.

52. What is User Datagram Protocol (UDP)?

The User Datagram Protocol (UDP) is a connectionless, unreliable service that operates at the Transport layer of the OSI model. UDP relies on the upper layer protocol for both error correction and reliable service. UDP messages can be lost, duplicated or arrive out of order. Also, packets can arrive at much faster rate than receiver processing rate. The major uses of this protocol are DNS and TFTP and delay sensitive deliveries like RTP.

53. Explain the TCP windowing concept.

A TCP window represents the amount of outstanding (unacknowledged by the recipient) data a sender can send on a particular connection before it gets an acknowledgment back from the receiver that it has gotten some of it. The primary reason for the windowing is for congestion control.

For example, if a pair of hosts is talking over a TCP connection that has a TCP window size of 128 KB (kilobytes), the sender can only send 128 KB of data and then it must stop and wait for an acknowledgment from the receiver that some or all of the data has been received. If the receiver acknowledges that all the data has been received then the sender is free to send another 128 KB. If the sender gets back an acknowledgment from the receiver that it received the first 64 KB (which could happen if the second 64 KB was still in transit or it might happen if the second 64 KB got lost), then the sender could only send another 64 KB since it cannot have more than 128 KB of unacknowledged data outstanding (the second 64 KB of data plus the third).

54. Explain flow control.

Flow control is a technique to properly match the segment transmission rate of sender to that of the receiver and the network. It is important for the transmission to be at a high enough rates to ensure good performance, but also to protect against overwhelming the network or receiving host.

55. What is CRC?

The CRC is a very powerful but easily implemented technique to obtain data reliability. The CRC technique is used to protect blocks of data called Frames. Using this technique, the transmitter appends an extra n-bit sequence to every frame called *Frame Check Sequence* (FCS). The FCS holds redundant information about the frame that helps the transmitter to detect errors in the frame. The CRC is one of the most used techniques for error detection in data communications. This technique gained its popularity because it combines three advantages:

- Extreme error detection capabilities
- Little overhead
- Ease of implementation

APPLICATION LAYER

56. What is Domain Name System (DNS)? What is the advantage of it?

DNS is Domain Name System that maps the human readable string into IP Address. It is difficult to remember IP Address for every internet site we browse. For example, it is easy to remember www.cisco.com that it is IP Address like 10.101.23.231.

When we type www.cisco.com, the browser will use the default DNS server configured in the machine to query the com server address and from com (Commercial Organization) server it collects the Cisco server's IP address.

57. What is Client/Server architecture?

The **client/server software architecture** is a message-based infrastructure that is proposed to improve usability, flexibility, interoperability, and scalability as compared to centralized, mainframe, time sharing computing. Client/Server model is the widely used in web technology.

Client application is the request provider, which is usually thin application. Client code is usually Web pages. Server application is the service provider/request responder which is usually thick application. Server application code is commonly called business logic.

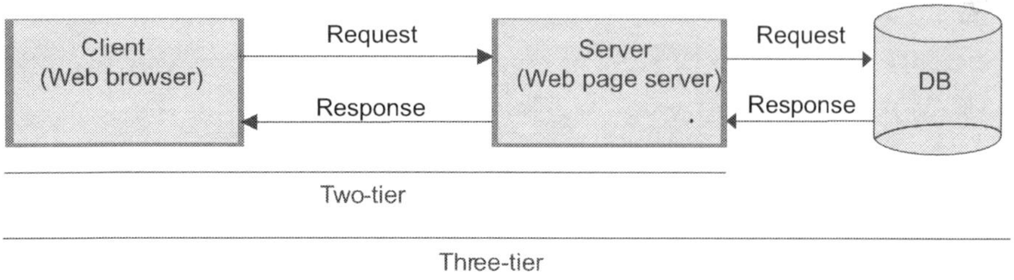

Note: Client/Server architecture is generally called **2-tier architecture.** If the database and server (business logic) are in different location then it is termed as **3-tier architecture**.

58. What is HTML?

HTML is Hyper Text Markup Language, a markup language defined by Document Type Definition (DTD). To a document writer, HTML is simply a collection of tags used to mark blocks of text and assign them special meanings

```
File: Test.html
<HTML>
   <B> this is bold information </B>
</HTML>
```

If you open the above file in a web browser, a webpage will be displayed with a message: **this is bold information**

59. What is telnet?

Telnet is a Terminal Emulation Protocol that allows you to make a terminal connection to other computers on the Internet. This requires that you run a telnet client on your computer and connect to a telnet server on the other machine.

To run a telnet client in windows, type telnet <IP Address> in the command prompt

60. What is an Element Management System (EMS)?

If number of devices in a network becomes more, it is difficult to manage them manually. To manage more number of devices, every equipment vendor provides management software to manage their network devices. This management application is known as **EMS**.

61. What is SNMP protocol?

The **Simple Network Management Protocol** (SNMP) is an application layer protocol that assists the exchange of management information between network devices.

An SNMP-managed network consists of three key components—managed devices, agents and element-management systems (EMSs).

A managed device is a network node that contains an SNMP agent and that resides on a managed network. Managed devices collect and store management information and make this information available to EMSs using SNMP. Managed devices can be routers and access servers, switches and bridges, or hubs.

An agent is an element-management software module that resides in a managed device. An agent has local knowledge of management information and translates that information into a format compatible with SNMP.

An EMS is an application that monitor and control managed devices. One or more EMSs could exist on any managed network.

62. What are the basic SNMP operations?

Managed devices are monitored and controlled using three basic SNMP commands: read, write and trap.

The read command is used by an EMS to monitor managed devices. The EMS examines different variables that are maintained by managed devices. There are three read commands:

- getRequest – for query Scalar objects
- getNextRequest – for query tabular objects
- getResponse – response for query objects

The write command is used by an EMS to control managed devices. The EMS changes the values of variables stored within managed devices. Write command is:

setRequest – update a scalar are tabular objects

The trap command is used by managed devices to asynchronously report events to the EMS. When certain types of events occur, a managed device sends a trap to the EMS.

63. What is SNMP Management Information Base (MIB)?

A Management Information Base (MIB) is a collection of management information that is organized hierarchically. MIBs are accessed using an element-management protocol, such as SNMP. They are comprised managed objects and are identified by object identifiers.

A managed object (sometimes called a MIB object or an object) is specific characteristics of a managed device. Managed objects are comprised one or more object instances, which are essentially variables.

Two types of managed objects exist: scalar and tabular. Scalar objects define a single object instance. Tabular objects define multiple related object instances that are grouped in MIB tables.

For example,

- sysName is a scalar MIB object under System tree that represents the device name.
- ifDescr is a tabular MIB object under interface tree that represents the device interface description. Interface is a tabular object since a device can have more than one interface.

64. What are the various SNMP protocol versions?

SNMP has three main protocol versions namely SNMPv1, SNMPv2c and SNMPv3.

65. Why is SNMP protocol good option for EMS?

The main requirements of an EMS application are as follows:

- Network should not have downtime even in seconds.
- Management protocol should not access more network bandwidth.

Keeping these conditions in mind, a good management protocol must be chosen. The reasons for choosing SNMP are as follows:

- It is running over UDP (connectionless protocol) so that not much bandwidth will be utilized.
- As the name suggests, it is Simple to implement.

SECURITY

66. What is a firewall?

A mechanism that isolates a network from the rest of the Internet, permitting only specific traffic to pass in and out is a **firewall.**

67. Why data encryption is required?

Data that traverses unsecured networks is open to many types of attacks. Data can be read, altered or forged by anybody who has access to the route that your data takes. For example, a protocol analyser (sniffer) can read packets and gain classified information. Or, an intimidating party can tamper with packets and cause damage by hindering, reducing or preventing network communications within your organization.

Encryption provides a means to safeguard network data that travels from one router to another across unsecured networks. Encryption is particularly important if confidential or critical data is being sent.

68. What is public key encryption?

Any cryptographic system uses two keys for encryption/decryption. Public key, known to everyone and a private or secret key, is known only to the recipient of the message. When Device A wants to send a secure message to Device B, it uses Device B's public key to encrypt the message. Device B then uses its private key to decrypt it.

An important element to the public key system is that the public and private keys are related in such a way that only the public key can be used to encrypt messages and only the corresponding private key can be used to decrypt them. Moreover, it is virtually impossible to deduce the private key if you know the public key.

The only difficulty with public-key systems is that you need to know the recipient's public key to encrypt a message.

69. What are digital signatures/certificates?

An attachment to an electronic message used for security purposes. The most common use of a digital certificate is to verify that a user sending a message is who he/she claims to be, and to provide the receiver with the means to encode a reply.

An individual wishing to send an encrypted message applies for a digital certificate from a Certificate Authority (CA). The CA issues an encrypted digital certificate containing the applicant's public key and a variety of other identification information. The CA makes its own public key readily available through print publicity or perhaps on the Internet.

The recipient of an encrypted message uses the CA's public key to decode the digital certificate attached to the message, verifies it as issued by the CA and then obtains the sender's public key and identification information held within the certificate. With this information, the recipient can send an encrypted reply.

The most widely used standard for digital certificates is X.509.

70. What is SSL?

SSL—Secure Sockets Layer, is a technology developed by Netscape Communications Inc. for encrypting data sent between clients and servers. SSL is the basis for Netscape's secure communication technologies.

COMMANDS AND UTILITIES

71. What does 'ping' command do?

Ping—Packet Internet Groper is the name of a standard network utility packaged with modern network operating systems. Ping command uses 'ICMP' protocol. This command can be used to determine if a remote device (such as Web or game server) can be reached on the network and, if so, roughly how fast the current connection is.

72. How do you get to know your MAC or IP address details?

UNIX: Type shell command 'ifconfig –a'

Windows: Type in command prompts 'ipconfig /all'

73. What does the UNIX 'traceroute' ('tracert' in Windows) command do?

Traceroute displays the routers that are passed through to reach the given destination IP address. This diagnostic utility determines the route taken to a destination by sending Internet Control Message Protocol (ICMP) echo packets with varying Time-To-Live (TTL) values to the destination. Each router along the path is required to decrement the TTL on a packet by at least 1 before forwarding it. When the TTL on a packet reaches 0, the router is supposed to send back an ICMP Time Exceeded message to the source system. tracert determines the route by sending the first echo packet with a TTL of 1 and incrementing the TTL by 1 on each subsequent transmission until the target responds or the maximum TTL is reached. The route is determined by examining the ICMP Time Exceeded messages sent back by intermediate routers.

74. What is the command to get the system information on Unix?

sysinfo. This command provides information such as RAM space, hard disk space processor speed, etc.

PROBLEMS AND SOLUTIONS

Exercise 1

You are given two addresses/mask combinations, written with the prefix/length notation, which have been assigned to two devices. Determine if these devices are on the same subnet or different subnets.

Device A: 174.16.17.30/20

Device B: 174.16.28.15/20

Subnet for Device A:

```
174.16.17.30 =      10101110.00010000. 00010001.00011110
255.255.240.0 =     11111111.11111111. 11110000.00000000

                    -----------------------| sub|----------------
```

Looking at the address bits that have a corresponding mask bit set to one, and setting all the other address bits to zero (this is equivalent to performing a logical "AND" between the mask and address), shows you to which subnet this address belongs. In this case, Device A belongs to subnet 174.16.16.0.

Subnet for Device B:

```
174.16.28.15 =       10101110.00010000. 00011100.00001111
255.255.240.0 =      11111111.11111111. 11110000.00000000
                     -----------------------| sub|-----------------
```

From these determinations, Device A and Device B have addresses that are part of the same subnet.

Exercise 2

Given the Class C network of 200.12.5.0/24, subnet the network in order to create the network in below figure with the host requirements shown.

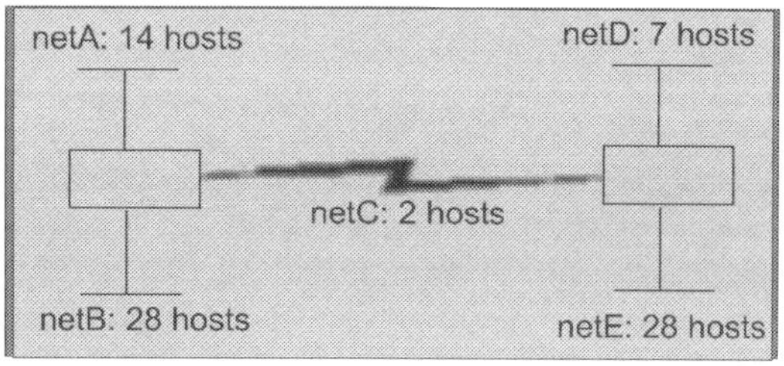

Figure 8.7 *Subnet example*

Looking at the diagram shown in Figure 8.7, we can see that we are required to create five subnets. The largest subnet must support 28 host addresses. To create the five needed subnets we need to use three bits from the Class C host bits. Two bits would only allow us four subnets.

Since you need three subnet bits that leaves us with five bits for the host portion of the address. With that we can support $2^5 = 32$ (30 usable).

Therefore, we have determined that it is possible to create this network with a Class C network. An example of how we might assign the sub networks is:

netA: 200.12.5.0/27 host address range 1 to 30 netB: 200.12.5.32/27 host address range 33 to 62 netC: 200.12.5.64/27 host address range 65 to 94 netD: 200.12.5.96/27 host address range 97 to 126 netE: 200.12.5.128/27 host address range 129 to 158

PROTOCOLS AND STANDARDS

75. What does an RFC mean?

The *Requests for Comments* (RFC) document series is a set of technical and organizational notes about the Internet. Memos in the RFC series discuss many aspects of computer networking, including protocols, procedures, programs and concepts.

The official specification documents of the Internet Protocol suite that are defined by the Internet Engineering Task Force (IETF) and the Internet Engineering Steering Group (IESG) are recorded and published as standards track RFCs. RFCs must first be published as Internet Drafts and then if accepted, it will become standards.

76. Mention some important internet protocol's application that are more frequently used.

FTP—File Transfer Protocol, an Internet client-server protocol for transferring files between computers.

SFTP—Secure File Transfer Protocol, is an interactive file transfer program, similar to ftp, which performs all operations over an encrypted transport layer.

TFTP—Trivial File Transfer Protocol is a simple form of the File Transfer Protocol (FTP). TFTP uses the User Datagram Protocol (UDP) and provides no security features. It is often used by servers to boot diskless workstations, X-terminals and routers.

DHCP—DHCP stands for "Dynamic Host Configuration Protocol". DHCP's purpose is to enable individual computers on an IP network to extract their configurations from a server (the 'DHCP server') or servers, in particular, servers that have no exact information about the individual computers until they request the information. The overall purpose of this is to reduce the work necessary to administer a large IP network. The most significant piece of information distributed in this manner is the IP address.

PPP—Point to Point Protocol, a communications protocol that turns a dial-up telephone connection into a point-to-point Internet connection. This is commonly used to run WWW (World Wide Web) browsers over a phone line.

SMTP—Simple Mail Transfer Protocol, an internet standard protocol for transferring electronic mail messages from one computer to another. SMTP specifies how two mail systems interact and the format of control messages they exchange to transfer mail.

HTTP—Hyper Text Transfer Protocol, an internet protocol used to transfer HTML information.

77. Mention some of the 802 standards that are widely used.

802.3—standard for Ethernet technology.

802.5—standard for Token ring technology.

802.11—standard for Wireless LAN (WLAN) technology.

802.15—standard for Wireless Personal Area Network (WPAN) technology

THINKER'S CHOICE

78. What is the difference among DHCP, RARP and BOOTP?

79. What is CIDR? Why is it needed?

80. What issues are involved with operating a packet sniffer on a switched Ethernet network?

81. Assume you are a System Admin for your campus. What are all the precautionary steps you consider to stop data hack?

82. What is VLAN? What are the advantages and disadvantages of it?

83. What is passive and active connection in TCP?

84. Write TCP segment, UDP segment and IP datagram formats.

85. Explain how TCP handles Out-of-band data.

86. What is Quality of Service (QoS)? Why is it needed?

87. What is Storage Area Networking (SAN)?

88. What are the differences between SNMPv1, SNMPv2c and SNMP v3?

89. Why is switching faster than routing?

90. What is Wireless LAN?

91. Given IP address as 172.17.52.16 and Subnet mask as 255.255.240.0, find

- **the number of subnets possible on this network**
- **the number of hosts possible on each subnet**
- **which subnet this address is on**
- **range of addresses on that subnet**

92. Given the network IP address 154.30.0.0, work out the following:

- **Create 8 subnets**
- **Compute the subnet mask**
- **Give the starting and the end address of any one subnet**

REFERENCES

1. Andrew S. Tanenbaum, *Computer Networks*, 4th edition, Prentice Hall.
2. Douglas E. Comer, *Internetworking with TCP/IP*, Prentice Hall.

Made in the USA
Monee, IL
25 March 2026

46885586R00166